PREPARING
FOR THE
GREATER
COMMUNITY

A BOOK OF THE
NEW MESSAGE
FROM GOD

PREPARING
FOR THE
GREATER
COMMUNITY

AS REVEALED TO

Marshall Vian Summers

PREPARING
FOR THE
GREATER
COMMUNITY

Edited by Darlene Mitchell
Cover and interior: Designed by Reed Summers

ISBN: 978-1-942293-55-2 (POD)
ISBN: 978-1-942293-56-9 (ebook)
NKL POD Version 7.06 ; Sv7.5 5/18/2020
Library of Congress Control Number: 2020905148

Publisher's Cataloging-in-Publication Data
(Prepared by The Donohue Group, Inc.)

Names: Summers, Marshall Vian, 1949- author. | Society for the New
    Message, issuing body.
Title: Preparing for the Greater Community / as revealed to Marshall Vian
    Summers. | Society for the New Message.
Description: Boulder, CO : New Knowledge Library, the publishing imprint
    of The Society for the New Message, [2020] | Series: New message
    from God.
Identifiers: ISBN 9781942293552 (POD) | ISBN 9781942293569 (ebook)
Subjects: LCSH: Society for the New Message--Doctrines. | Communities--
    Religious aspects. | Social evolution. | Summers, Marshall Vian--
    Religion.
Classification: LCC BP605.S58 S866 2020 (print) | LCC BP605.S58 (ebook) |
    DDC 299/.93--dc23

Preparing for the Greater Community is a book of the New Message from God and is published by New Knowledge Library, the publishing imprint of The Society for the New Message. The Society is a religious non-profit organization dedicated to presenting and teaching a New Message for humanity. The books of New Knowledge Library can be ordered at www.newknowledgelibrary.org, your local bookstore and at many other online retailers.

The New Message is being studied in more than 30 languages in over 90 countries. *Preparing for the Greater Community* is being translated into the many languages of our world by a dedicated group of volunteer student translators from around the world. These translations will all be available online at www.newmessage.org.

The Society for the New Message
P.O. Box 1724   Boulder, CO 80306-1724
(303) 938-8401   (800) 938-3891
011 303 938 84 01 (International)   (303) 938-1214 (fax)
newmessage.org   newknowledgelibrary.org

It is time to prepare. The Greater Community Way of Knowledge is the only Teaching in the world that can prepare you for the Greater Community. It is the only Teaching in the world that can present to you what Knowledge and Wisdom really mean within a larger arena of intelligent life. It is the only Teaching in the world that can activate your Knowledge and give it full expression within the context of the world's evolution.

It is a New Revelation. It is a new gift to humanity. It is the gift humanity now needs in order to emerge out of its isolation and face the realities, the difficulties and the opportunities that await it in the Greater Community.

The Creator would not leave you alone or unprepared for the Greater Community. The Creator would not leave you without a means for discovering the greater purpose that has brought you into the world.

Receive this gift. Hear this calling. Find your deepest response. Go beyond your thinking and your ideas. Go beyond your preoccupations and attachments.

There is something great living within you. It is needed within the world now. It is being called for at this moment. It is a calling to awaken.

From: *Preparing for the Greater Community,*
Chapter 17: Beginning the Preparation

PREPARING
FOR THE
GREATER
COMMUNITY

TABLE OF CONTENTS

INTRODUCTION

Preparing for the Greater Community is a book of Revelation from the Creator of all life given to prepare us for the reality of Contact with extraterrestrial life and for humanity's emergence into a "Greater Community" of worlds in the universe.

Contact has begun, yet it is not Contact of a beneficial form for humanity. We are facing an alien Intervention into human affairs and this represents a threat to our freedom and survival as a race. And yet it also represents a great opportunity. Our isolation in the universe is now over, and humanity's emergence into the Greater Community has begun. This is perhaps the greatest event in human history and it is happening right now, in our time. Yet we are unaware and unprepared.

In addition, Contact is occurring at a time when we are racing towards a dangerous and uncertain future in our world. Humanity is outstripping the Earth of its life-giving resources at an alarming rate, changing the climate of the world and destroying the natural environment as never before. At the same time, political, social and religious conflict and division are escalating, fracturing the human family when instead we must be working to find a real and functioning unity to ensure our collective survival. We are divided, and this makes us vulnerable to outside influence and intervention from the universe around us.

Preparing for the Greater Community was given because humanity has reached this critical threshold in its evolution, a time of convergence when the reality of a changing world and the reality of Intervention from the universe collide. This book is here because the Greater Community is here—forces from the Greater Community are in our world now. With this comes the urgent need to prepare mentally, emotionally and spiritually for the realities of engaging with life on a larger scale. It is to present this preparation that this book is now being made available to the world.

For over 30 years, Marshall Vian Summers has been receiving a communication from the Creator of all life. This communication has been translated into human language by the Angelic Presence who watch over our world, who then speak this message through Marshall in the Voice of Revelation. The voice was recorded and then transcribed and presented in the text of this book, and the other books of the New Message. And from the beginning, this New Message from God was centered on the reality of the Greater Community and humanity's emergence into a larger universe.

Revealed in 1997, *Preparing for the Greater Community* was the first text of the New Message to reveal the larger reality of the Greater Community in which we live and to present a comprehensive preparation for life in this new and challenging environment. Here the Creator of all life is revealing what awaits humanity in the universe at large, the challenge and complexity of interaction between worlds, and the essential tools humanity will need to navigate its engagement with forces from beyond our world. Here the human family eclipses its millennia-old isolation in the universe and learns to interact wisely with other forms of intelligent life. This interaction will greatly expand how we view ourselves, God and our place in the universe.

Marshall Vian Summers received the very first revelation about the Greater Community on March 13, 1987 which is now the third chapter of *Wisdom from the Greater Community: Volume I.* This process continued in the years following, especially in 1989 with the revelation of *Steps to Knowledge*, a core book of spiritual practice and development, and then *Greater Community Prophecy*, a prophetic revelation about humanity's place in the Greater Community.

Then in 1993 came *Greater Community Spirituality*, the theology of Contact and a revelation of what religion and spirituality are like in the Greater Community. Four years later, the Allies of Humanity arrived with their first Briefing, opening a whole new chapter in this process. And just days after that came the book *Preparing for the Greater Community*, in response to the future need for many people to prepare themselves in light of what the Allies of Humanity had revealed.

Therefore, the 1980s and 1990s were a seminal period in the revelation of the Greater Community in our world. And yet few at that time were ready to hear and respond to this message and to begin the preparation themselves. It is now that this book and others from that period are being presented to the world for the first time. It is especially important this happen now because of the great need for humanity to prepare and respond to the growing presence of the alien Intervention in our world.

In addition, there are people in the world today who are innately connected to life in the universe and are now ready to begin their inner and outer preparation for humanity's emergence into the Greater Community. The connection and awareness they hold is kept within their Knowledge, the deeper spiritual Mind within them. The New Message from God provides the key to unlocking this Knowledge and with it your deeper nature and heritage beyond the world in order for you to serve the world now as it undergoes Contact and emergence into a larger arena of intelligent life.

Preparing for the Greater Community provides this key to you. This opens for you an essential stage in your preparation for a new life, in a changing world, in a greater universe beyond. Humanity's success and survival in the future depend on you and others like you undertaking this preparation.

This will enable you to participate in the world in a new way, as guided by the power of Knowledge within you and playing your part in a greater coordination of people working together to support humanity in making this great evolutionary step forward. This may be the greatest step humanity has ever taken and it is no accident you are here at this time.

ABOUT THE NEW MESSAGE
FROM GOD

The New Message from God is an original communication from God to the heart of every person on Earth. It is not for one nation, one tribe or one religion alone. It is a Message for the entire world, a world facing very different needs and challenges from those of ancient times.

Throughout history, God has given Revelation and Wisdom to meet the growing needs of our world at great turning points in the evolution of humanity. Now God is speaking again, delivering a New Revelation to meet the critical needs of humanity as it faces Great Waves of environmental, political and economic change and contact with a Greater Community of intelligent life in the universe.

God's progressive Revelation is continuing anew through a New Message from God, of which *Preparing for the Greater Community* is a part. The words of this text are a direct communication from the Creator of all life, translated into human language by the Angelic Presence that watches over this world, and then spoken through the Messenger Marshall Vian Summers, who has given over 30 years of his life to this process of Revelation.

This divine communication is here to ignite the spiritual power of humanity, to sound God's calling for unity amongst the world's nations and religions, to prepare humanity for a radically changing world and for its destiny in a larger universe of intelligent life.

The New Message from God speaks on nearly every aspect of life facing people today. It is the largest Revelation ever given to humanity, given now to a literate world of global communication and growing global awareness. Never before has there been a Divine Revelation of this size, given by God to all people of the world at once, in the lifetime of the Messenger.

Yet the New Message from God has not entered the world through the existing religious authorities and institutions of today. It has not come to the leaders of religion or to those who garner fame and recognition. Instead, it has been given to a humble man chosen and sent into the world for this one task, to be a Messenger for this New Message for humanity.

The Messenger has walked a long and difficult road to bring the New Message from God to you and to the world. The process of Revelation began in 1982 and continues to this day. The Messenger's story is one of perseverance, humility and lifelong service to others. His presence in the world today represents an opportunity to know him and receive the Revelation directly from him.

At the center of the New Message is the original Voice of Revelation, which has spoken the words of every book of the New Message. Never before has the Voice of Revelation, the Voice that spoke to the Messengers and prophets of the past, been recorded in its original purity and made available to each person to hear and to experience for themselves. In this way, the Word and the Sound of God's Revelation are in the world.

In this remarkable process of spoken Revelation, the Presence of God communicates beyond words to the Angelic Assembly that oversees the world. The Assembly then translates this communication into human language and speaks all as one through their Messenger, whose voice becomes the vehicle for this greater Voice—the Voice of Revelation.

The words of this Voice have been recorded in audio form, transcribed and are now available in the books of the New Message. In addition, the original audio recordings of the Voice of Revelation are available for all to hear. In this way, the purity of God's original spoken Message is preserved and given to all people in the world.

At this time, the Messenger is engaged in compiling over three decades of spoken Revelation into a final and complete text—The One Book of the New Message from God. This book of Revelation will ultimately be divided into six volumes and possibly more. Each volume will contain two or more books, and each book will be organized by chapter and verse. Therefore, the New Message from God will be structured in the following way: Volume > Book > Chapter > Verse.

Preparing for the Greater Community is a book in Volume 2 of the New Message from God and contains 17 individual revelations (chapters) revealed to the Messenger over a 14-day period in 1997, as well as one additional revelation received in 2008. The Messenger has compiled these revelations into the text you see today.

In order to bring this spoken communication into written form, slight textual and grammatical adjustments were made by the Messenger. This was requested of him by the Angelic Assembly to aid the understanding of the reader and to convey the Message according to the grammatical standards of the written English language.

In some instances, the Messenger has inserted a word not originally spoken in the Revelation. When present, you will often find this inserted word in brackets. Consider these bracketed words as direct clarifications by the Messenger, placed in the text by him alone in order to ensure that possible ambiguities in the spoken communication do not cause confusion or incorrect interpretations of the text.

In some cases, the Messenger has removed a word to aid the readability of the text. This was usually done in the case of certain conjunctions (words such as *and, but*) that made the text unnecessarily awkward or grammatically incorrect.

The Messenger alone has made these slight changes and only to convey the original spoken communication with the greatest clarity possible. None of the original meaning or intention of the communication has been altered.

The text of this book has been structured by the Messenger into verse. Each verse roughly signals the beginning or ending of a distinct message point communicated by the Source.

The verse structure of the text allows the reader to access the richness of the content and those subtle messages that may otherwise be missed in longer paragraphs of text that convey multiple topics. In this way, each topic and idea communicated by the Source is given its own standing, allowing it to speak from the page directly to the reader. The Messenger has determined that structuring the text in verse is the most efficacious and faithful way of rendering the original spoken revelations of the New Message.

Through this text, we are witnessing the process of preparation and compilation being undertaken by the Messenger, in his own time, by his own hands. This stands in stark contrast to the fact that the former great traditions were rarely put into written form by their Messengers, leaving the original messages vulnerable to alteration and corruption over time.

Here the Messenger seals in purity the texts of God's New Message and gives them to you, to the world and to all people in the future. Whether this book is opened today or 500 years from now, God's original communication will speak from these pages with the same intimacy, purity and power as it did the day it was first spoken.

Though it appears to be a book in the hand, *Preparing for the Greater Community* is something far greater. It is a calling and a communication from the Heart of God to you. In the pages of this book, God's Presence calls to you and to all people, calling for you to awaken from the dream and nightmare of living in Separation apart from your Source, calling to the presence of "Knowledge," the deeper spiritual Intelligence that lives within you, waiting to be discovered.

Preparing for the Greater Community is part of a living communication from God to humanity. Remarkably, you have found the New Message from God, or it has found you. It is no coincidence that this is the case. This opens the next chapter in the mystery of your life and of your presence in the world at this time. The door opens before you. You need only enter to begin.

As you enter more deeply into the Revelation, the impact on your life will grow, bringing a greater experience of clarity, inner certainty and true direction to your life. In time, your questions will be answered as you find growing freedom from self-doubt, inner conflict and the restraints of the past. Here the Creator of all life is speaking to you directly, revealing to you the greater life that you were always destined to live.

The Society for the New Message from God

CHAPTER 1

WHAT IS THE GREATER COMMUNITY?

The Greater Community is an environment in which you live. It represents the greater physical and spiritual universe into which humanity is now emerging. You have always lived in the Greater Community, but your relative isolation in this world has not given you the experience of the greater context into which you are now emerging. It is this greater context that will give you the clarity and the understanding that you will need to discover the greater purpose that has brought you into the world.

The Greater Community into which humanity is now emerging represents a vast network of communities and cultures in the physical universe. This vast network represents the evolution of intelligent life in all of its manifestations, from the very primitive to the very advanced. It encompasses cultures that possess a wide array of values, motivations, beliefs and associations.

The Greater Community is not united. It is diverse and often contentious, yet magnificent beyond what you can now possibly imagine. An emergence into the Greater Community will not be the result of your journeys into space but rather the result of visitors coming to the world. Many of these visitors are in the world today. They represent different organizations and associations. In essence, they are competing for influence in the world.

Humanity's emergence into the Greater Community represents the greatest threshold that humanity has ever faced as a race. It poses tremendous risks; however, it offers the possibility and the opportunity for humanity to unite and to gain a greater vantage point in life.

As you enter into these pages, you will begin to learn about the reality of the Greater Community, a reality that is very different from what many people in the world believe in today. And you will come to see that humanity is at a great threshold, and that you are connected to this threshold. Here your spiritual life and your spiritual reality will become illuminated and will finally have the context necessary for you to realize why you have come, who you must meet and what you must do.

When you look out into the skies above you at night and you imagine how vast it is, it is important to understand that this universe is full of life. It is not that life only exists in remote and rare outposts amidst a vast desert of emptiness. Though there are many, many worlds that are uninhabited and uninhabitable, life has anchored itself and established itself throughout the Greater Community.

Therefore, answer for yourself once and for all the question of whether you are alone in the universe. How impossible this is. How preposterous to even think that this could be the case. This kind of thinking is born of the fact that humanity has evolved in a state of relative isolation and has not had the advantage of direct contact with intelligent life from beyond the world, except recently.

In ancient times, Greater Community explorers came to your world to gather biological resources and, in rare situations, to hide things. Their encounters with native peoples were quite rare, for they were not here for that purpose.

WHAT IS THE GREATER COMMUNITY?

From a Greater Community standpoint, your world is like a greenhouse, a great biological storehouse in the universe, and this is rare. For this reason, it has been used over the span of time as a place where biological resources could be gathered. Yet visitations were rare and the native peoples, though they witnessed some of these visitations, were not the primary focal point of the visitors.

A great turning point for humanity came in ancient times with the seeding of greater intelligence through interbreeding. This is what gave rise to modern man in a very short period of time and set the stage for humanity to emerge within this world as the predominant race and species, and to develop slowly the world civilizations that you see here today. This was largely the result of Greater Community intervention, an intervention that was destined to happen and has given you many of the great advantages that you experience here today, and many of the great problems that you face now as a race.

When We say relative isolation, We mean that [though] you have grown up in a world preoccupied with human ideals, human values and human endeavors, the Greater Community has had a profound effect upon your evolution and development. Yet this has not been part of your experience, for humanity has seemed to evolve alone in the universe, drifting through space, unaware of the greater forces that are shaping life and are shaping the destiny even of this world.

In this way, you are like villagers deep in the jungle. Your religions reflect the range of your perception and understanding. Yet you are largely unaware of the greater forces that are functioning in your world and will likely be greatly unprepared for the coming of visitors from that world.

Using this analogy, you can begin to see the great predicament that humanity is in at this time, for you are like villagers in a remote jungle who are about to be discovered by the outside world. Humanity is about to be discovered by divergent forces from the Greater Community who are here for their own purposes. Here your isolation will be rudely interrupted, and the discovery that you are not alone in the universe, or even within your own world, will come in shocking waves of revelation.

Many people feel there is a great movement in the world today, that [they] are at a great turning point. Some speculate that this will lead to a great disaster for humanity, others to a great awakening. It is as if the ground is moving beneath your feet, and within yourself you feel a great turbulence, as if something is driving you forward towards an unseen and unknown destiny.

In response to this great movement, people project their ideas, their beliefs, their hopes and their fears. And from their perspective, the world is either filled with angels or with demons, as they speculate that the great times of change will fulfill the ancient prophecies or will begin new ones.

This is the result of people experiencing the evolution of the world, of experiencing living at a time of great change. This is the result of people experiencing the world's emergence into the Greater Community. Yet how few people in the world today really understand what they are experiencing.

Humanity is emerging out of its isolation now. It is emerging into a Greater Community of life. It is entering a larger physical and spiritual universe, of which it has always been a part.

Here you will encounter the reality of other forms of intelligent life, but they will not be angelic, and they will not be demonic. They will be races of individuals who are facing the same problems of survival and competition, advancement and control that humanity is struggling with within the world. Though their technology seems to be beyond comprehension, that does not mean that they have magical powers. They are here for their own purposes, very little of which has anything to do with human reality or human history.

The Greater Community is in the world today. When We say this, We mean that there are a few groups who are here. They certainly do not represent the entire Greater Community. Yet their presence here brings with it the reality that life will change forever within the world, and that all that humanity has developed in its life in isolation will undergo a profound change and challenge, tremendous growth.

This is the most difficult thing that could happen to humanity at this time, and yet it is the most beneficial. For it will take the presence of the Greater Community to finally bring humanity to realize that it must unite, that it must preserve the world, that it must protect its citizens, and that it must become strong and capable in order to function within a Greater Community environment.

Why is the Greater Community here in the world today? The Greater Community has been called here and brought here for different reasons and different motivations, but primarily each group is responding to humanity's development and the prospect of humanity's emergence into the Greater Community. Some are here to gain advantage in the world. Some are here to observe you. Some are here to offset your dangerous and aggressive tendencies. And some are here because they support your emergence into the Greater

Community, and they value your existence and they wish to assure your advancement.

Clearly, you can begin to see that you are entering a very complicated environment, a very complex situation. You are entering an environment where humanity is not the primary race, is not the strongest participant, is not the ruling party, and this gives rise to fear and anxiety.

Humanity's great world wars in this century [20th century] and the development of nuclear weapons have given a great signal to those in the Greater Community who are aware of humanity's existence that their intervention must take place now. This is also stimulated by the deterioration of the natural environment here, an environment which is highly valued by others. With the exception of those few races who are aware of humanity, who seek to assure and protect your advancement, all the other races are here to serve their own interests, to preserve the world for their own uses. They are here primarily to control humanity.

Within the Greater Community, you have allies, you have enemies, and you have competitors. Your allies are not here directly. They are not here to control humanity. They do not wish to take over or to influence human government or human affairs. Instead, they wish to present something that will enable humanity to prepare for the Greater Community and to learn to gain wisdom and discernment in this larger arena of life that at the outset seems so daunting, so immense and so confusing. They watch you from afar, and they send their counsel to those who can receive them. They do not represent great military forces, for that is not their strength and their wisdom.

In the Greater Community you have enemies. That is not to say you have enemies at this moment, but there are those who will oppose your ventures into space, and they will certainly oppose your ventures beyond this solar system when that threshold is reached.

According to Greater Community values, at least amongst nations that trade and interact, a world such as yours can claim dominion over its own solar system but not beyond. Given human values and the generally anthropocentric view that the universe is there for the taking, this will create great problems for humanity in the future and will create adversity. You are only a century away from being able to go beyond your solar system, a very short period of time in the larger scheme of things.

Your enemies will oppose you because they have their own interests, which they wish to protect, and because they do not regard the aggressive nature of human communities as they exist today in a positive way. Those who are potential enemies of humanity that live within the proximity of this world beyond your solar system are aware of your existence and will seek to defend themselves against humanity if it becomes necessary. They have no interest in human affairs except to defend themselves against it.

Next, you have competitors. These represent races of beings who want to have some kind of interaction with you, but for their own purposes. Some will seek to establish trade; some will compete with you for the resources of this world. None of them will have your best interests at heart except insofar as it serves their own purposes. They will collaborate only for advantage, and they will oppose you and attempt to manipulate you if you are competing for the same things. They are not enemies in the sense that this will generate warfare, but it creates very subtle forms of adversity, with which humanity is quite unprepared to contend.

Within the great scope of the Greater Community, there are very, very few races who are aware of humanity's existence. By very few, let Us say 20 or 30. Very few.

For the Greater Community is vast. Space travel is relatively slow. It takes a long time to get around. The distances are vast. There are huge areas that are unexplored and uncharted. [In] the Greater Community, large regions are called sectors. Within a sector, there may be several thousand solar systems, many of which are uninhabited.

The sector that your world exists in is very densely inhabited. What that means is that if 12-15% of solar systems are inhabited, that is considered densely populated in the Greater Community. So your world, rather than being in some far corner of the universe, is actually right in the thick of things. This means that humanity will have to contend with the realities of Greater Community trade, commerce, cooperation and competition to a far greater extent than if your world were in a remote and uncharted region of the Greater Community.

Greater Community forces are in the world today because humanity is destroying the world and because humanity is at the threshold of emerging into space. Here humanity is suddenly thrust into a greater environment representing greater forces, some of which are even competing with each other for influence here.

It is like the remote villagers finding themselves within a larger human community representing forces, empires and nations of which they are totally unaware. Yet how much more inexplicable will the Greater Community seem to you than the outside world of humanity would seem to the remote villagers who are finally discovered.

This is the great turning point. This is the great threshold. This is why you have come into the world—to be a part of this, to learn about this and to make a positive contribution to humanity and to the world.

And yet how far and beyond human comprehension, human concern and human belief are the very things that shape and will shape and have always shaped human destiny and human evolution.

Humanity's encounter with the greater forces is imminent now and is being greatly felt by many people around the world. Some retreat into their ancient religions, prophesying the end or the beginning. Others go into a state of prolonged confusion and ambivalence and are unable to function, even in the affairs of daily life. And others try to move forward, try to break the bonds of the past and enter a greater and new understanding.

These represent the three primary responses that any person can have to great change, and they are demonstrated on a mass level. Faced with great change, you can either go away from it, you can go against it or you can go towards it.

To go away from great change is to enter fantasy and confusion and to become preoccupied with little things to the exclusion of everything else. This represents all of the addictive behavior of humanity and the many manifestations of human preoccupation.

To go against great change means to hold fast to old ideas and to oppose the emergence of change, to fight against the tides of change, to completely identify with something in the past and use it to resist the present and the future.

To go towards great change requires that one break free of the bonds of the past sufficiently to be able to gain a new understanding, to break new ground psychologically and emotionally, and to attempt to extend and to open to new possibilities.

Each of these three responses is inherent within each person, yet one will always be predominant. That is to say, people are capable of responding in any one of these ways to great change, but they will tend to respond primarily in one way.

Each of these responses has certain benefits and certain liabilities. Each has great risks. That is why it is necessary to learn The Way of Knowledge and to develop the wisdom to experience Knowledge and to express Knowledge.

It is essential now that you accept that your world is emerging into a Greater Community and to accept that this is beyond your comprehension and to accept that you are not prepared for it.

This realization, which is so fundamental and essential for your well-being and your ability, may give rise to great anxiety. But if seen correctly, it will give rise to great promise, and will call forth your greater abilities, and will enable you to prepare for a new life in a greater world. This is the great challenge and the great opportunity that faces you and that faces people everywhere.

Humanity will be led forth by the few who can respond and who can prepare. Everyone else will become victims of change rather than the beneficiaries. They will succumb rather than advance. Your history has proven this again and again at times of great upheaval.

It is for this reason that there is a great calling in the world today, a spiritual calling—calling people forth out of their fantasies, out of their ancient beliefs, out of their fixed viewpoints, to gain a greater vantage point and a greater position in life, and from here to be able to prepare for the changing of the world and the coming of the Greater Community. It is this calling that this book represents. Take courage, then, and enter into these pages with the desire to learn and with the confidence that Knowledge within you, the great knowing Mind, will respond.

What you will learn here you will not be able to learn in any other book, for this is a teaching about the Greater Community. This is the preparation for the Greater Community. It is a spiritual teaching because it calls upon the greater powers within you that you have brought with you into the world from your Ancient Home. And yet it is a teaching about how to be in the world, how to live life every day, how to deal with all the mundane manifestations of life, and at the same time how to penetrate the great mysteries that will reveal to you your purpose in coming here and what must be accomplished by you specifically.

It is with this understanding that you will come to see that the Greater Community represents a very practical form of salvation for humanity. For without emergence into a larger arena of life, humanity would simply deteriorate here in the world, unable to overcome its deficiencies and its conflicts, its history and its cultural adversities. The Greater Community, with all of its challenges and all of its problems, provides the context for humanity to recognize that it is one, and that it must unite, and that it must preserve and develop its resources if it is to survive and to advance in a greater arena of life.

If you are a person who has become aware that you are undergoing a spiritual development, you have also come to realize that spiritual development often is most greatly furthered through experiences of difficulty and adversity. You have had the opportunity to learn that some of the greatest gifts come amidst the most difficult and challenging times.

This is how intelligence is strengthened and expanded. This is how spirituality is discovered and expressed. This is how individuals everywhere, both within your world and throughout the Greater Community, are able to rise beyond their personal self-preoccupations to enter a greater life and a greater service.

We invite you, therefore, to take this great step forward, to learn about the meaning of your life, your purpose for coming to the world, the evolution of the world and the coming of the Greater Community.

Take this step with courage and with humility. Take this step realizing that you are at the beginning of a great journey. Take this step realizing and recognizing the tremendous limitations under which you currently live. And take this step with the understanding that the opportunity unlike any other is presented before you to become a greater human being in a greater world in a greater universe. It is from this point forward that you can begin your education in The Greater Community Way of Knowledge.

CHAPTER 2

THE GREATER COMMUNITY PRESENCE IN THE WORLD

Humanity has evolved primarily to deal with its environment and to learn how to interact and compete with itself. This means that human intelligence, discernment and capability have evolved largely in response to living in the natural environment and in dealing with other human beings.

From within the isolation of your world, it appears that the differences between people are very great. The differences between individual capabilities and comprehension are significant. Yet from a Greater Community perspective, the difference between human beings is very slight. The difference between their comprehension and abilities is very small.

Because human beings have primarily evolved to only deal with each other as other forms of intelligent life, they are very limited in their capabilities. These limitations are quite evident in human affairs and have given rise to the great problems and failures that humanity has experienced in a compounding way since the last century [end of the 19th century]. The presence of divergent races from the Greater Community in the world today gives you and humanity as a whole the opportunity to develop its intelligence and to expand its capabilities in order to adapt to a changing situation.

Yet most people in the world today are still so fixed in an anthropocentric view of life, in a human-centered universe, that they can only conceive of other forms of intelligent life in an adjunctive way. In other words, they can only consider the meaning of an extraterrestrial Greater Community presence in terms of how it benefits or complements human understanding. That is why from a human viewpoint, the heavens are often filled with demons or angels rather than real beings.

Without the intervention of Greater Community presences here, regardless of their intentions, human beings would not develop beyond the limited adaptive situations that they create for themselves.

That is why many people in the world today think that there must be floods or tidal waves or earthquakes in order for something new to happen, in order for a breakthrough to happen in human understanding. For it is generally recognized that if nothing significant happens to humanity, nothing significant will change. And because people still believe they are living in isolation, they imagine all kinds of physical calamities in order to provide the stimulation and the context for the expansion of human intelligence and capabilities.

This is all the result of living and thinking in isolation. Yet it does hold a seed of truth. The seed of truth is recognizing that unless you encounter a greater intelligence or a greater set of circumstances, to which you are [not yet] adapted, you will not be able to grow and expand individually or as a race. This is why individuals occasionally go out and do really extreme things in the world—climb mountains and sail across the oceans alone—in order to push themselves into a situation where they will have to grow and adapt because under normal circumstances, there would not be the necessary stimulation. Well, congratulations! You have been born into the world at a time of great challenge and great change.

THE GREATER COMMUNITY PRESENCE
IN THE WORLD

The Greater Community is not here because of your spiritual needs. They are here because of larger circumstances. They are not here for you, but you can benefit from their presence. It is only in the presence of a greater intelligence that your intelligence can grow. It is only in proximity to another race that has greater capabilities that your capabilities can expand and grow.

Humanity has been slowly evolving its technology and social development, but it has been very incremental, only accelerating in the recent two centuries. Yet now faced with the reality of Greater Community life in the world and Greater Community intervention in human affairs, you are faced with a situation that will require the development of a greater intelligence and greater spiritual capabilities. You cannot rely upon your old ideas or upon the talents that you have developed so far. Here everyone is a beginner regardless of what they think they have accomplished so far in life. Here human mastery becomes quite relative to the circumstances in which it is expressed.

That is why We say there are no masters living in the world because mastery is relative to the circumstances in which it is expressed. Within a Greater Community context, human mastery is not very significant—promising, but not significant.

This indeed has a humbling effect, an equalizing effect, for everyone is in the same boat now. Everyone is at the same starting place. There are none who are way, way, way ahead of everyone else. Now many people cannot even get to the starting place, but there are only a handful of people in the world who are beyond the starting place, and they are not very far indeed.

This is the environment in which you were born. This is the world that you have come to serve. This is the situation for which you have been preparing all your life. This is the great set of circumstances that will either defeat you or elevate you.

If you can consider these things without fear or apprehension, if you can take this position, however difficult it may seem in the moment, you will begin to see something you could not see before. You will be able to gain a sense of life and your place in life beyond the extremely limited parameters of personal preoccupation. And here you will see that personal preoccupation is the prison house in which everyone lives and which everyone builds for themselves. And you will see that liberation exists beyond this prison house. It exists beyond individuals being preoccupied with themselves—their wants, their fears, their needs.

For when you are engaged in a greater life, you begin to live a greater life. When you can face a greater reality outside of yourself, you will begin to experience a Greater Reality within yourself. If you live in isolation in a human world, with human ideals, human values and human preoccupations, that is all you will experience.

That is why people go to nature—to try to experience a greater reality—for nature is a greater reality than human culture. They will go there for liberation, for refreshment, and for insight and for reasons that We will describe later in this book when We talk about the mental environment.

The Greater Community presence in the world poses the greatest danger that humanity has ever faced. That must be clearly understood. And as you read these pages, you will begin to see why.

Yet the Greater Community presence in the world provides the greatest opportunity, the greatest contrast, the greatest stimulation, the greatest need that humanity has ever faced—all of which will enable people to rise beyond their personal preoccupations and their tribal conflicts and their ideological warfare with one another to recognize that they are living in a greater situation and must prepare for it accordingly.

So on the one hand, the presence of the Greater Community poses an ominous risk to humanity. On the other hand, it is the greatest possible thing that could happen at this time. Humanity, at the brink of a great decline—culturally, environmentally, economically, at the brink of a tremendous decline—is now faced with the very circumstances that will rejuvenate it, that will unite its citizens everywhere and give them a common purpose and a common focus, to bring them into the present time to deal with real situations now and in the future, which will elevate them beyond their national, tribal and religious identity sufficiently to establish bonds of cooperation within the human family that have never been established before. These great problems that the Greater Community brings humanity have within them a saving grace that could not be established in any other way.

At present, humanity is in a very adolescent stage of its evolutionary development, adolescence that, in a sense, is beginning to experience its power. It is beginning to experience its authority over its affairs and its environment. Yet it is adolescent in the sense that it is irresponsible, that it is not accountable, that it does not recognize the consequences of its actions, that it does not think in long terms, that it is preoccupied only with itself and its gains.

This adolescent state, which is so chaotic and hazardous for young men and women, is being experienced by the entire race. Humanity is gambling its future by destroying the very resources that support it in the world, hoping its technology will somehow save it in the eleventh hour. It is risking its inheritance, and it is creating a situation where only calamity can come. It is amazing that so many people in the world today cannot even see this, yet many people feel this and are anxious [about] it. They either seek escape, confrontation or advancement as a result.

Humanity is faced with a situation where it will have to unite and elevate its capabilities and its inherent skills in order to preserve its self-determination and its pre-eminence in this world.

Some people feel, "Oh, this is such a fearful way of looking at it. This is such a fearful prescription! I want to see a happy universe. I want to see a happier situation. It really isn't going to be like that." And We say, "It is not about love and fear. It is about seeing clearly, without preference, without denial. It is about seeing what is there and then responding to it appropriately."

People face the problem of preference and denial every day in how they manage their lives and affairs. That human beings possess such great possibilities for intelligence and creativity is completely thwarted by such attitudes and approaches.

It is not a question of whether you see a happy universe or a fearful universe, it is a question of whether you see or not, whether you can see what is there or what you want to see, whether you see the reality of life beyond yourself or your own thoughts. That is the critical question.

We bring to you life as it is and not as you may want it to be. Very few people will want the presence of the Greater Community here, but many people feel that something has to happen to change the course of human history and destiny.

Here, within you, you have to rise above preference and fear to gain a position of greater objectivity and clarity so that you can see. If you can see, you can know. But if you are filled with protecting what you have, protecting your ideas, protecting your vision of the world and the happy outcome that you prescribe for yourself and others, or the fearful outcome that you prescribe for yourself and others, you will not be able to see and you will not be able to know. It is a question of whether you can see, not how you see.

There are several allied races who are in the world today who are attempting to biologically and genetically bond with humanity in order to gain the adaptive ability to live and to function in this world. If they are able to do this effectively, then they will become the rulers of mankind.

Why does it take them so long to adapt to being here? Because most technologically advanced races live in sterile environments, and this world with its millions of different kinds of organisms poses a tremendous adaptation problem. Technologically advanced societies, particularly those that travel a great deal, are primarily adapted only to live in either sterile or near-sterile environments. Bring them into a world of biological diversity, and they can only dwell here for very short periods of time while employing great precautions. But gain the human adaptive advantage, which is not only a biological adaptive advantage but also an intuitive adaptive advantage, and you can bring your greater intelligence or your values into a human situation.

Humanity at present is in a very vulnerable position. It is ripe for domination. Human cultures are filled with superstition. They are embittered against one another. They are self-seeking, often very primitive in their outlook on life and very tribal in their orientation, which means they only relate to their group. They are easily persuaded, very very vulnerable to persuasion and to influence. How easy it is to get everybody to buy the same products, to use the same cars, to go to the same places, without a great deal of variety.

Human beings have been trying to influence one another forever, since time began here in the world. This is practiced in the Greater Community, but at a much higher level of skill and effectiveness. Humanity is so vulnerable in its diversity, in its superstition. The great threat to humanity will not come by great armies landing here and taking over. That is barbaric and destructive. That is not how influence will be cast over the human family.

This is a calling not for fear and retreat, but for courage and preparation. If humanity will prepare adequately, if enough people will become strong in their understanding of the Greater Community and the development of Greater Community Knowledge and Wisdom, this domination will not take place. It will be offset and overcome.

This is the great turning point. Everything is at risk—everything you value, everything you hold dear. And yet how foreign this seems from people's concerns and preoccupations. It seems outrageous to consider such things: "How could anything take over our ability to think and determine what we want for ourselves? How could anything affect our priorities, our values, our emotions? How could anything take over? And if we even think of such things, we think of someone coming over and blowing everything up—primitive style, the way we do things here."

This is thinking in a tribal way. This is the result of living in isolation. But isolation is over. You are right in the middle of the Greater Community. The Greater Community is here. This is the great turning point. This is the great calling. This is the great spiritual emergence, not because the Creator is going to come and save you, but because the Creator has given you the wisdom and the skill and the inherent intelligence to be able to prepare for such a great undertaking and to serve a world in transition.

What does this have to do with you? This is the greater context for understanding who you are, why you are here and what you must do. You can only understand the greater questions and the greater reality by understanding the context in which they are truly meaningful. People so often try to create their idea of who they are and what their purpose is based only on their desires and interests, but this is never sufficient. You must understand the context to understand the purpose that has meaning within that context.

The greater context for the world now is the world's emergence into the Greater Community. Into this greater context, the reality of who you are, why you are here and who sent you will become revealed to you with such clarity. Your spiritual power and nature will become ignited and will begin to express itself through your activities every day.

You may say, "Oh, this seems too great! I cannot even comprehend it. It is too much of a challenge." It may be too much for your thinking mind, but it is perfect for your Being and your nature. You will absolutely thrive within such a greater context. But if you were to retreat and just try to focus on your personal preoccupations, you will stay small, and your spiritual reality will be dormant within you, and your sense of being alive and the vitality that is a natural inheritance will be muted and hidden within you, and you will suffer all of the emotional and psychological problems that result from this. Therefore, this has everything to do with you. It is life's gift to you. It is life's calling for you. If you can rise above your preoccupations, you can begin to feel this in every fiber of your body.

Is it not clear that people rise beyond themselves in times of great tribulation or emergency? People do extraordinary things. They exhibit extraordinary courage and self-determination. They act in a selfless way. They go beyond their normal state into a greater state. This is so very evident.

You live in a world now that is entering a great state of emergency, the very state that will redeem you and elevate you, give you strength and vitality and enable you to experience your own value, your courage and your ability. It will call upon you to develop those abilities that are so important, but that are as yet latent within you.

This is the world that you have come to serve, but you must understand the context in order to understand the service. Therefore, We endeavor to bring to you and to illustrate to you the greater context as it truly exists in the world today. Without this context, you will have the question, but you will not be able to find the answer. "Who am I? Why am I here? What must I do?" These are the fundamental questions in life. But to find them [the answers], you must find the context that gives them meaning, value and direction. Otherwise, you will try to answer them out of your ideas and your beliefs and all the social conventions to which you have adapted.

In the Greater Community, you have allies, you have enemies and you have competitors. Your enemies are more adversaries. They just oppose you. Your competitors try to use you. And your allies try to support you.

How will you be able to tell them apart? How will you be able to respond appropriately to each one? How will you be able to maintain your self-determination in the face of greater forces, not just technologically greater but with greater mental power and focus?

Surely this must call upon something very great within you, something inherent within you, something you do not simply learn but something that you already have, that you must learn to express and experience. Surely this must call upon a strength within you that even the Creator recognizes is there.

The Creator has given you everything you need to live life fully, and to prepare for the Greater Community and to learn about the Greater Community. This was not given to your grandparents or your ancestors, for that was not the need of their time. But it was given to you, and it will be given to your children and their children because this is the great need of your time and will be the great need of their time.

The world's emergence into the Greater Community is not something that simply happens in a year or in a decade. It is a greater emergence than that, and yet its manifestations will be so tremendous and so challenging. They will seem within themselves to be great thresholds, but they are all part of a great shift, a great movement out of isolation and into a [larger] arena of life.

You will now have the opportunity to learn about the Greater Community, to begin your Greater Community education, to learn what Knowledge and Wisdom mean within the Greater Community and to bring this learning into your everyday life—to rise above your preoccupations, which will solve many of your personal problems, and to engage with the greater power that the Creator has given you, which is calling upon you, which is waiting to be discovered.

This greater power We call Knowledge. It is within you at this moment. It is here on a mission in service to the world. Experience this. Unite with this power. And you will recognize that its mission is your own, and this will part the veil of confusion and ignorance that could only blind you before.

This Greater Power within you is directly connected to the evolution of the world because that is why it is here. Though people invest greatly in their personal interests, comforts and security, that is not why they are here. People are not simply here to be consumers or to be comfortable. Where you came from is where you are comfortable. Where you will return to is where you are comfortable. That is where you are known. That is your Ancient Home.

You did not come here to build a sweet nest for yourself. You came here to accomplish something important. That is what makes you important. That is what makes your life important. That is what gives you vitality and strength. That is what gives you the greater energy to create, to demonstrate. This is fulfillment. Fulfillment is never the result of a desire for comfort and pleasure. It is never the result of personal indulgence. It is the result of embracing a greater life, a greater challenge and a greater reality.

There is so much confusion in the world today regarding this. People are trying so hard, they are working so hard to be fulfilled by trying to get for themselves what they want. And they pay a huge price, and their rewards are pathetically small. Moments of happiness for years of suffering and strife.

Look around you. You can see this. It is manifest everywhere. People trying so hard to be happy, trying so hard to feel vital and meaningful. But they are not looking in the right place. They do not have the right context. And so they have to invent the context.

The real context for happiness, for vitality, for fulfillment, for awakening, for awareness, all exist in your dynamic involvement in the world. It is here that the needs of the world and your inner need have finally come together, for they are directly related.

This is finding the context for happiness in the natural by-product of your activity. For fulfillment is the natural result of your accomplishment, where vitality is generated because it is needed every day, where awareness and awakening occur because you are seeing beyond personal preoccupation, which is the source of all mental illness. Here you use what you have, and you rely upon who you are, and from here you are able to build relationships of strength that represent a greater dynamic in life.

Find the greater context, and you will find your greater self and your greater purpose and your greater meaning. The context exists. It is here. It is real. It is now. It is all around you. You do not see it day to day because what you see is a result of people's personal preoccupation. But if you can step outside of the cacophony of personal strife and ambition, you will be able to feel the movement of the world. You will feel it within your heart. You will feel it in the ground beneath your feet. You will feel it as you look up into the sky at night.

But this is only the beginning. To learn about the Greater Community, to gain a Greater Community education, to learn about Knowledge and Wisdom within the world, you must have a preparation. You must engage in a form of education that is not available at any university in the world, that is not available in any book that you have found until now. You cannot get from here to there without taking the steps. You cannot emerge out of isolation and [out of] tribal mentality without a preparation.

This preparation cannot be a human invention. It must be something given to humanity. It must come from the great spiritual Source. It must teach you to gain the strength, the perception, the perspective and the abilities that you need to fulfill your purpose for coming into the world. It must connect you with the reality of the Greater Community and the great needs of humanity at this time. Then your purpose, no matter how mundane it may be in its manifestations, will be directly related to furthering humanity's ability, self-determination and competency within a larger arena of life.

Therefore, ask yourself, "What does this have to do with me?" It has everything to do with who you are, why you are here and who sent you. It may have little to do with who you think you are and what you are preoccupied with at the moment.

The Greater Community is in the world today. Humanity's isolation is over. There is now competition for pre-eminence in the world. It is happening on the mental level. It exists throughout the world. It has everything to do with you and everything to do with why you are here and what you value.

CHAPTER 3

ESSENTIAL TRUTHS ABOUT THE GREATER COMMUNITY

In presenting the reality of the Greater Community and its overall importance to humanity at this time, We realize that We challenge many of the most preferred ideas and cherished ideas in human cultures today. We stimulate many questions and perhaps a great deal of confusion. But this is the reality that must be presented, and people must find a way to understand what it means and to outgrow their former ideas if they prevent them from doing this.

Because humanity is in a very adolescent stage in its development, it is filled with many ideals and superstitions that have nothing to do with reality. Instead, they represent the desires and fears of human consciousness. So strongly can these be adhered to that it can be very difficult for people to hear something new. It can be very difficult for them to see clearly and understand clearly what is being presented in this book.

We understand these difficulties, and We will attempt to clarify the realities that We are presenting as clearly as possible. Yet you must still understand that you have to do the work to gain the vantage point where you can see for yourself. It is not enough simply to believe what is being presented in this book. You must experience it for yourself, and you must be able to see it clearly. In this, you do most of the work.

If you stay immersed in your preoccupations, if you stay immersed in human ideals and beliefs, you will not be able to see the bigger picture, and you will not be able to recognize the greater forces, both within yourself and within the world around you, that are shaping your life and your destiny. Therefore, We bring a great challenge with Our message. We understand how great it is.

Humanity is but one more race emerging into the Greater Community. Across the vast network of societies and cultures in the Greater Community, there are at this moment other races that are in various stages of emerging into the Greater Community. Some of them are ahead of where you are now. Others are far behind.

So this is a very natural process, as it is a very natural process to grow from adolescence into adulthood. As you personally have an evolutionary progression in your life, so humanity as a race has an evolutionary progression. This is manifested in human society, human culture, human ideas and human education.

This is going on everywhere in the universe. By its very nature, intelligent life must grow and expand. This is what sets it apart from other forms of life, which play a different role in the great fabric of the universe.

Both within yourself and within the world are great forces moving this evolution forward. To keep pace with this, you must be able to go beyond your former education and set aside ideas, even if they have served you thus far. For what is education but learning something new, going beyond what you knew before, experiencing new revelations and so forth?

Therefore, as We present the Greater Community reality to you and its tremendous importance to you and to humanity as well, We also are presenting a greater learning opportunity, the most important learning opportunity that you could have at this time.

ESSENTIAL TRUTHS ABOUT THE
GREATER COMMUNITY

In order for you to begin this process of education, to begin the process of gaining a greater vantage point in life from which you can see what you could not see before and know what you could not know before, We must present certain essential truths about the Greater Community, about your world and about your essential spiritual nature, for they are all directly connected. What We are about to present may seem difficult to understand at first. Even if you think you can understand it right away, you still do not yet have the vantage point from which you can see it and know it fully.

In order to prepare you for the Greater Community, there are certain things you must understand. If these things are not recognized and understood, if they are not seriously considered, then you will not be able to understand the Greater Community, and you will not be able to prepare for it.

First of all, the Greater Community that We are speaking of primarily represents life in the physical universe, though it also includes the greater spiritual panorama which We shall speak on later. At this point We are primarily concerned with physical reality.

When We speak of life, therefore, in the Greater Community, We are speaking of physical life and physical existence. We are talking about intelligent life in the physical universe. It is necessary to understand that Greater Community encompasses intelligent life at all stages of evolution—cultures in a state of early emergence, early development, adulthood and decay.

We are not talking about enlightened beings. We are not talking about angelic forces. We are talking about real physical beings such as yourself, who have grown up and emerged in environments far different from your own and who have had to face the same difficulties in life: the difficulties of survival, competition and relationship.

The very fact that they have dealt with [this] in very different ways accounts for the different results that they experience. But it is important for you to know that there are certain things you hold in common with them and with all intelligent life in the physical universe.

It is very important not to confuse the physical and the spiritual realities. This is frequently done, and as a result your ability to discern clearly what you are dealing with becomes greatly obstructed. The physical reality is quite different [from] the spiritual reality. It operates according to different laws. It has different manifestations and a different purpose.

One is temporary. The other is permanent. One is primarily focused on education and service. The other is primarily focused on contribution. One is the realm of doing. The other is the realm of being. One requires tremendous forces of conflict and competition, and in the other these things do not exist.

This is such a primary area of confusion for people that We must emphasize again and again that you are dealing with physical forces and physical beings. The fact that you will need to call upon greater spiritual forces to assist you is essential, but do not confuse them with the forces from the Greater Community with which you must learn to contend.

Next, it is important to understand that when We use the word Greater Community, We are not talking about a unified community, a great brotherhood out there in the universe. We are talking about a vast array of individual cultures and individual worlds [that] have developed and, to certain degrees, have had to interact with each other. Some of this interaction is peaceful and harmonious. Some of it is contentious and full of adversity.

This is so very important because for centuries people have looked to the skies for salvation, thinking that out there there must be a better life, there must be a resolution to all of their problems, there must be a way of living where the problems of greed, violence and hatred simply do not exist.

But this only exists in your Ancient Home, from which you have come and to which you will return. And it only exists in the Greater Community amongst very small and isolated communities of Knowledge.

Great technological societies rarely possess and demonstrate real spiritual Knowledge and advancement. Their focus is on control and uniformity. Individual freedom is rarely prized in such societies. Rather, they seek to create a one-dimensional form of interaction, highly regimented and regulated.

For many who read this book, this will be profoundly disappointing, for they have thought: "There must be idyllic worlds out there somewhere, and those from the idyllic worlds will come to teach us how to be idyllic ourselves."

This is a very deep-seated hope and expectation, but it must be corrected at the outset, or you will be blind to what is happening in the world, and you will misconstrue your own experiences as well as the experiences of others.

There are societies that have achieved a high level of spiritual awareness and intellectual capability, but they are rare. They are the exception. Do not confuse this with technological advancement.

Technological advancement and spiritual advancement and achievement are not at all the same. This is so easily confused, for if someone has a technological capability that seems magical to you, you will tend to think that they are magical beings, or that they are very highly evolved, or that they are very altruistic, or that they have great compassion and love. But this is not the case.

After all, human beings today have great technological advantages that were unthinkable only a couple of centuries ago, and yet has humanity evolved significantly in a spiritual way? Has violence been erased from the human experience? Has greed been corrected? Has cooperation and compassion manifested throughout human societies? The answer to these is obvious. And yet technologically, humanity has far exceeded even its own expectations.

Therefore, there are great technological societies in the Greater Community, and there are many of them, for technology can be learned and traded and exchanged and brought into the realm of commerce.

But development in The Way of Knowledge, which in the Greater Community means spiritual development, is rare, just as it is rare within your world. For instance, every person can own a computer, perhaps, but how many people understand the inner workings of the human spirit or have the scope to realize the great dynamics in human relations or the mental environment which affects their thinking? Therefore, an essential truth is to understand that technological advancement and capability is not the same as spiritual advancement and capability.

Understand as well that you are dealing with real, physical, mortal beings. They have not mastered death. And because there are limits to what technology can do in the physical universe, they are not omnipotent. They may seem godlike to you in certain respects because of what they are able to achieve, but they are no more godlike than you are and in fact are beset by the same kinds of psychological and cultural conditions that limit and restrict your ability.

Next, it is essential to realize that the presence of the Greater Community in the world, and their arrival at this time, and their work and activity in the world have nothing to do with human spiritual evolution. In other words, they are not here to fulfill human mandates or human destiny directly. The fact that human destiny prescribes that humanity must eventually emerge into the Greater Community does not mean that the Greater Community forces who are here support that.

As We have said, they are here for their own purposes. This also is a very difficult idea for people to understand because they think that anything from the skies must be angelic or demonic, and must have something to do with fulfilling ancient human prophecies, and must be about humanity because from a purely human viewpoint, humanity is the center of the universe and everything revolves around that. And if there is Greater Community here, it must be about humanity; it must have come to support humanity or do something for humanity.

This is a fatal error. Do not make this mistake. The Greater Community's presence in the world today is the result of their own activities, motivations and projects and humanity's emergence as a technological society with capabilities to go beyond its own borders.

The attempt to control human destiny now from the outside has to do with this evolutionary stage, but it is not about human spiritual advancement per se. Human spiritual advancement will be the result of preparing for the Greater Community. And it will be the result of becoming a greater and more compassionate and effective human society.

Your visitors will not give this to you. As a matter of fact, most of your visitors are not even as spiritually advanced as you are. They have greater technology and social cohesion, but they do not have the rich spiritual traditions that humanity has here on Earth for the most part. They are here for more prosaic reasons.

Often people try to incorporate their awareness of the Greater Community, however small it may be, into their world vision or their spiritual understanding of life. Here there is a great deal of confusion between levels, a great deal of confusion between the spiritual and the physical. People try to make everything one and the same. Life is one, but it operates differently at different levels of existence, and you cannot confuse the levels if you have any hope of understanding what exists within them.

Next, you will not be able to understand Greater Community intelligence, Greater Community motivations, or the Greater Community reality from a purely human perspective. You must gain a greater vantage point.

This is possible because of what the Creator has given you. If you look at this purely from your own human ideas, you will not understand. That is why a preparation is necessary—a stairway to take you to a higher plane, to a higher vantage point on the mountain of life so you can see the lay of the land, so you can see beyond the treetops, so you can see where you really stand and what is really happening.

I could not expect you simply to understand everything We are presenting here in this book, but you must have a certain understanding to begin—to begin that journey, to find that higher vantage point.

Likewise, you cannot turn to human religion to provide the answers for this, for these are religions that were established in a state of isolation and cannot account for a Greater Community of life.

The great spiritual teachers in human history, though predominant within the world, though outstanding in their performance and demonstration, are, within a Greater Community context, very small figures. For the Greater Community also represents a greater spiritual reality. And your whole notion of who the Divine is and how the Divine functions in manifest life will undergo profound changes as you gain a Greater Community perspective and understanding.

Therefore, do not turn to the ancient texts to try to understand the meaning of the Greater Community or why it is here, for they cannot tell you. That was not the learning at that time. That was not the message that was needed at that time.

The ancient traditions, though rich with virtue, were primarily concerned with establishing compassion and cooperation as the foundation of civilization. They were not focused on preparing humanity for its emergence into the Greater Community. Instead, they were focused on enabling humanity to even begin to prepare for the Greater Community. In other words, they laid the foundation for where you are now. But this is a new beginning. This is a new threshold.

Next, understand that in the Greater Community all races are dealing with survival issues, as is humanity. Highly technological societies in the universe often destroy their own natural environment, such as humanity is doing now. This requires that they travel to other worlds to gain resources and begin the process of engaging in certain contexts for trade and commerce. This profoundly affects their cultures. In many cases, they are overtaken by stronger races. In other cases, they are able to survive and to maintain their own identity. They have not mastered the physical requirements of life, such as is so hoped for here in the world. They must deal with their own physical requirements. They must deal with security issues regarding other races. And they must become functional in the mental environment, which is something that We shall speak about later on.

In fact, the physical requirements have become greater because they need more resources. They need greater insulation in the Greater Community. They often have to rely upon other races to provide primary materials. It is a more challenging and difficult existence in many ways.

Despite the fact that technology can solve many little problems, it creates many more big ones. That is why in the Greater Community, the Wise remain hidden for the most part and do not engage in a great deal of travel and trade. There are some very fundamental reasons for this, which We shall speak about later.

But for now, it is important for you to understand that the races that you will be encountering, in fact most of the races in the Greater Community, are not thoroughly self-sufficient and have to deal with tremendous problems in terms of relations with other cultures and environmental problems of their own.

This is a crucial understanding because here you begin to realize why they might be here in the world. They are not traveling around the universe doing good works. They are looking for things that they need. They are looking to extend their power, their security, their resources and so forth.

And because this world has been an important resource for many local cultures [in the Greater Community] over a very long period of time, it has great attractiveness and importance. And because it is in a highly populated area of the Greater Community, relatively speaking, it also has a strategic importance, of which humanity has no awareness at all.

Consider the analogy of the little tribe in the jungle. Do they have any understanding of how important their location or their resources might be to an outside culture? And yet this has been the motivating factor for these cultures being discovered, polluted and forever changed. We have such a situation now.

Therefore, what has motivated your visitors is not care and concern for human happiness, but the need for resources, the need for security and the need for power. The only exception to this is your Allies, who are fundamentally concerned with your integrity and your ability to survive in a Greater Community context. But they do not represent [the forces] who are in the world today, as they do not represent the majority of forces in the Greater Community.

This is an essential part of your Greater Community education, and it may be very difficult to consider at first. For there is so much hope and expectation, so much belief and fantasy considering the reality of other forms of life and their hoped-for benefit for humanity that this can be a very difficult thing to consider.

But this brings with it the need for self-reliance, the need for development, the need for education and the need to become stronger and more competent, mentally and physically. This is what humanity needs. And this is what is required.

There are greater spiritual forces that are here to help humanity to prepare, but they do not constitute your real [physical] visitors from the Greater Community.

The Greater Community is a vast network of communities—some of which are involved in commerce and trade and some of which are not. Some live in isolation in remote parts of the galaxy; others live in more highly inhabited areas.

It is not expected that you can understand how vast this network is or how it functions, but it is vital that you understand that certain realities exist in the Greater Community and will have direct bearing upon the future of humanity.

Let Us say again that when We present these ideas, We are dealing with a set of expectations and beliefs that do not exist within the human culture, which make it very hard to understand or see these things clearly.

Some people think that there are terrible forces out there, warlike and destructive. Others believe that they are all angelic brothers who are here to help humanity into a new dimension. And between these extreme points of view, there are all kinds of different interpretations.

But you must learn to see clearly and to understand clearly. It is not [a choice] between having a loving perception and a fearful one. Again, We say it is about whether you can see or not.

At all great events in human history that have been recorded and that have existed, certain people could see what was happening and many people could not. Certain people could see the emergence of a great conflict; many could not. Some could see the outcome of a great conflict; many could not. Some could act accordingly and responsibly and take a positive and contributing role; many could not.

Such will be the case now. As the Greater Community reality becomes more evident in the world, people will become more polarized in their positions and in their attitudes. There will be greater opposition, greater denial, greater fantasy because so many people will not be prepared to deal with this greater reality. They will retreat into their old ideas and habits, and some will deny its existence altogether. But it has always been like this in human affairs.

However, it is essential that a certain number of people become educated [about] the Greater Community and learn how to approach it wisely and with discernment. That will make all the difference in the outcome.

The next essential thing to realize is that humanity at present is not prepared for the Greater Community. It is not prepared psychologically. It is not prepared politically. It is not prepared in terms of its religious traditions, which, within this context, tend to hold people back.

The need for this preparation is so great and so profound, and many people feel the need to do something to prepare, to take a positive course of action, to become stronger and more competent, to become wiser and more discerning. But until now there has been no preparation for the Greater Community.

For as We have said, you cannot use human religion, you cannot use human psychology to learn about life in a greater panorama. You need a Teaching from the Greater Community about the Greater Community. You need a Teaching whose source is from the Creator to guarantee its purity, its power and its necessity in life.

The preparation is here now. But the question is, "Will people prepare? Will you prepare?" Or will you fall away to go find a place to hide, to go live in a happy place in the world where everything seems pleasant and content, to surround yourself with beautiful objects, beautiful sights and sounds and think beautiful thoughts about the world that is entering into a dire situation?

Even if the Greater Community were not here, this would still be the case. For the world is in decline, and humanity has not taken responsibility for this. But because the Greater Community is here, it changes the entire situation and provides the impetus that people everywhere will need to rise above their preoccupations, to rise above the tendencies for denial and fantasy, to grasp a real situation. And because the preparation is here in the form of The Greater

Community Way of Knowledge, people finally have the means to prepare and to prepare directly.

Humanity is not prepared. If you think about this, if you look about and see where people are investing themselves; what preoccupies people everywhere; where they devote their time, their energy and their resources; what they think is important and what predominates their attention, you will see that very few people can yet bear witness to the great events that are occurring now and that will come.

Another essential truth that must be recognized is that the Greater Community will not give humanity technology unless it wants humanity to become dependent. This is an essential idea. Again, many people who have thought about this think that the visitors will bring life-saving technology to humanity, which will solve so many of humanity's problems because technology is seen now as the saving grace. In earlier times, providence was considered the saving grace. Now it is technology.

However, technology tends to create more problems than it solves. But it is important for you to understand at the outset that should any technology be given to human governments, for example, it will not be for the benefit of humanity as much as it will be an appliance or an avenue to gain control over human affairs. After all, if a great piece of technology were given to humanity and humanity needed it and became reliant upon it, but its source were from outside the world, then you see you have given away a great deal for really very little.

The real gift that the Greater Community has to give to people is the reality of its presence and the reality of its intention. This is a call to awaken and to prepare. It is not a sign that more free things will be given to humanity. Humanity must awake from its slumber and become mature, become adults in a Greater Community of life.

Greater Community forces will not come and solve the world's problems, at least not for humanity. They will emphasize the preservation of the physical environment, but that is for their use and not for yours primarily. Attempts are being made now and have been underway for decades to replicate human, plant and animal forms, to preserve them for future use.

Therefore, do not come to the Greater Community forces with open hands, begging and pleading, greedy for their power, greedy for their technology, for this will trap you and this will blind you. Here you will lose your free will.

Next, it is important to understand that Greater Community influences will be focused on the governments of the world primarily. We shall speak in depth on this when We give Our discourse on the mental environment. But it is important for you to know that the influence will not likely be directed upon you as an individual because you do not have that much influence in the world as a whole, but [it will be directed] upon world leaders, upon influential people, upon those who possess tangible forms of power. They will be the focus of the influence. That is not to say that all authorities, all governments, are under the influence directly, but this is the focus. This is where the influence will be focused and is being focused now.

Now there are other manifestations of this that We will describe later on, but it is important for you to understand this. If you can realize that the Greater Community forces in the world today are being driven by their own needs, needs that you can also relate to and understand, this will give you a much clearer understanding of why they are here. Then you will not see them merely as good or bad; you will be able to understand what drives them and what their concerns are. Here we get out of a romantic view of the universe and come into a real relationship.

Next, it is important for you to understand that all intelligent life has a spiritual nature, but this spiritual nature can be as latent and undeveloped in them as it can be in human beings. In many highly technological societies, which are often the societies involved in travel and trade, this spiritual reality can be very subdued and very controlled.

After all, a highly technological society that must coordinate their activities over vast [distances] cannot be run by highly individualistic beings who have their own personal motivations to guide them. The manifestation of this varies considerably throughout the Greater Community.

Here again it is essential to realize that those who have traveled here to visit you physically do not represent highly evolved spiritual beings—intelligent, capable, technological, powerful in the mental environment, capable of mental persuasion, yes. But spiritually advanced, no.

Here you can begin to gain an understanding that the Greater Community is like the world except vastly larger with many of the same problems. Rather than being a saving reality that simply gives you everything you want and solves all of the problems of the world, it creates a whole new set of problems and a whole new set of opportunities. Its opportunities are what are saving. That is its saving grace. But you can only take advantage of these if you prepare accordingly.

Next, it is essential to understand that the primary focus of Greater Community activity in the world today is in two primary areas. We have already mentioned that there will be a focus on world governments. The second is on world religions.

It is in the realm of religion that people are most vulnerable, the least objective, the most easily persuaded. It is here that people will act against their best interests for inexplicable reasons. Do not think that these reasons and these motivations cannot be discerned and used.

There are forces in the world today from the Greater Community that could create the image of Jesus appearing at the foot of your bed. How would you discern if it were real or not? They could produce the mental image and project it into your mind. How would you know if it were real or not? Many would simply follow, yield, fall down on their knees, give in, dedicate themselves to whatever the image directed them to do.

Who has the discernment? Who has the capability to recognize reality from simple projections such as this? Who has the capability to recognize what is real and distinguish it from what is not? Everyone in the world has this potential. You have this potential. But is it developed sufficiently? Will you become an individual who simply cannot be fooled regardless of how persuasive the presentation may be?

Human religion is the wellspring of greater virtue and greater promise for humanity. But it is also the arena of greater superstition, greater mistrust and misunderstanding.

As governments use religions for their own purposes, the Greater Community can use religions for their own purposes. This will be focused on very large denominations of religions that have tremendous impact over many, many people. Here you need only influence a few to influence the many. Do not think it is difficult to do this. From a Greater Community standpoint, it is not difficult.

That is why in the Greater Community itself, those cultures and nations that have been able to preserve or cultivate any spiritual tradition at all have had to guard it carefully against the intrusion of others. This is a reality in the Greater Community. It is a reality that you must come to understand.

All that We are presenting in this discourse is to give you a foundation, to give you a foundation in truth and understanding. It is not to frighten you. It is to give you a solid foundation, which is actually very difficult to have in the world.

Most people cannot distinguish between reality and fantasy. They cannot discern the nature of their own thoughts. And they do not know what is influencing them in the mental environment.

Therefore, We understand that this is challenging, but it must be given simply and clearly as it really is, or you will succumb to persuasions that you cannot possibly understand, and you will not be able to distinguish what is happening within you, within your thoughts and emotions, nor what is happening in the world around you.

You must think in a very big way with very clear eyes. You must hear clearly without coloring the information to make it more favorable or pleasant. It is obvious that this is necessary, but it is so difficult for so many people. And everyone has some difficulty with this.

The world is emerging into a very real situation. What has been going on in the Greater Community has been going on since before humanity as a race even existed in this world.

And the spiritual work that the Creator has been undertaking throughout the Greater Community has been going on since before, long before, human religious traditions were ever started.

Because the Greater Community represents such a formidable set of circumstances, the Creator has set in motion a formidable set of powers and abilities and has generated a great network of service, both within manifest physical reality and beyond it as well.

If you can come to deal with these Greater Community realities, with these essential truths, then you put yourself in a position to begin to learn about the nature of the Creator's Work in the world and why you are the way you are.

CHAPTER 4

GREATER COMMUNITY INTELLIGENCE AND THE MENTAL ENVIRONMENT

We have saved one of the most essential truths about the Greater Community for this chapter. It has to do with the mental environment. The mental environment is the environment of thought. It is the environment in which you think. Invisible to the eye and to the senses, it nonetheless casts as great and sometimes an even greater influence upon you than does your physical environment, which you see, sense and touch.

The mental environment is an environment that is a true frontier for humanity. Very little has been learned here except in recent years, and even here the education in the mental environment is only in its earliest stages.

Walk into any person's home and you will experience the mental environment of that place. It is filled with that person's thoughts, feelings and memories. Walk into any group meeting or any assembly anywhere, and you will experience the mental environment of that place. It too will contain the thoughts, the emotions, the feelings and the memories of the people present. The mental environment of certain places can be so firmly imprinted upon the physical landscape that even years after a traumatic event has occurred, you can still feel it in that place.

People everywhere, who were either born with a greater sensitivity or have developed it subsequently, have begun to experience the reality of the mental environment. Yet everyone exercises themselves within the mental environment and is influenced within the mental environment.

The home you grew up in was a mental as well as a physical environment, and it shaped your thoughts and your attitudes and your feelings. Wherever you go, there is a mental environment.

It is not only people who create a mental environment. For instance, many people love to go into nature to experience its mental environment. It is how it feels to be there. It is not just how visually pretty it might be or how it tantalizes the senses, but it is how it feels there. The forces in nature in terms of the mental environment are not as strong as the forces in a human environment, as least not as far as humans are concerned.

People everywhere are always creating and responding to the mental environment. If there are many people present, it can take quite a while to develop a mental environment, and even here it is usually the product of a very focused attention.

Go to a political rally, for instance, where attention has been focused on a certain person or a certain set of ideas, and it will be a unique mental environment. However, if you walk into a train station, where people are going everywhere, preoccupied with themselves and with their own concerns, you will not experience a clear mental environment there.

Animals create their own mental environment, but its effects are far too weak to be felt by most people. Wherever there is thought, there is the mental environment.

This brings Us to a very important and essential truth about the Greater Community. Races that interact, trade, cooperate or compete with each other have all had to develop skill in the mental environment. Technology, because it is widely traded and exchanged and copied, ceases to become the critical factor.

The real power, the real essence, the real skill, is in being able to influence others. If you can influence others, you can persuade them to do what you want. You can read their secrets. You can receive their impressions. With skill, you can discern their nature, their temperament, their predispositions, their strengths and their weaknesses.

Amongst nations that are highly technically advanced, the critical factor becomes development and skill in the mental environment. Not every nation or race that trades or travels is highly skilled in the mental environment, but they all know about it and define it in their own terms, in their own ways. Yet it is known to them all.

This is a critical factor in terms of humanity's encountering Greater Community races and forces. They all have at least basic skill in the mental environment. Humanity does not have skill in the mental environment.

While it is true that people do attempt to persuade each other, the forces of persuasion are still very simple and crude. Salesmen and advertisers around the world are trying to persuade you to buy their product or their service and so forth. This is an effort to influence the mental environment, but this is still very basic.

You may try to influence someone to like you or to love you. You may try to influence someone to do business with you. You may try to influence your children to behave the way you want them to. This is all an effort to affect the mental environment. It is much more effective than force and far less destructive. And though humanity has been practicing the art of persuasion in the mental environment since time began because people are thinking beings, still humanity's skill in this arena is quite undeveloped.

If you consider this seriously, you will see that a Greater Community presence involving a small number of individuals can over time generate a significant impact upon human thought and priorities. Because in the Greater Community, cultures and races that travel often utilize a pooling of intelligence called group mind, they can exert tremendous influence. In practicing group mind, they do not all attempt to think identically to each other all the time, but they do become focused on one arena, and to this they dedicate their total and complete concentration.

This is very important to understand because in reality a visitor from another world may have no more intelligence than you do, but if they practice group mind, their impact upon the mental environment can overcome you. It will be far more powerful than anything that you as an individual could possibly generate.

That is why in the Greater Community there are rarely very few powerful individuals. Power is measured in terms of group mind, not in terms of individual will or capability. Here is one of the great differences between reality within your world, living in a human environment in isolation, and living within a Greater Community of life. There is no individual in the world who could overcome the group mind of another race if it was capable and powerfully focused.

Indeed, people experience this within the context of human life—
the power of the group, the will of the group, going where the group
goes. Does this not have a powerful effect upon you? And yet this is
a crude expression of what group mind really is and what it can
really do.

People's persuasion upon each other is often very emotionally based
and has a great deal to do with rejection and acceptance. But in the
real practice of group mind, it is focused on a deeper part of the
mind. It does not cater to basic emotions like this because in the
Greater Community, people realize if their emotions are being
affected [they] can learn to counteract this.

In Greater Community involvements, the exercise of group mind and
manipulation of the mental environment is far more sophisticated.
For example, if two different beings from different races are
interacting and they wish to influence each other, they both have
certain skills. They both can feel when they are being scrutinized.
They both can feel basic efforts at manipulation or influence.
Therefore, they must utilize skills that are far more subtle.

Another example within the world of focusing the mental
environment and the use of group mind is in the arena of prayer. If
you are praying for someone or with someone, you are attempting to
focus the mental environment and create a greater power between
the two of you by joining your minds together in a focused activity.
Here for a moment at least, you transcend your individuality and
create a greater mind. When large numbers of people are praying or
focusing, this creates an even greater power.

So the demonstration of group mind and the importance of the
mental environment are manifest throughout people's lives here,

but the great difference is in the degree of magnitude and the degree of skill. Here humanity is at a great disadvantage. Emotional, superstitious, preoccupied, people are as frightened by their ideas as by anything that could possibly happen to them on the outside. The situation, then, is ripe for a very potent form of manipulation.

Now you might think, "How can it be possible that someone could influence my thoughts directly? My thoughts are my own thoughts. There are certain boundaries over which no one can trespass. There are certain limits to how much you can influence someone!" There may be great limits in terms of how much you may influence another person, but these limits do not exist in reality. They only mark the extent of your skill and ability.

In recent years, governments around the world have attempted to use forms of manipulating the mental environment, and focusing, and viewing and so forth with some degree of success. This is partially stimulated by the fact that certain people in positions of power are aware of the Greater Community presence and of the power of these presences to create group mind and to focus it. That is why there is a great deal of activity in developing these skills in secret ways amongst secret organizations. This recognizes a fundamental need and a great disparity between the skill of your visitors and your own skill.

Contrary to popular notions, the visitors are not here to blow things up or to land vast armies. They do not need to use physical, brute force. Their numbers are really small. There are not vast armies of beings visiting the world. There are only small groups, but their activities are highly focused and integrated. They come to the world with a clear intention, with a mandate, with clear objectives, to which they are focusing all of their activities and interests.

But humanity does not have a clear mandate. Humanity does not have clear objectives. Humanity does not exert itself in a way that demonstrates an awareness of a unified purpose and mission. And so while your visitors may be no more intelligent than you are individually, their approach and their ability to exercise group mind and their awareness and understanding of the dynamics of influence in the mental environment put them in a highly superior position to produce results, results that they themselves do not have to physically demonstrate.

You simply influence people to have them do what you want. You create a mental condition. You create imagery. And they begin slowly and even very subtly to think along the lines you want them to think. Clearly, this is a form of mind control. The important thing to realize here is it is a fundamental exercise of power in the Greater Community.

It is an interesting thing that in the Greater Community amongst many interacting races, there is great care not to destroy technology, natural environments and so forth because these become rare and valuable. There is not the destructive violence that you see here in the world where things are wantonly destroyed. There is much more care to preserve resources in the Greater Community because resources are valuable. Instead, the competition for power is far more focused upon the mental environment.

In an adversarial situation, you are no match for the one who can influence your thoughts. It is remarkable, but your world could be overtaken without firing a shot. It will not be overtaken simply by exerting a group mind focus; it will be overtaken by permanently influencing the nature of thought.

This will not be done by introducing alien kinds of thinking or concepts. It will be done by taking advantage of traditional thinking. There is so much conflict and contentiousness in the world today, and the roots of this run so deep in the history of culture and consciousness that one has only to direct these powers and forces to gain desired results.

To accomplish this, human beings have been studied extensively in the last half century—psychologically, emotionally and physically. Because human beings do not have a great deal of strength in the mental environment, they can be made ready subjects for study. Their minds can be overtaken. They can have extensive experiences of contact with little or no conscious memory. And yet they are forever changed to a slight degree. If these contacts continue over time, a person's psychological capabilities will be greatly hindered, and they may in fact begin to think according to the will of their investigators. The change here is very subtle, but very complete.

The fundamental education for every human being is to begin to learn that they live in a mental environment and to have a sane and a sober approach to this. You as an individual have certain natural boundaries, but these can be transgressed. People influencing people, there is a great deal of limitation in the power of the effect, but in the context of relationship with Greater Community forces in a Greater Community reality, the contrast becomes much greater. The power of the mind over the power of the body is significant.

Therefore, it is important to remember that human beings have only evolved to interact with one another as intelligent life forms. Other forms of intelligent life in the world have either been subdued and destroyed or are generally ignored as having no competitive threat.

Therefore, your skill with one another may seem to be very great, but in a Greater Community context, it is not significant.

If you could but consciously remember or meet those visitors, you would see by their physiology, by their manner, by their demeanor, by the nature of their physical existence how much priority they give to influencing the mental environment.

You are physically stronger than most of them. You have much greater adaptive ability in the world. You can live far more successfully in terrestrial environments. You have much more physical strength, are much more robust, much stronger, but they seem to have the advantage.

Here We have a serious problem. If you consider this and realize the predicament that it puts humanity in, if you see the predicament it puts you in in terms of just dealing with other human beings, coming to terms with the fact that you are greatly influenced and trying to find out what the influences are and how they are affecting you, you will see that this represents a new threshold in education, and a vital one at that.

Here the ability to focus the mind and to control the vital energies becomes essential. This is not necessary spiritual development. It is intellectual development. It is developing power of the mind, which is different from power of the Spirit, as We shall soon describe.

You may ask, "Well, given these grave situations and given our tremendous disadvantages, why is not the Creator intervening on our behalf? What is here to save us? What is here to enable us?"

The answer is fundamental. The Creator has given you an intelligence that cannot be influenced in the mental environment. It cannot be persuaded. It cannot be dominated. It is entirely freethinking within you.

We are not talking about your thinking mind now. We are talking about a greater Mind that exists beyond your thinking mind. This is the Mind We call Knowledge. It represents your ability to know. It is the only part of your consciousness that is truly free in the mental environment. It is the only part of your consciousness that cannot be persuaded and dominated by greater forces.

This is why Knowledge becomes the focal point of spiritual development in the Greater Community. In essence, Knowledge is your spiritual reality. It cannot be influenced by anything in physical reality, thus again demonstrating that physical reality and spiritual reality are fundamentally different.

Why is the Creator not intervening? Because the Creator has put the answer within you and within each person. Knowledge exists in the Greater Community forces, Greater Community races, but in highly advanced societies it is fairly deleted from the individual's experience.

As We have said, in many societies of this nature individuals are taught to think according to certain codes and ethics and to strictly adhere to them under all circumstances. That is why their adaptive capability is so weak. That is why they need human resources in order to survive in the world because they cannot adapt to it.

This is their weakness and your strength. They want your strength because they need it if they are to become permanent residents here.

This is why the preparation for the Greater Community is so focused on learning The Way of Knowledge, on bringing your thinking mind and the greater knowing Mind within you together and uniting them. This completes you as a person and makes you whole. And this gives you strength and power in the mental environment. This puts you in a position to see, to know and to act with authority and with strength.

This is the great hope for humanity. This would be the great hope for humanity even if the Greater Community were not here. For there will never be a culture, a religion or a political system upon which everyone can agree. But everyone's Knowledge is in alignment, for there is no individual Knowledge—your Knowledge, my Knowledge. There is only your interpretation and my interpretation. At the level of Knowledge, it is all one.

In the mental environment, Knowledge is critical. It is the greatest power—greater than technology, greater than group mind. But to have this greatness, an individual or a group of individuals would have to develop a very high functioning capability in Knowledge. This is a great challenge, and this represents the essential education.

But Knowledge is only part of the education in the Greater Community. You must also learn Greater Community perspective and also learn how the Greater Community functions. This represents a tremendous education, but Knowledge still represents the core of the curriculum.

People ask, "Well, is this intuition?" No, this is greater than intuition. It is where intuition can come from, but it is greater. It is entirely another mind within you. It does not think like your personal mind. It does not deliberate. It does not choose. It does not go into prolonged states of confusion and uncertainty. It does not weigh this against that. It does not use reasoning as you think of it. It simply knows and waits for the moment to act.

Humanity is centuries away from having a social cohesion necessary to utilize group mind in a truly functional way in the Greater Community, though it is possible for individuals and small groups to develop these capabilities. But for society as a whole, it is centuries away and perhaps even longer. You are centuries away from having the technology to meet your visitors face to face on equal terms.

Therefore, the most important thing of cultivation is to gain a Greater Community education and perspective and to develop as a man and woman of Knowledge. This will require that you gain a basic education in the mental environment, something which unfortunately you cannot find in any college or university in the world. For this you need a special preparation, which is being provided here.

In learning about the mental environment, you begin to discern the mental environment of your own personal life and the forces that are prevalent there. You begin to understand the dynamics of relationships and how people influence each other. You begin to take responsibility for who and what is influencing you and to arrange them accordingly. You begin to see the negative effects of inappropriate persuasion and the positive effects of helpful persuasion. You begin to realize that there are no neutral relationships, that everyone is either strengthening you or weakening you to some degree. This is primarily important in terms of your primary relationships.

Here you begin to break [new] ground in learning the real mysteries of life. Here you gain strength and capability. Here you replace fear with skill. Here you replace judgment with compassion.

If you learn about the mental environment, and this is governed by Knowledge and wisdom, then the result will be very different from what your visitors can demonstrate. But people are superstitious. They do not distinguish the mental from the spiritual environment. They cannot differentiate between the different realities of which they are themselves a part. They cannot distinguish between subtle forms of manipulation and spiritual acknowledgments and empowerment. They cannot distinguish between these things until the results can be proven, and by then it is too late.

Again, if there were no Greater Community in the world, it would still be your primary education—if you seek to become wise and compassionate, if you seek to become whole and complete within yourself. But the presence of the Greater Community makes the situation far more demanding and makes the requirement for education far greater. In this it has a saving grace.

There are many people in the world already who have been contacted by the Greater Community forces. Where they may attempt to exert influence upon the political and religious institutions that govern the society, they nonetheless are seeking to gain influence amongst people everywhere through direct contact. This is so behind the scenes and people are so preoccupied, they cannot see this happening. But it can be felt.

You have had experiences of discomfort and unrest that perhaps you attributed to your immediate circumstances or to your own emotional states, but which in reality were the result of you experiencing something in the mental environment that was either directed towards you or directed towards something near you.

You can feel the presence of the Greater Community. They are very good at concealing themselves, but you can feel their presence. And beyond this, you can learn to know who they are and why they are here, for this can be known at the level of Knowledge.

To prepare humanity for the Greater Community, a great Teaching is being brought. Its Source is the Creator, and it is supported by your Allies throughout the Greater Community, who support the emergence of Knowledge everywhere and who seek to keep Knowledge alive in the universe.

This is called The Greater Community Way of Knowledge. It represents a tradition of learning and transmission that is older than humanity itself. It is being given to humanity to prepare humanity to unite its world, to rescue its environment, to elevate its consciousness and abilities and to prepare for its new life in the Greater Community. It is unlike any other Teaching in the world. It represents the wisdom of the ages that human traditions have kept alive, but beyond this it represents Wisdom of the Greater Community, which has never been learned in the world before.

The great need of humanity has brought a great response from the Creator. It has brought a great promise, a great opportunity, a great need. Only a Teaching from beyond the world could prepare you to engage with life from beyond the world and to enter an arena that goes beyond the former limits of your isolated state.

This book serves as an introduction to The Greater Community Way of Knowledge, but it also presents the great need and calling in life today, greater than all of the chronic problems that have plagued humanity through the ages.

There are many things in the world that need great attention at all levels of existence, in all places. But fundamentally humanity must maintain its integrity as a race and its self-determination within the world. These are being directly challenged by the presence of the Greater Community and will be increasingly challenged as time goes on.

This is not something that you can ask someone else to do something about. It is your responsibility. It is the responsibility of each person. It is the responsibility of those especially who can feel and who can know the great need and calling of the time and who can respond to the education in The Way of Knowledge that is required. They can rise above their fears and their desires and their preferences to take action and thus gain the great benefit of living a life according to truth and to purpose. And they will learn for those who cannot learn, and they will contribute to the world where others have not been able to contribute.

This is the work of Knowledge. This is the work of the Divine within you. This is what Divinity means within the Greater Community. When you take away culture, tradition and all the edifices of religion, to the very essence of what spirituality really is, when you take all of it away, what you have is Knowledge, the driving spiritual intelligence and force that oversees the universe and that gives beings everywhere promise and true capability.

Yet just as in your world, Knowledge is being thwarted and denied throughout the Greater Community. And just like in your world, real wisdom, real skill and the great healing powers are there and unique.

So while We prepare for something so beyond the current limits of human understanding, We must also return to the very essence of who people are and what they have brought with them into the world from their Ancient Home.

Thus, what is great within you responds to what is great within the world. If you only respond to what is small in the world, you will only know what is small within yourself. But if you can respond to what is great within the world, you will find what is great within yourself. This is because your inner and outer reality are directly related.

Knowledge within you has come to the world to give. It is directly connected to the evolution of the world. It is not governed by human desire, human fear or human wishes. It is not governed by these things in any culture or race in the Greater Community. It has its own focus and purpose.

If you are afraid of this, you are but afraid of your true Self and afraid of the Greater Power and the greater life that has brought you here.

What could be more important than this? This is the source of all selfless activity. This is the source of all contribution and creation in the world. What could be more important than this? The times in which you live call for this now more powerfully than ever before.

The Greater Community is in the world. It is exerting its influence in the mental environment. It is demonstrating its skill among a great population of human beings who do not have this skill and cannot respond with wisdom.

To find your way, you must find the forces that support you and the forces that hinder you, many of which are felt but that are unseen. You must learn to become responsible not only in the physical environment in the world of people, places and things, but you must become responsible and competent in the mental environment, which is the realm of thought and influence.

This will give you strength and integrity as a person and will enable you to harmonize and balance your life by balancing the influences that affect you directly. And this will, over time, teach you how you can positively influence others so that they too may become men and women of Knowledge.

All this is part of the world's emergence into the Greater Community. All this is part of the turbulent and difficult times in which you live. All this is part of your great calling. All of this is part of your contribution to the world, in whatever form that it may be exercised.

CHAPTER 5

RESOURCES, TRADE AND COMPETITION IN THE GREATER COMMUNITY

In order to give you a clearer understanding of what life is like in the Greater Community, and more specifically what motivates most of those who are coming to visit your world, it is important that We speak further on this subject.

In the Greater Community, societies that have developed technologically and have expanded their empires always outstrip their own world's natural resources and therefore must seek resources from beyond their own boundaries. This brings them into the realm of trade and commerce. As a result, they are involved in a very competitive environment with other worlds that seek the same kinds of resources. This has led overall to a very complicated set of relationships and involvements, alliances and so forth, amongst nations and races that are involved in trade and commerce.

The need for resources and the nature of the competitive environment account in large part for the motivation for most of those groups who are visiting your world at this time. They are primarily concerned with gaining resources from your world— biological resources, mineral resources and genetic resources. They are driven by this need.

Here again We must emphasize that they are not here because they are connected to spiritual traditions upon the Earth. They are not here to fulfill ancient prophecies. They are not here to spiritually uplift humanity. They will take advantage of spiritual ambitions and spiritual traditions if it meets their need, but that is not their purpose for being here.

Here you must come to understand that your world is recognized as a rich biological storehouse, a world that represents tremendous resource capacities. This naturally makes it interesting to those on the outside. What human beings take for granted in their natural environment, what they spoil and neglect here, is in fact highly prized by others who are aware of it.

Here again We draw upon the analogy of the ancient dwellers in the jungle, who find themselves discovered for purposes that they cannot even fathom. They are discovered because others are looking for resources. They are looking for wealth. They are driven by their own needs and by the competitive environment that they live within. In the history of this world, how often has this been demonstrated, and how often has the native population been decimated or forever changed as a result?

In the Greater Community, not all nations trade. Not all nations seek to have relations beyond their own borders. There are small enclaves of individuals, small groups, that seek to be self-sufficient and not become involved in the complicated affairs of the Greater Community. They seek to remain hidden, to not have their world's resources discovered. They do not welcome resource explorers. They do not want involvement in the Greater Community.

This is a privilege: the ability to be self-sufficient, the ability to remain outside the sphere of commerce, trade and competition. It is a right that is difficult to achieve and difficult to maintain, particularly if your world's district or area is recognized to have great assets.

In the case of your world, it is far too late to achieve this autonomy though it is possible to secure it in the future. The resources of the world have already been recognized and have been utilized for centuries. Now that humanity has become the pre-eminent race on the Earth and poses within itself a potential threat as a potential participant in Greater Community affairs, those who have been using these resources are now taking an active effort to influence humanity, to take advantage of humanity's weaknesses and to capitalize on humanity's strengths.

Still others have visited your world merely to observe you—to observe your behavior, to observe your tendencies. And, as We have said earlier, you also have Allies who seek to support the emergence of Knowledge within the world, to support the development of Greater Community Spirituality within the world, to help to lift humanity above and beyond its tribal conflicts and identities so that it may become a responsible and cooperative global race, able to maintain its own resources and to establish its self-determination.

It is again very important to recognize that the Greater Community is a physical environment primarily, governed by physical laws of which you are aware. Races of nations everywhere must contend with their fundamental survival needs, which becomes very complicated when you are involved in commerce and trade with other races.

If your world is recognized as being rich and valuable, this poses many problems, for others will contend with you for it. Though outright conquest is discouraged among civilized nations, there are subtle means to achieve the same ends. This involves skill and focus in the mental environment and a careful understanding of diplomatic affairs between worlds.

Of course, humanity has none of these skills. It has not developed capabilities in the mental environment. It has not been able to establish a group mind experience that is adequate to meet the situation at hand. And it has no diplomatic skill in terms of dealing with other races.

And yet humanity dwells upon a world that is immensely rich. It is like the native village deep in the jungle, living on top of a great mineral wealth unknowingly, a mineral wealth that draws the rest of the world to it. Such is the case with humanity in the world today.

Therefore, again realize that your visitors are here for very prosaic reasons. They are not Divine, and they are not evil. They are simply driven by their own needs. They recognize your weakness and your incompetence, the degradation of the environment, and they seek to establish themselves here to maintain those resources that they desire and to take advantage of humanity's skills and adaptive abilities.

Should humanity be able to emerge successfully into the Greater Community, it will have to deal with the issue of trade and commerce. This is a very complicated issue and one that requires great skill and discernment on the part of the participants.

Here humanity will find itself thwarted in its attempts to go beyond its own solar system, for it will come to find that the regions that it wishes to explore have already been laid claim to. Instead of being seemingly alone in a great empty universe, it will find itself coming up against the properties and interests and priorities of other races.

There are Greater Community establishments even within this solar system, but they are primarily established to observe affairs upon Earth. Within the Greater Community, amongst trading nations there are certain ethics and standards that are generally followed and honored, though there are notable exceptions. One of these ethics stipulates that a race has primary rights to all worlds within its solar system and that these cannot be violated by force by any outside race. The violation of these ethics brings severe repercussions and can in fact disrupt the flow of trade and commerce, leading to contentiousness and conflict.

There is also an ethic in the Greater Community that stipulates that should a race spoil its own natural environment, then other races have the right to come and displace it. Though this is a controversial clause and is rarely acted upon, it is still generally held amongst most races that are involved in trade and commerce.

Now the Greater Community is very vast and usually nations that are involved in trade and commerce only have one or two or three trading partners. Everyone does not trade with everyone else. It is far too vast for that. And so when We speak about ethics in Greater Community trade and commerce, We are talking about something that is reinforced for practical reasons, but not by everyone who is involved. We mention this here so that you understand that there are certain standards that govern behavior and are generally recognized, particularly by races in this region in which your world resides.

Because humanity is in the process of rapidly destroying its natural environment, this gives others the motivation to become involved and to take self-serving action to preserve their interests here and to attempt to offset humanity's tendencies.

There is an ethic in the Greater Community within trade and commerce that stipulates that military force will not be used amongst trading nations. Violation of this creates disorder and becomes very difficult and costly for those who are involved. And because many nations are skillful in the mental environment, they have found other ways to gain advantages and usually regard use of physical force, such as [that which is] so commonly demonstrated here in the world, as barbaric and unnecessary.

This brings Us to a very important point, which We have referred to earlier, but which now requires some explanation. It is very important for you to understand, given what We have presented thus far, that nations that are involved in trade and commerce generally do not represent civilizations that are spiritually advanced. Let Us elaborate on this.

In the Greater Community, the ability to exercise Knowledge is recognized as a great skill and asset. And there is generally an attempt to gain access to those who have these skills and to employ them for your own purposes. Therefore, the Wise must retreat to maintain their abilities and the integrity of their own societies.

Those groups and nations that are spiritually advanced, therefore, rarely are involved in trade except in a clandestine manner and attempt at great cost and difficulty to maintain insulation within the Greater Community environment. They have come to recognize everywhere that demonstrating their skill and prowess only invites inquiry and intervention.

This brings Us to a very fundamental idea in learning The Greater Community Way of Knowledge and in preparing for the Greater Community itself. This idea is that the Wise remain hidden. The Wise remain hidden to remain wise. If they do not remain hidden, they are exploited and overtaken.

Therefore, it is important to understand that nations that are involved in resource exploration, commerce or the acquisition of properties do not represent those who are spiritually advanced. They do not represent those who are strong in Knowledge. For Knowledge, being the spiritual intelligence, would not promote or allow this to occur amongst those who are bonded to Knowledge and who are close to Knowledge.

Therefore, you must understand that except for your Allies, who watch you from afar, those who are involved in this world today do not represent the spiritually advanced races of which We speak. There is a great deal of confusion about this, and this confusion will have tragic consequences if it is not corrected.

Consider this idea that the Wise remain hidden. Is this not also true within your own world? You will find that the wisest teachers, those who are considered strong and saintly, live in seclusion and are not readily accessible to many people, except in rare situations. And in those rare situations, the skill and ability of these individuals bring upon them great difficulties, considerable scrutiny and intervention, which is very difficult to contend with.

Thus, within your own world, the Wise remain hidden. The greatest teachers within the world are hard to find. Though they may publish their works in a written form, they reserve their greatest talents and gifts for the serious students who have taken the pains to find them and who have committed themselves to study, to learn the greater ways of Knowledge.

This is even more true in the Greater Community, where intelligence is recognized as a resource and is sought after and highly valued. Thus, those who are wise and strong in The Way of Knowledge attempt to find retreat in the Greater Community. They attempt to insulate their societies, and to protect and preserve their mental integrity, and to fortify [themselves] against outside intervention from interfering with the mental environment they have taken such great pains to create and to maintain.

You can think of many examples within your world—between the individual who is the salesman and the individual who is the saint. Which takes a strong public stance and which withdraws to remain hidden?

Therefore, do not make the critical and fatal error of thinking that those who are visiting the world are spiritually advanced. Because they have skill in the mental environment, because they may be able to communicate without words and have great skill in influencing those whom they encounter does not mean that they are spiritually advanced or that they are guided by Knowledge itself.

This is a critical understanding. Here you begin to realize both the strengths of your visitors and their weaknesses. And here you can more fully understand the strengths that humanity already has. For humanity—despite its tribal conflicts and its self-preoccupation and its destructive tendencies—has been able to maintain rich spiritual heritages within the world. Knowledge has been kept alive within the world, to a far greater extent than it has within the Greater Community itself. Again, you must distinguish technological advancement and skill in the mental environment from spiritual awareness, understanding and capability.

Those who develop skill in Knowledge will seek to preserve their skill and will have to learn to recognize all the forces around them that

seek to intervene and to prevent their skill from being cultivated and
expressed appropriately.

For example, if you were an individual who had a great capacity to
know, to foresee events to come, to discern relationships, and to have
ability in the mental environment, would not others seek you out for
their own advantages? If it became known that you had these skills,
would you not then be sought after?

Everyone would want you to help them with their problems, and
though you may want to contribute to others and to bestow your gifts
upon them, over time you would have to learn to become discerning
as to where to give your gifts and where to withhold them, who is the
real recipient and who merely wishes to use you for their own
purposes.

In the Greater Community, this education becomes vital for survival,
for there is skill in the mental environment, and others will seek to
use you for their own benefit. What little rewards you may receive
from them are far outweighed by the loss of freedom, the loss of
ability and the ultimate promise of collapse that their involvement
will bring for you.

In the world today, those who have great sensitivities, who have
cultivated their psychic abilities, either for pleasure or for profit, and
have attempted to make these skills known, put themselves at great
risk. They do not realize what jeopardy they place themselves in.

This is attempting to have power without wisdom. Wisdom always
tries to protect the gift of the giver and to direct the giving where it
can be most effective.

In the world today, the Greater Community forces who are present are especially interested in those who have great psychic abilities, who have made these publicly known and available. You may wonder why people are receiving so many messages from so many places and why there is such confusion and conflict between the messages that people receive. And you may wonder, "Where do these messages come from?" Let Us speak on this now.

It is important to understand that people in the world have very little skill so far in being able to distinguish the mental environment from the spiritual reality. There is a great deal of level confusion here.

People think if they are intuitive and have psychic experiences that this is spiritual in nature, but that is not true. For those who have absolutely no spiritual awareness or foundation can learn to exercise great skill in the mental environment. They can read and interpret the thoughts of others, and they can cast an influence on the environment so that others over time will come to think the way they want them to think.

There are many people in the world today who feel they have had spiritual contact when in fact they are in contact with those in the Greater Community. It is not difficult for the world's visitors to utilize the spiritual superstitions and imagery that are present today to make contact and to gain influence.

In fact, in the world today there is great effort amongst your visitors to gain access to those who are spiritually sensitive, who are mentally sensitive and to cast an influence upon them. Here the emphasis is to align these individuals with the source of the message, to pacify them and to put them in a state of pliant receptivity.

This has tragic consequences, for the persons who are affected over time will lose their personal will. They will lose their self-determination. They will lose their ability to discriminate and to discern. They will be encouraged to be constantly open to whatever is given to them, and over time they will not be able to discern whether what is being given to them is correct or not. They will be enthralled, but they will also be enslaved. This then represents subtle manipulation of the mental environment.

Please do not be confused in thinking that all people who are receiving spiritual counsel are being affected by the Greater Community, for this is not the case. There is also a great deal of work being done by the forces of the Creator to enlighten humanity, to direct humanity, to uplift humanity. But if you step back and look at the whole picture, you will see that both of these activities are going on, and there is a great deal of confusion.

So how do you sort this out? How do you make sense out of this? How do you say, "Well, which is true guidance and which is a form of manipulation?" The key question and the key element in answering this and resolving it for yourself has to do with the reclamation of Knowledge.

Any spiritual teaching that fortifies the individual's ability to see, to know, to discern and to act represents a true teaching and a true counsel. Any teaching that encourages the person to acquiesce, to become pliant, to become indiscriminately receptive, to give up their self-determination, to acquiesce, to become entirely subjective in their viewpoint, these individuals are suffering from a form of manipulation. Regardless of the emphasis on spirituality, Knowledge is being taken away from them. They are being encouraged to be divorced from what they know and what they most deeply feel.

You can see the manifestation of both of these tendencies in the world today, and it will take great care and discernment to be able to tell them apart. For the language used may be very similar. The ideals presented may seem to be one and the same. But the entire emphasis of the teaching is different.

As We have said, the Greater Community forces who are in the world today, who are seeking to gain dominion here, will attempt to use two fundamental arenas of human authority—the institutions of government and the institutions of religion. These represent the two great power centers in human affairs, and these are where most of the attention will be focused.

Yet it is important to understand that any individual who demonstrates a unique and greater sensitivity also becomes a target of inquiry for those from the Greater Community. For remember, greater sensitivity, greater insight, is something that your visitors are looking for. It is something they need.

They need these natural intuitive capabilities in order to establish themselves here, for they do not have an intuitive connection to this world. They do not have an intuitive connection to life forms and the forces of nature. They are not connected to the elements of the Earth, so they need these capabilities and will seek them out in individuals wherever they can find them. And those who are the most open and the most indiscriminate are the most vulnerable for this kind of intervention.

In learning The Way of Knowledge, men and women are encouraged to develop great sensitivity and the ability to focus, but they are also prepared to be very discerning and to learn to understand the greater forces within themselves and within their immediate environment that affect them and how these effects are brought about. They are encouraged to take a very sober approach to relationships and to interactions in the world.

How different this is from the great romantic ideals that are promoted within certain spiritual circles. How different this is from those who become swept up in the glorious images of themselves in the world or in their strict ideologies that were established long ago.

The man or woman of Knowledge must learn to see and see clearly, must learn to discern where to open themselves and where not to open themselves, where to give their gifts and where not to give their gifts. They must come to recognize the greater forces, those forces that are beneficial and those forces that are not beneficial, both within the world itself and within the Greater Community into which your world is now emerging.

People who promote the development of sensitivity without this discrimination and without this training and preparation are encouraging people to be at great risk. Even if the Greater Community were not here, this would still produce great risk. For if you become too sensitive without discernment, it becomes very difficult to live within the world. The world becomes too irritating, too harsh, too grating to experience, and you are forced to withdraw, not to cultivate your strengths but simply to avoid the vicissitudes of life. Here the individual becomes weaker and weaker, less capable. They lose strength, they lose self-determination, they lose the ability to interact with life.

This is happening in the world today. It is being accelerated by the presence of the Greater Community, who have the power to neutralize the human spirit. They have the power to gain control over the prevailing ideas and beliefs of people here.

The only real defense against this is the cultivation of Knowledge and the development of a Greater Community perspective and understanding. Here men and women require skill—the skill to find Knowledge within themselves, the great knowing Mind that you have been endowed with from the Creator; the skills to discern interactions, to discern the mental environment and to discern the greater forces that are affecting humanity and that are moving you within your own life.

It is quite remarkable, but people do not realize the extent of influence upon their lives. There is a general belief that people are the captain of their own ship, and yet when you visit their ship there is no captain to be found. There is no authority; there is no determination. The ambivalence and passivity that you see within people is evidence that they are not in charge of their affairs and have not taken responsibility for their lives or for their destiny.

The mental environment of people everywhere has been dominated by forces that are generated from beyond themselves to such an extent that they cannot even discern what is theirs and what is not theirs. In fact, there is very little original thinking within the human family at this time. This is both sad and tragic. It is sad because the human spirit is creative and wonderfully endowed. And it is tragic because this brings grave possibilities for humanity as it undergoes its emergence into the Greater Community.

To be within the Greater Community, you must be smarter than you have ever been, more discerning than you have ever been, more responsible than you have ever been, and you must become strong with Knowledge.

If you could go beyond your world and travel about the Greater Community, you would see how races everywhere have been enslaved and dominated because they have not developed these fundamental capabilities. There is very little freedom in the Greater Community. There is very little personal freedom in the Greater Community.

This is difficult to accept, perhaps, but it is essential for your education. Freedom is the result of gaining these skills We have indicated and to cultivate them within yourself and within your relationships and within your communities. The failure to do this naturally leads one and naturally leads one's society to become dominated. In the Greater Community, the strong do rule the weak, as is the case within the world.

Within Greater Community commerce and trade, there are many, many societies that are merely client states of other races. They have lost their self-determination, both through the contracts that they establish with other races and through their ability, or lack of ability, to maintain their focus and their determination within their relationships with others. This is prevalent in the Greater Community.

Indeed, if you could travel about widely, you would see that it is rare when you find a race that is truly independent and self-determined. This is the result of lack of training and ability, and in part it is the result of engagement with other races and of becoming interdependent with them.

Therefore, the Wise remain hidden in the Greater Community and within your world. But humanity is not hidden, and it is not yet wise enough to maintain its insulation or to discern intervention from the outside.

So here again We come to a situation. We come to find that humanity is at a great disadvantage, that humanity is extremely vulnerable, that humanity does not have the skill or the discernment or the cooperation within its own family to maintain a strong and self-determined position in the Greater Community.

And here We find that humanity is dwelling upon a world whose wealth and value it does not yet fully realize. It has not had the exposure to the Greater Community to understand its wealth or its grave predicament. This is the unfortunate result of living in isolation for so long.

But now there is a great calling around the world for people to gain strength, to become strong individually and collectively, to gain the power of Knowledge, which is their greatest endowment and natural birthright, to gain the foundation for cooperation in union with others and to unite the world beyond tribal and cultural differences.

For it is only a united humanity that will be able to survive and to prosper in the Greater Community. A world warring in divisive groups and tribes can only fall under the domination of outside forces who will take advantage of these conflicts and of these identifications and of these preoccupations for their own advantages.

To prosper and to survive in the Greater Community, to maintain your freedom and self-determination within this larger environment of life, humanity must become unified. This will be a great, difficult and painful process, but life requires it, your circumstances require it, the presence of the Greater Community here requires it.

This will be fostered by the growing realization that humanity is in a grave situation and that everyone everywhere within the world is in the same situation and has the same fundamental problem. This problem will be generated by the deterioration of the natural world, by the loss of the world's resources, and most fundamentally by the presence of the Greater Community.

It is unfortunate but true that only a threat from the outside will be able to finally unite humanity and to establish a common need and a common cause here that will enable people to step above and beyond their tribal differences and identities.

A world full of divisive tribes cannot survive in the Greater Community. It cannot maintain its self-determination, for it will not be strong enough. It will not have the cooperation and the strength necessary to contend with other races who have achieved a state of uniformity and who represent a group will.

Knowledge within you makes this possible, but there must be a way to Knowledge, a Greater Community Way of Knowledge that can prepare you to understand the Greater Community, to understand your true nature, to enable you to gain your essential strength and to claim your greatest endowments for the restoration and the protection of the world.

Because of humanity's degradation of its natural environment, it will be forced in the future to seek resources from beyond its separate shores. This will place requirements upon the human race and will require the cultivation of significant and tremendous skills and abilities, for you will not find that the universe is there for your taking.

It is as if the world were a house and your solar system represented your yard. You may go around your yard as you please, but if you seek to go beyond it, you enter someone else's property. You trespass on someone else's interests or establishments.

Here you will find that trade and commerce are largely self-regulated. There is no one great organization that rules and manages everything. That is not possible in a Greater Community environment. Certain ethics and standards are maintained for practical reasons—to maintain peace, to maintain continuity of trade and to establish an environment where most nations can prosper, even if a few suffer as a result.

Here humanity will find itself in the midst of a larger interaction of life, in a situation that has been long established and will not be changed by humanity's entrance. It is like the young child entering the world. They may have great ideas about themselves and great expectations about what life will give them, but once they enter the real world, it is quite different.

Humanity here is like the adolescent venturing out into life for the first time, filled with ideals, filled with expectations, filled with a sense of omnipotence and divine appointment, but what awaits humanity in the Greater Community is a difficult and sobering learning process.

Yet for humanity to even have this opportunity to participate in the Greater Community, to engage in trade and commerce, which will become necessary in the future, it must develop the foundation, it must have the strength and the environment of cooperation within the human family to even be able to begin.

You may ask, "What does this have to do with me? I am just a person. I am just an individual. I have to go to work tomorrow. I have to take care of my own affairs!"

This has everything to do with you because the greater purpose that brought you into the world is directly related to the evolution of the world and to the greater needs of humanity. Whatever your gift may be, however it may be expressed, everything We are presenting in this book is entirely relevant to your ability to comprehend your true nature and to express it effectively.

Here within the realm of your own life, you will find that the precept, "The Wise remain hidden," is entirely true and valid. Here within the context of your own life, you will see that you too have to maintain and establish your own mental environment, and learn how to do this and how to maintain it in a world that will always be seeming to break it down. Here you too, within the context of your own life, will have to learn what the foundation of real relationship is and how greater harmony and cooperation can be established in your affairs with others.

Everything that is true in the Greater Community holds true within the sphere of your own life. But even as you come to realize this, should you undertake the preparation in The Way of Knowledge, you will also find that it is necessary for you to understand the greater panorama of life in which you live.

It is not enough simply to take care of your own personal affairs and to maintain yourself, for you have a greater responsibility and a greater opportunity in life. If you seek to know your true nature, if you seek to experience and to express the greater purpose that has brought you into the world, then you must step beyond your self-preoccupation. You must not only manage your affairs harmoniously, but see what awaits you beyond that, what calls to you to respond.

There are no great rewards in leading a small and self-centered life. There are only small rewards and great costs. But entering into a greater life, there are great costs but great rewards, far greater than the costs involved.

You can only know this to be true by taking the steps yourself and by discovering what they mean for you. We can only point to the greater environment in which you live and to the greater forces that are shaping your life and your future and destiny. But you yourself must find out.

Here We give you the perspective and the understanding that will enable you to truly comprehend the nature of your presence here and the greater events that are shaping the destiny of the world.

CHAPTER 6

THE MEANING OF SPIRITUAL DEVELOPMENT IN THE GREATER COMMUNITY

Because the Greater Community represents such a vast network of societies and such a tremendous variety of environments and races and natures and so forth, spirituality must take on a more universal character, a more essential nature. If it is encrusted with cultural images, if it is intertwined with the social history of certain cultures alone, then its essential nature becomes clouded and more difficult to access.

For spirituality to be shared in the Greater Community, the artifices of culture and history, which are genuine within themselves, must be set aside to deal with the essential elements of what spirituality really is and what it is here to do. While each of varied nations, at least those that have maintained a spiritual tradition, might have their own local customs and ceremonies, in order for them to share this with other races or to communicate about it with other races, they must share the essential nature of what spirituality is and what it is here to do.

This enables you to have a great opportunity to find out the answers to these fundamental questions for yourself. When We speak of spirituality, We are talking about the essence of what spirituality is. We are not speaking of the institutions that have been built around it or that seek to use it or to manipulate it. We are not speaking of tribal culture and history. We are speaking of an essential force that lives within you, a force We call Knowledge.

Because the Greater Community is so vast and so varied, only what is essential can be translated from one world to another. We call this a translatable spirituality. It is this very translatable spirituality that must become the focus now of human religious study and inquiry. You can never agree on culture, history and values, but at the level of Knowledge, people resonate together. People are united at the level of Knowledge, for Knowledge is one throughout the universe. It is the great peacemaker. It is the foundation for true cooperation and recognition. It is the greatest medium for communication and understanding.

Yet within the Greater Community and within the world, the experience and the expression of Knowledge are rare and precious. As We have said, there are many many technologically advanced races in the Greater Community who have no tradition of spiritual practice or study at all. For them, technology is a religion. For them, their social goals and objectives are their religion. Theirs is the religion of the state, of the group, of the authority that they establish for themselves. However, the Greater Community contains tens of thousands of advanced races, even within your sector, even within your local universe. So there is great variety here.

But what is essential to all intelligent life? What is essential spirituality? What can be translated from one world to another where the environment, the history, the culture and the values are so different and so varied? What holds true for everyone regardless of their form, their society, their world and their orientation?

This is the essence of spirituality. This is translatable spirituality. This is what We call Knowledge. The development of Knowledge focuses on the person's ability to know beyond belief, beyond speculation, the ability to recognize what is true and to respond to it appropriately.

Here you do not learn how to know. Instead, you learn how to reclaim what you know and the ability to know. But here you must learn wisdom—the wisdom to recognize Knowledge, to discern it from the other forces within you; the wisdom to know when and how to express Knowledge; the wisdom to know who possesses Knowledge and who does not and how to participate with them accordingly; the wisdom to know the role of Knowledge within your life and your intrinsic relationship with it; the wisdom to practice forbearance, insight, discernment, compassion and contribution according to the wisdom and grace of Knowledge itself.

How rare this is in human life and yet how rare it is in the Greater Community as well. What a precious commodity. What a precious reality—so precious in fact that it is greatly sought after by those who are aware of it.

As the Creator works behind the scenes within the world and within your life, the Creator works behind the scenes within the Greater Community as well. Here there are Unseen Forces that further and stimulate the cultivation of Knowledge everywhere where intelligent life exists, utilizing all available opportunities to achieve this. Yet in so many places in the Greater Community, in so many civilizations and cultures, the opportunities are few.

At the basis of the preparation for the Greater Community, of your preparation for the Greater Community, there must be the focus on the development of this essential spirituality, for this represents not only your greatest abilities and skills, but your ability to be free within a Greater Community where freedom is rarely known.

It is important for you to realize here that the freedom that you enjoy as human beings in the world today is far greater than the freedom that most individuals enjoy in the Greater Community. Your freedom, therefore, is precious even if it is not well utilized. It presents remarkable opportunities even though these opportunities are neglected.

Therefore, never take for granted that life in the Greater Community offers many opportunities for personal freedom, for this is not the case. Within this difficult learning situation in the Greater Community, the Creator and the Unseen Forces that represent the Creator must work behind the scenes to stimulate individuals of promise and to develop groups or communities of Knowledge.

In certain places, this has been achieved to a very high level of ability. There are small communities of Knowledge and individuals of Knowledge in the Greater Community that have achieved great heights of understanding and ability, but as We have said, these are not communities that are involved in trade and commerce. These are not communities that expose themselves to the difficulties of life in the Greater Community. Instead, they are hidden and secret, hidden far away, hidden so that they may work within their respective worlds without repression and hindrance.

Yes, in many worlds there are state religions, highly codified and highly regulated, but these do not represent communities of Knowledge. Throughout the Greater Community, communities of Knowledge and individuals of Knowledge must maintain in great secrecy their true nature and capabilities to avoid being manipulated, to avoid being controlled, to avoid having their great gifts utilized by the powers of state, by the powers of another group will.

Here you can begin to realize that there is a great distinction between what spirituality is and what religion becomes. Yet religion is also necessary, for there must be a tradition and there must be a mechanism, a medium, through which spirituality can express itself and become available. Therefore, do not malign religion, but understand that if religion becomes public and well known, then it is merely taken over; it is used; it is manipulated by the powers of state, by the powers of society, wherever it becomes manifest.

In the Greater Community, the real communities of Knowledge, the true adept individuals, are in nearly all cases hidden away—out of view, beyond the reach of commerce and trade, beyond the reach of the great manipulating forces that are so active in life today in the Greater Community.

Therefore, do not look to the religions of your world to find these communities though there are communities of Knowledge in the world today. You will not find them in the public places of worship. You will not find them in the public organizations. You will not find them at the surface of life where they can be easily seen and greatly affected.

This requires the development of tremendous discernment and discretion, fundamental skills in learning how to live life effectively and successfully. Look here to the Greater Community for your examples, for humanity has only manifested the reality of these matters to a certain degree, but in the Greater Community they have been lived out completely.

The successes and the failures involved have been pronounced and profound. Entire worlds have fallen into bondage because of indiscretions and lack of discernment. Entire religious traditions, so promising, have fallen under the control of their own states or the states of other nations because of a lack of discretion and a lack of discernment. And how many great and promising individuals have lost their promise, have lost their gifts, have lost their lives because of a lack of discretion and discernment in their affairs with others.

These examples are prevalent within the world, but within the Greater Community their prevalence is so great and their demonstration is so important that We must focus your attention here.

Of course, there is great hope amongst many people in the world today that those who are advanced in the Greater Community, who have come to the Earth, represent spiritual mastery—they are spiritual masters, and they will come to enlighten humanity, to relieve humanity of its age-old problems and give humanity a new life within a greater spiritual brotherhood.

There is much fanfare and fantasy about this, much hope and expectation. Yet the truth itself is very sobering. Yet the truth itself is also liberating. For to live in hope and fantasy can only blind you and deny you access to the greater spiritual reality that lives within you, and disable you from expressing this reality effectively, as it should be expressed.

You cannot be invigorated in a state of fantasy. You can only be invigorated in a state of truth and clarity. And invigoration is the essence of health and is the true context for spiritual emergence, both within the world here and throughout the Greater Community.

The Creator works in the Greater Community in a very fundamental way. It is exactly the same way that the Creator works within the world. When you are dealing with essential spirituality and are not caught up in all of the romance and glory that people try to create to keep themselves inspired, when you are focused on essential spirituality and translatable spirituality, the work of the Divine becomes ever more apparent. Here it is established in reality and not in hopeful expectation.

Throughout the Greater Community, the emphasis is upon the cultivation of Knowledge. When We use the word Knowledge, We are not talking about ideas or a body of information, but the profound ability to know. This experience is the very essence of your spiritual reality. For the Creator can only be known. Your greater purpose for coming into the world can only be known. The world's emergence into the Greater Community can only be known. The realization of your true gifts and their meaningful expression can only be known.

Hope, fear, belief, speculation cannot replace the reality of Knowledge itself. This is the fundamental difference between the institutions of religion and the pure experience of spirituality.

When We use the word Knowledge, We are talking about spirituality in the Greater Community. We are talking about universal spirituality, a spirituality that you share with all sentient beings everywhere.

Yet this holds true in every facet of your life within the world, for the Greater Community is simply a larger picture of your life within the world. It is vastly greater. It has far greater variety, but the essential elements of spiritual reality hold as true there as they do within your world, and vice versa.

Within the Greater Community, spirituality is advanced through the development of Knowledge within the individual and the development of communities of Knowledge. Knowledge within you will always seek to join in meaningful [relationship] with others with whom you share a greater destiny. This is true of beings everywhere in the Greater Community.

It is not about different levels of existence. It is not about going in and out of different dimensions. That is not the focus in the advancement of spirituality in the universe. That more represents the human imagination. It is far more simple than this and far more essential.

The Creator's focus in the Greater Community is the cultivation, the expression and the protection of Knowledge. Wherever Knowledge can emerge, contribution is made. Intelligence is increased. Cooperation is extended. And peace and harmony become established.

Wherever Knowledge is absent or is being thwarted, divisiveness rules, power is based upon will and ambition, subjugation and enslavement become the essence of relationship.

With Knowledge, all true things are possible. Without Knowledge, all problems arise. How fundamental and yet how mysterious this is.

As We have said before, technological advancement is entirely different from spiritual advancement. This you are coming to see in your own time, as even the ancient tribal religions are recognized for possessing remarkable wisdom despite the fact that they had very little technology.

THE MEANING OF SPIRITUAL DEVELOPMENT IN THE GREATER COMMUNITY

And yet to find the essential wisdom, you must go forward; you cannot go back. For your life is moving forward; it is not moving back. You are heading into the future. This is where you need to give your full attention. Attempting to relive the past can never be successful, for it will deny you the present and disable you from preparing for the future.

The Greater Community is your future. It is part of your present experience even though you cannot yet account for it. Spirituality within the Greater Community is fundamental and real, as it must become fundamental and real within your own experience if you seek to find your true nature and your true purpose in life.

Therefore, the essence of Greater Community Spirituality is the cultivation of wisdom, the reclamation of Knowledge and the development of a Greater Community perspective and understanding. Every emerging world throughout the Greater Community must face this. It must outgrow its tribal traditions with their emphasis on culture and history to find essential and translatable spirituality and to begin to live it and to receive its great empowerment.

What humanity is facing at this moment has been faced by every world that has had to emerge into the Greater Community. It is part of the evolution of all races. It will occur sooner or later regardless of the preferences or the beliefs of the society involved. Just like every child must grow up, every isolated world must have some exposure to the Greater Community.

The Wise who choose to withdraw from the Greater Community do so because they have learned what the Greater Community is and have learned how to respond to it, how to discern it and how to understand its mechanisms and its relationships.

Just like you cannot become an adult by hiding away from the world, you must enter the world and learn about the world and then find your seclusion within it. But seclusion does not mean that you are not participating within it or are not contributing to it in a genuine and direct way. All communities of Knowledge throughout the Greater Community are primarily focused on contribution, and their focus for contribution is not upon [their] world alone, but upon life within the Greater Community itself. For it is the relationships in the Greater Community that must become enlightened.

Here again We have a fundamental difference between human understanding of spirituality and the Greater Community reality itself. Many people in the world today are preoccupied with their own personal enlightenment, but in Greater Community Spirituality this is never the emphasis. It is always the cultivation of Knowledge and the establishment of relationships of destiny.

What can an enlightened individual do if they are not united with others? Their enlightenment is an illusion if they cannot substantiate it with their relationships, if they cannot enter community and establish a group mind in service to Knowledge itself.

For in the Greater Community, there are no powerful individuals. There are only powerful relationships. There are only powerful communities. This may be very difficult for you to understand given the pre-eminence given to individuality in the world today, but individual power is impotent compared to the power of relationship and the power of community.

Every individual throughout the universe who is developed in The Way of Knowledge has entered a greater Community of Knowledge. This is because Knowledge is always focused on relationship and bringing the individual into meaningful and purposeful relationship.

The obsession with personal enlightenment is antithetical to true spiritual advancement, for the person you are trying to enlighten is the thing that is standing in your way. You are trying to enlighten the person, but the person can never be enlightened. Knowledge is already enlightened. The enlightenment is uniting with Knowledge and uniting in relationships of Knowledge.

And it is an enlightenment that does not take you away, does not elevate you outside of life. It is an enlightenment that brings you into active engagement to contribute to the realities of manifest life for as long as you are here.

Your only purpose for coming into the world is contribution. You are not here to correct old mistakes. You are not here to pay old debts. You are not here to relive old lives. You are here to find Knowledge and to allow Knowledge to express itself through you. That is the essence of spirituality in the Greater Community, and that is the essence of spirituality in the world.

How simple and how powerful this is, and yet it is unfathomable. You can never exhaust its mystery or its reality. Do not let its simplicity fool you, for you can never exhaust it.

Within the Greater Community, there is no such thing as sainthood or mastery. Sainthood is a form of recognition that others may give to you, but within itself, it does not mean anything. It may be a sign of recognition for achievements made, but it does not signify real mastery.

Because of the emphasis on the individual in the world today and the lack of true communities of Knowledge, mastery is seen as an individual accomplishment. In some cultures, it is called mastery. In some cultures, it is called sainthood. People are called avatars. They are called masters. They are called saints. But what does this mean?

In the Greater Community, there is no such recognition, at least not in communities of Knowledge. Yet every state religion, wherever it may exist, has its saints, its spiritual or religious authorities, because that is part of government.

But in communities of Knowledge, mastery has no meaning because Knowledge is the master, and it is always greater than the person or the individual who is its vehicle. How can you be a master when Knowledge is the master? As long as you are a person in the world, you are not totally united with Knowledge. There is still a part of you that is a person in the world. How can the person in the world be the master when the master lives within you and works through you?

This confusion has led to many grave and unfortunate results throughout human history, and yet the emphasis on mastery and sainthood is still very prevalent in the world today. But in Greater Community Spirituality, it has no meaning because there is only contribution and achievement.

When you return to your Ancient Home, you can be who you really are, and you will be recognized there. But while you are in the world, you must do the work of Knowledge. You must fulfill what you came here to do. That is the essence of meaning and value, and that is the essence of fulfillment for the individual.

Within Greater Community Spirituality, there are no creation stories. There are no final resolutions to the problem of good and evil. There is only an arena where contribution is either made or not made, where Knowledge is either found or not found, where relationships of Knowledge are either established or not established. And as long as Knowledge is not found and relationships of Knowledge are not established and contributions are not made, beings will continue to exist in manifest reality and experience the difficulties and ravages of time and all of its inherent problems.

There is no beginning, and there is no end. There is only what is happening. If you need a beginning and an end, then you can imagine them for yourself. Or you can believe in what others have imagined for themselves.

In reality, there was a beginning and there will be an end. But the beginning is so long ago and the end is so far in the future, it is irrelevant to where you are now. When the work is done, that will be the end, but there is a great deal of work to do.

In Greater Community Spirituality, then, many of the things that are predominant in human religions are simply not present at all. However, they are present throughout the Greater Community where religion is used by the authorities and by the state to promote adherence, obedience and cooperation, to establish a focus for individual will and intelligence.

But in the real communities of Knowledge that live hidden throughout the Greater Community, this is not the emphasis. These are the communities that practice and contribute true Greater Community Spirituality.

In Greater Community Spirituality, there is no one individual who is a great hero that all should subscribe to. Because there are no masters, because there are no individuals that are completely advanced in manifest life, the whole issue of hero worship and mastery is happily avoided.

The only thing that will save you is Knowledge, and for that you must dedicate yourself, and you must lay the foundation for Knowledge to emerge within your life and to express itself according to the great purpose that has brought you into the world.

There are great teachers. There are great demonstrations. There are great sacrifices. But no one individual is the God for everyone else. This is a true and appropriate understanding.

Hero worship denies the reality of Knowledge within everyone else and is actually a cruel form of recognition for the person so elevated. They can only be hated and maligned. They can only be crucified because they cannot be experienced. If you cannot join with them, then you are apart from them. And this will bring a cruel result for you and for them.

Communities of Knowledge in the Greater Community want to keep the spiritual focus pure and wholesome. They want to keep it beyond the reach of the manipulations and machinations of world governments and societies.

They understand the parameters of religion, but they must keep the Fire of Knowledge alive and burning brightly, for this is the fire of purification. This is the fire of redemption. This is the great fire of empowerment that will enable you to have the strength and the energy, the commitment and the determination, to carry out the great activities that are destined for you.

In Greater Community Spirituality, Knowledge is the foundation for freedom because it is the only part of your Being that cannot be influenced and dominated in the mental environment. It may be difficult at first to recognize the importance of this distinction, but if you are to develop in your Greater Community education, if you are to develop in your spiritual reality and understanding, over time you will come to see how fundamental this is and how essential this is.

That is why Knowledge is at the very heart of preparing for the Greater Community, for you may prepare your intellect, you may develop your ideas, and over time you may even be able to establish greater institutions, but all of these can fall under the sway and domination of more powerful forces. And no matter how powerful you become in the Greater Community, there are always other groups or nations that are more powerful than you. The quest for power is insatiable.

In Greater Community Spirituality, there are no Heavens and Hells: if you are a good person, you go to Heaven and if you are a bad person, you go to Hell. That is tribal mythology.

Your Hell is living without Knowledge, and you live it every day. That is Hell. More Hell is living more without Knowledge. Hell can go on for a long time, but it cannot last forever. For eventually you will find Knowledge, and you will express Knowledge while you are in manifest life because in between, when you leave this world, you will go Home to your Spiritual Family in your Ancient Home, and you will realize, "Well, this is it! But I forgot. I must return!" And you will return with important things to do.

You can begin to see here that without the weight of history and culture, spirituality is very simple and direct. Yet it is also mysterious and unfathomable. You cannot understand it. You can only experience it and express it and learn to understand your experience and your expression. But your intellect cannot grasp the full reality of what Knowledge is and what Greater Community Spirituality means.

It is necessary in the world today for humanity to learn a Greater Community Spirituality. This is not meant to replace the world's religions, but to give them new hope and new promise and the ability to survive within a Greater Community context.

If you are to prepare for the Greater Community, if humanity is able to maintain and keep Knowledge alive within the world and to gain its strength and power, which are its natural inheritance, then it must learn Greater Community Spirituality. Earth-based human religious understanding cannot provide these things because it is Earth-based, and because it is focused on human beings alone, and because it is buried beneath the weight of culture and history.

Greater Community Spirituality is essential to learn in the world today. Though not everyone will be able to learn it, it is essential that a critical mass of people be able to learn and to experience what it means, and to be able to receive the great rewards that it will bestow upon them in every aspect of their lives. For with this simplicity, this power, and this clarity, the obsessions and the problems that plague you will begin to fall away and a greater power and strength will emerge within you.

Without hero worship, without Heaven, without Hell, without all
these attendant beliefs that are so much a part of all of the Earth-
based religions, you can begin to find your way and your purpose.
And you can begin to gain a clear understanding of the forces in life
that support the emergence of Knowledge within you and the forces
that oppose it or seek to manipulate it.

If humanity is to be able to maintain Knowledge in the world and
have any promise for the reclamation of Knowledge in the future, it
must learn Greater Community Spirituality as it really is. Otherwise,
humanity will become another technological society, a society of
people who are governed mentally, whose lives become uniform and
totally conformed to the established standards. And this society will
fall under domination from other races, who will simply use
humanity as a great work force, as a client state.

Already within the world today, technology is viewed by younger
generations as being the god, the saving grace, the true inspiration.
You worship the technology because it seems to do miraculous
things for you, and yet it puts you in bondage, and you lose your
inner authority as a result.

People say, "I cannot live without this appliance!" or "I cannot live
without this machine," and "How could I possibly function [without
this]?" And as a result, people everywhere lose their natural instincts.
They lose their natural associations with the world. And over time,
they begin to lose their ability to have profound experiences of
insight and Knowledge, which heralds the emergence of Knowledge
within the individual.

It is time to learn what Greater Community Spirituality means. This
book serves as an introduction, which is the great need to prepare for

the Greater Community and the need to learn Greater Community Spirituality.

The great teaching on Greater Community Spirituality is presented in another one of Our books entitled Greater Community Spirituality. You are encouraged to make it your study. In so doing, you will find that it will illuminate all that is most natural within you. There is nothing foreign or alien about it, for it calls upon the great endowment of Knowledge that you already possess, and it teaches you how to gain a greater vantage point in life from which you can begin to discern the movement of the world and the presence of the Greater Community here and all that that entails.

As you can begin to see, the meaning of spirituality in the Greater Community is very different than it is within your world, and yet its fundamental elements, being universal, hold true here as well.

The great spiritual speakers, the great teachers in your world, they too sought to bring humanity back to the essential meaning and experience of the Divine nature and purpose. Yet to the extent that these teachers have become public, the teaching has become maligned and corrupted, has become a tool of the state. The natural process of transmission has been thwarted and interfered with.

Yet you can also see that there are great differences, [such as] spirituality without a final reward of Heaven, for Heaven is guaranteed anyway. You do not need a Hell now to motivate you to become responsible. That is why Hell was created: to motivate people, to make them work, to make them obedient, to make them take seriously what was intended for them, what the state wanted them to accomplish.

Here there is a complete denial of people's natural motivation, for what could be more motivating than finally coming to realize that living without Knowledge is intolerable, that having relationships without Knowledge can have no success or satisfaction, that being unable to experience your true nature and express it creates all the disabilities under which humanity now suffers. Is this not motivation enough for the person who is finally coming to terms with their true inclinations in life?

You do not need a Hell now. You are already living in Hell. You need a way out of Hell. That is great enough motivation in and of itself.

Looking into the Greater Community with this perspective, you can begin to understand the work of the Divine. The Divine influences; it does not intervene. The Divine works through individuals, both seen and unseen because the Divine is too great within itself to be an individual. And there are Unseen Forces working throughout manifest life to bring individuals everywhere to realize the need for Knowledge, and to help them to discover Knowledge and to express Knowledge and to fulfill Knowledge.

This is the essence of the Creator's work throughout the universe. Understand this and you will begin to gain a perspective that will allow you to see how the Creator is working in the world today— reclaiming the separated through Knowledge, establishing relationships of Knowledge, establishing communities of Knowledge, enabling each individual who is involved in this great reclamation to contribute their unique gifts and contribution in all avenues of life.

This is the great spiritual work. It has been going on in the Greater Community since the beginning of manifest life, and it will go on until the end of manifest life. For there is a beginning and an end. But the beginning was not yesterday, and the end is not tomorrow.

Your task now here is to contribute, and to be able to contribute is to find the source of your contribution within yourself. Learning about the Greater Community will teach you how to do this, for its demonstrations are clear. Becoming a student of The Greater Community Way of Knowledge will teach you the way to reclaim Knowledge and will teach you how to prepare for the Greater Community and learn the meaning and essence of Greater Community Spirituality.

Here your humanity is not replaced but is rejuvenated and reactivated. For as a human being, you were given what you needed to fully participate and contribute to the world at this time. The work of the Creator is to bring you to this contribution and to prepare you and enable you and inspire you to provide this contribution to the world so that you may find your fulfillment here. There is no other fulfillment in being in the world.

CHAPTER 7

THE GREAT CHALLENGE AWAITING HUMANITY

There are very many people throughout the world today that feel a great change is upon humanity. They base this not only upon the substantive change they see in their societies and cultures, but also in terms of their deepest feelings. Some are hopeful; many are fearful; some only speculate that greater rewards and success await humanity, while others forecast a great calamity is coming.

Many people in the world today are very worried. This is all the result of living in a period of transition, a period of great change. Throughout history during these periods, many great spiritual proclamations have been made: some predicting it is the beginning of a golden age, others the downfall and end of human existence. These kinds of prophecies and the legitimate concerns that people have are all part of living at a great turning point.

In response to this, many people try to retreat into ancient traditions, trying to recapture and relive what they believe was a golden or more pure era of human existence. Others become lost in fantasy, unable to deal with their own inner experiences or the substantive experience of change around them. Still others attempt to move forward, bravely going they know not where, but trying to move beyond the past and all that it represents.

These three responses demonstrate that humanity is living at a great turning point. The evidence of this is everywhere if you but look. But where is humanity going? What is really occurring? What is propelling the momentous change that people experience around them? And why are people restless and uncertain? What is generating this anxiety, this concern and this excitement?

To find the answer to these questions, you must look beyond the hopes and fears of the human family. You must look beyond the prescriptions for unbridled success or complete downfall that many people [predict]. In all of the different forecasts in between these two extreme perceptions, you must look beyond yourself first into the Greater Community.

It is quite evident that people have not looked towards their destiny in the Greater Community. For many of the forecasts for the future that you read about or are aware of in the world today do not contain any mention of the Greater Community because many people believe that humanity will merely continue in its state of isolation, trying to overcome its problems, trying to capitalize on its strengths, trying to adjust to the difficult change at hand and the difficult change to come.

Where do you see, in all the bright and dismal prospects for the future, any mention of the Greater Community, any mention that humanity's age-old isolation is coming to an end? People are still thinking in a state of isolation. They are projecting their ideas, their beliefs and their aspirations within a state of isolation.

Most people in the world today do not realize that their isolation is over and that the Greater Community is here. But day by day, the evidence grows that something important is happening, something significant is changing, something that is not the product of human error or human invention. Something beyond what the human family is creating is generating a great change.

Day by day the evidence grows. Day by day more people are becoming aware. But there is still tremendous ignorance and denial. There is still tremendous manipulation of the evidence. It is very hard for people to gain any reliable information now.

The governments of the world will not tell you what they know. The religious institutions of the world cannot help you. People are filled with superstition. They are filled with hope. They are filled with wild expectancy. But who can see clearly? Whose thoughts are clear and unaffected by the prevailing attitudes and beliefs of society?

The answer is both outside of you and within you, not just one or the other. You must look into the world, at the greater movement of the world. You must look beyond the human inventory of hope, belief, fear and aspiration. You must look beyond the human family to find that humanity is no longer alone, even within its own world; to find that the Greater Community is here and that your isolation is over; to find that the world of [humanity] is preparing for a great turning point, a turning point that will forever change the destiny of humanity and the outcome of human endeavor.

You must look into the world with new eyes, not with eyes of hope and longing, not with eyes of fear and trepidation, but look to see what is there, to take the time and the energy to really look and see what is there. Most people will not give this time. They are too afraid of their own uncertainty. They do not want to experience the confusion that anyone would experience as they are trying to penetrate the mysteries of life. They will simply choose a position that is agreeable and maintain that blindly and without thought or consideration.

Look into the world. Feel what is happening there. Ask yourself, "Are we alone in the world? Is humanity alone in the world? Is humanity now fully in charge of its destiny?"

And look within yourself—not to what you think and believe, but deeper, into your deeper mind, into the mind of what is truly known within you. Here you will find the substantiation as well, for what is most true within you is connected to what is most true outside of you, just as what is untrue or false within you is connected to what is untrue and false outside of you.

But to look in this way, you must look and be patient. You will not have the answer immediately. You must penetrate; you must go deeper; you must understand; you must take the time. This is necessary even to begin to comprehend and to experience what is happening and to prepare for a future that will be so unlike the past. Who will give this time and consideration to the meaning and destiny of their life and to the reality and destiny of humanity as a whole?

To see in this way, you must have young eyes. If you are trying to substantiate a life full of learning and ideas, you will primarily seek to substantiate what you already believe and what you already hold to be true. If you look out into the world, but your mind is made up about the nature of reality and the destiny of humanity and the causes for human change and evolution, you will not see the evidence even though it is all around you.

To see truly, you must see with open and young eyes. That does not mean that you have to be young, but it does mean that you have to be willing to be shown something you have never seen before, to see something you have never seen before, to feel and experience something you have never seen and experienced before and to have your own ideas challenged, no matter how much you have invested in them.

If you cannot see, you cannot know. If you cannot know, then you will not know how to respond correctly and appropriately. If you do not know how to respond, then you will respond like everyone else, in a predetermined and prescribed manner, according to your conditioning or according to the influences that influence you even at this moment.

It is incredible that people are not free, but they think they are free. They believe they are free, but they are not free. Just because you are not in prison; just because someone is not standing guard at your door; just because you have some rights within your society does not mean you are really free.

If you cannot see; if you cannot know; if you cannot experience what you most deeply experience; if you cannot see what is happening in the world around you, in the bigger picture beyond your own little personal sphere; if you cannot see these things and feel these things, you are not yet free. And freedom is calling for you.

The challenge for you is to see and to know and to act and to build a foundation for Knowledge within your life, a foundation for your spiritual reality, a new foundation. Here you do not embellish what you already know, you build a new foundation. You start anew.

Only what you can bring forward that will be helpful will be part of your future. Everything else, stage by stage, bit by bit, will be left behind. This is your challenge. You do not do this only for yourself. You do it for humanity. For yourself alone, you will not mount the effort; you will not make the commitment; you will not face the difficulties and the uncertainties. But for humanity, there is a greater calling and a greater responsibility.

That is your challenge. But that is not all. Because your inner reality is connected directly to your outer reality, you must find out what is happening and learn how to prepare. You must learn about the Greater Community. You must learn what Greater Community Knowledge and Wisdom really mean. You must experience Greater Community Spirituality to find your own and bring this into your traditions and into your experiences of daily life. You must learn about the Greater Community, and you must take the Steps to Knowledge. That is the great challenge awaiting anyone who is prepared to meet their great challenge.

Often people want the result: "Well, I just want to know what my purpose is, and I will do it. Maybe." They do not want to go through the process of finding out, which is the critical thing. They just want to have the answer. They want to have the result. So they give themselves the answer. They prescribe for themselves a result. And it is based upon their vacillating feelings, their hopes, their fears, their desires, their concerns.

They cannot make a commitment to anything, for they have no foundation to make a commitment upon. And so today they firmly want this, but next week, well, it changes. And then a month later it is something else. And they cannot become focused, and they cannot choose a direction and move there clearly with wisdom and discernment.

The great challenge facing humanity is to prepare for its emergence into the Greater Community, to prepare to deal with the reality that its isolation is over and it must now contend with other races who are themselves interested in what humanity values, and in the resources and opportunities within this world.

But to meet this challenge, people like you—people who are reading this book, people who are responding—must take the challenge within themselves. Here you do not follow a leader. Here you do not idolize a teacher. Here you do not assume a rigid form of belief or set of precepts.

Instead, you begin the mysterious and fundamental journey towards Knowledge. You take the Steps to Knowledge. You learn The Way of Knowledge. You become a student of Knowledge. You seek the preparation that you yourself cannot provide for yourself. You take responsibility for your development. You respond to the calling within you. You do not accept the passive and idle assumptions that people all around you will make and are making now.

Humanity is made up of individuals, and humanity has always been furthered by the determined effort of a small percentage of its populations. What furthers humanity is men and women of good will and true inspiration joining together to carry out important tasks to meet problems that are existing and to prepare for problems that are emerging on the horizon.

Humanity does not simply prepare. It is the individuals who prepare. Do not look to your government. Do not look to your religious institutions. Do not look to your social service organizations. Do not say, "Somebody should do something about this!" It is you. The calling is for you. The calling is for anyone who can respond, and who can prepare, and who can accept the challenge, and who can meet the responsibilities.

Yes, they are great, but this is the way you find greatness within yourself. You never find greatness living a little life preoccupied with little things. You find a greater life by taking on a greater challenge and responsibility, by calling upon a greater power and energy within yourself and by staying with it and moving through the thresholds of learning, developing your skills and your awareness.

As We have said, humanity is not prepared for the Greater Community. It is not prepared intellectually; it is not prepared psychologically or emotionally; and it is not prepared spiritually. You cannot call upon human institutions or human traditions to provide this preparation, for the real preparation will go beyond what they have achieved thus far to meet a new set of circumstances.

Here it is essential to realize that what the great Teachers provided millennia ago cannot fully be sufficient to meet a new set of circumstances. That is why the evolution of religion constitutes a successive wave of new Revelations. They do not happen every day or every year, but rather every century or every millennium. And they occur to meet the changing circumstances of life and to prepare for the future.

The Christianity or the Buddhism or the Islam of 2000 years ago [or 2500 years ago], or 1500 years ago, of antiquity cannot meet the challenges of today without a new wave of Revelation. The Revelation is here. It is the teaching about the Greater Community. It is the means for learning Greater Community Spirituality. It is The Greater Community Way of Knowledge.

This is what will breathe new life into the ancient traditions here. This is what gives new promise to humanity. But the real responsibility still rests upon you the individual. What will you do? Knowledge knows what you must do, but you do not yet know what Knowledge knows. That is your opportunity. Knowledge has the power and the strength and the wisdom to guide you towards your fulfillment, but you must have the courage to take such a journey.

Humanity is emerging into a far greater arena of intelligent life. And everyone will feel a little smaller as a result. This is always the price you pay for moving into a larger context. Instead of being an important person in your village, you are now a small person within a larger community.

Everyone will feel very small and vulnerable as they come to realize that their isolation is over and that the Greater Community is here. They will recognize their helplessness. They will see that they cannot control events. They will see that they cannot even control their responses. And that is why there is so much denial in the world today. People want to maintain their sense of control and authority even though the circumstances of their lives have changed dramatically.

Who can face this? Who can face this with the understanding that this is a saving grace? It is easy to become afraid. It is more difficult to engage with your own courage.

Humanity is way behind schedule in its preparation for the Greater Community. It was hoped by the greater Spiritual Forces that are overseeing the well-being of humanity that more progress would have been made. But humanity is lagging. Its self-preoccupation is so complete that it cannot see beyond itself.

For instance, it has only been in recent years that it has finally taken any responsibility that it lives in an environment that must be rejuvenated and protected. There are individuals who for centuries have known this. Every good agriculturist knows this. Every good woodsman knows this. But finally there is a collective sense of responsibility. And how long has it taken for this to come about? And how late is its emergence?

If you feel restless, if you feel something is moving within you and you cannot get comfortable, and no matter how many pleasures and enjoyments you give yourself, you cannot seem to settle down. If this is the case for you, then you know something, and you are responding to something. And perhaps there is a sense of urgency within you that you cannot account for personally because you seem to have enough in most arenas to be a relatively satisfied person.

Why the restlessness? Why the sense of urgency? Why the care and the caution? Why the disturbing feelings and emotions? Is it because you are fundamentally flawed? Is it because you had an unhappy childhood? Is it because your life is not perfect?

No. Look beyond. Look deeper. You feel that you are responding to something. This is what it means to be responsible: to be able to respond. And it is responding to something within yourself very deep and something beyond yourself way beyond the parameters of your personal life.

Before it begins to storm, the animals in the forest become quiet and seek refuge. They change their behavior. They respond even though the storm has not begun. You respond, too, but your responses often go unheeded and unfelt. This is your natural honing device that keeps you connected to your environment, but within modern peoples especially, this natural instinct, this natural capability, has been greatly diminished and damaged. It goes unrecognized.

People will go about their daily lives as if nothing is happening even though the entire circumstances of their lives have changed. People do not prepare for the future. They do not prepare for growing older. They do not prepare even for the necessities of their lives because they are not responding to the signs and the cues that they need to respond to.

The Greater Community is in the world today. It is hidden, but it leaves its evidence everywhere. It is there for you to find, but you must look. You will not see it in your newspapers, for they are not allowed to print such things by and large. There is a general amnesia over human society, particularly in the more developed nations that one would think would be more educated and more well-informed.

The great challenge awaiting humanity is not only the presence of the Greater Community, but the requirement that humanity begin to account for its changing circumstances and to become aware of the elements in its environment and circumstances that are producing such a fundamental change. This leads you right to the Greater Community.

It leads people everywhere to consider something they have never had to consider before. Your parents did not have to consider this. Your ancestors did not have to consider this. They had other problems, some of which you no longer experience. But you have problems that they never had to experience.

To be able to respond internally, you must go beyond all of the conditioning that you have received in your education and in your life in the world, which is very substantial. You have to rise above it. You have to go deep beneath it to find that responsibility within yourself.

The Greater Community brings great risk to humanity, but it also brings the saving grace requiring a greater education, a greater spiritual attunement and a greater set of abilities. It puts everyone in the world in the same boat—rich or poor. No matter what country you are from, you are faced with the same problem. This equalizes the inequities that exist and provides a foundation for cooperation that simply did not exist substantially enough before.

The reality of the Greater Community, the need to create a Greater Community understanding and perspective and the need to learn Greater Community Spirituality are the very things that will provide the foundation for cooperation for humanity. It is not simply that humanity everywhere is facing a grave threat; it is also that you have now the opportunity to develop the foundation that will solve most of the world's problems today and will prepare and enable you to deal with the greater problems that are awaiting humanity in its emergence into a Greater Community of life.

If you respond to the Greater Community just with fear and anxiety, you will not be in a position to know. Yet if you respond to the Greater Community with unbounded optimism—thinking that everything will work out fine, it is just a process, God is in charge of everything, I just have to play my part, and it will all be fine—you will not be able to know, and you will not be able to prepare.

Instead, you must take the middle ground. Fear and hope have their own attractions, but they both have grave liabilities. The man or woman of Knowledge does not indulge themselves in either but takes the middle ground so that they can see clearly. They find the balancing point within themselves. They stand over the fulcrum of balance, and they look, and they discern.

Look around you. You will see that people are vacillating between unbounded enthusiasm and complete anxiety. They go from one extreme to the other. They do not know how to find the middle ground.

From a position of fear, optimism looks wonderfully liberating, so you go there. "Everything is going to be fine. Everything works out fine. We can deal with this. God is in charge. I can relax. It's not as bad as I think. In fact, it is all wonderful." And you live there for a while and you find out, "Well, that does not really match my experience of reality at all," and so you sink back into anxiety and apprehension.

You must find the middle ground. This is where clarity is achieved. This is where balance exists. It is not running from one set of emotions or expectations to another. It is finding the middle ground. This is following The Way of Knowledge, for Knowledge is not captivated by promises of hope and prosperity and happiness. And Knowledge is not captivated by the dark [draw] of fear or the attractions of anxiety.

Fear is easy. It takes very little effort to experience it. Optimism is a little harder, but it too is easy because you can fill your mind with wonderful expectations and tell yourself all kinds of things about reality around you and within you. But Knowledge is harder. Finding the balance point is more difficult. It requires determination, effort and preparation.

Within these pages, We are giving you a clear view of the bigger picture, a clearer view than you will find anywhere else. We do not say all this to overwhelm you, but to incite a deeper response and a deeper knowing within you, a knowing that you already have. We are calling upon what you know, not giving you something new to believe. This is part of the great challenge awaiting humanity.

It is a curious thing in human society and in many other societies in the Greater Community that there is a propensity for letting things deteriorate to a point where resolution becomes absolutely necessary, beyond everyone's expectations and preferences. People allow conditions to deteriorate, and then they are forced to do something, but by that time their actions become desperate and are very costly and often are not very effective.

Whereas the man or woman of Knowledge seeks to eliminate the problem once it is first recognized, the person without this great foundation will allow things to deteriorate and then will make drastic efforts to address it, often without good results.

This propensity demonstrates a lack of responsibility and a lack of inner awareness. It demonstrates a lack of social cohesion in human societies and a lack of respect for the great impact of your environment—your mental environment and your physical environment.

The coming of the Greater Community will change all this. It will require it. When people simply want something, well, that is not quite enough, but when it must be done, it must be done. That creates the impetus. The man or woman of Knowledge is governed by what must be, not by what they want or prefer. Desires are weak and vacillating. Preferences are based upon personal wishes. They are not based upon the realities of life or the movement of Knowledge within the person.

The great challenge is this: Humanity must prepare for the Greater Community, and must gain a greater and more pure spiritual foundation, and must establish a basis for cooperation and union amongst the human family if it is to survive and maintain its self-determination in the Greater Community.

It is a must situation. It is not something where you say, "Well, it is a problem, but we will get to it some day." With that approach, by the time people wake up, it will be too late, and the damage will already have been done.

It is the same challenge in so many other areas of human life—the degradation of the natural environment, the extent of poverty and social unrest in the world, the improper distribution of resources. These are all problems that are growing in scope day by day, and there is not enough responsibility in the human family to fully face and resolve them. The torch of truth is being carried by individuals who are ignited with the truth, but their numbers, though growing, are still not strong and great enough.

The great challenge awaiting humanity is not simply the challenge to become aware of something, to become aware of the Greater Community, but the challenge to prepare and the challenge to act. This must come from a clear understanding of the situation at hand, and it must be powered by Knowledge to be truly effective and to have truly beneficial results.

This great challenge facing humanity is the same as the great challenge facing you—the challenge to find who you are, to find what you came here to do, to find the foundation of truth within you, and to begin to live it.

You were born with the Knowledge of what you must do, where you must go and what you must become. It is time to find that Knowledge and begin to live it. That is the great challenge facing you. It is the same as the great challenge facing humanity.

There are greater things for you to do in your life. There are greater things for humanity to do. There are greater things for you to become aware of. There are greater things for humanity to become aware of. There are important things for you to know and to realize. There are important things for humanity to know and to realize.

It all begins with the individual. Do not look to your governments and institutions. They are paralyzed by the past. They are paralyzed by their belief in the past, and often they are not free to respond to the future, for they are being influenced and dominated themselves. It comes from the individual. This is where innovation occurs. Whoever you are, wherever you work, whatever your circumstances in life, this is your great challenge.

The Greater Community is in the world today. It is seeking to gain influence to establish itself here. It is affecting people in the mental environment, and it is genetically attempting to bond with humanity. It will take advantage of the conflicts in human governments and the contradictions in human religions to gain influence here, to pacify those who have greater strength and ability and to maintain the current illusions of humanity so that it may continue to build its presence here without human intervention.

Yet you also have Allies in the Greater Community, and We shall speak on them later in this book and their importance to you as an individual and to humanity as a whole. For you will not be able to emerge into the Greater Community without their assistance, and you will not be able to prepare for your new life in a greater arena of intelligence without finding the preparation that will make this possible.

Let Us now focus on the preparation itself and what it involves, what it requires and the great rewards that it offers you. To be aware of something is not enough. You must prepare to meet its challenge and its opportunity. Then you will be able to deal with the Greater Community and benefit from its presence, and use it to gain strength and integrity, and use it as a foundation for union and cooperation in the human family. And you shall use it to build relationships that are strong and focused and are not governed by personal desires and fears. This is all the result of preparation, and this is what We will address now.

CHAPTER 8

DEVELOPING A GREATER COMMUNITY PERSPECTIVE AND UNDERSTANDING

In life, people see what they can see based upon their vantage point and based upon what colors their perception. Clearly, if you reach a higher vantage point on the mountain of life, you are able to see more. You are able to see things you simply could not see before because you did not have the position from which to look. Previously, you could believe anything, but you could not see.

The important thing here is to reach the vantage point where you can see for yourself. You can see and know clearly. Using the analogy of the mountain, you could stay down below in the woods and cultivate any point of view you want, but you cannot yet see where you stand. You cannot see your position on the mountain. You cannot see what surrounds the mountain. You cannot see how great the mountain is. And you cannot see how far along you are.

This is why the idea of mastery is so relative. You may say, "Well, I am a master! I am so far beyond, so far above where I was before!" But then finally you turn and look, and you see that the path keeps going, and you have to move along, for your journey is not done yet. So each thing you master sets a new beginning. Each thing you complete establishes a new beginning.

It would not be enough for Us to provide all of the insight, perspective and information that We are presenting in this book if We were not prepared to take you to that vantage point from which you could see. Our intention is not simply to give you a wonderful and grand perception of life, a grand idea, a bigger belief system, a whole new set of ideas to adhere to and to identify with. That would only compound your problem and increase your burden.

Instead, We are telling you that you can see and know what must be seen and known if you reach the vantage point from which you can see and thus know. From a higher vantage point, things are simply obvious, but until you reach this vantage point, you must consider them as possibilities.

Knowledge within you knows what it knows already. The closer you become to Knowledge, the more you will know what Knowledge knows. But you still must make the journey to see with your own eyes the real circumstances of your life and the greater circumstances that are affecting the course and destiny of humanity.

This brings Us now to discuss developing a Greater Community perspective and understanding. Here We are not advocating that you have an alien point of view, but simply that your eyes can learn to see in a larger way and that you can learn to think in a larger way and that your perception and experience can be more encompassing and more authentic.

An alien viewpoint may be just as jaded as a human viewpoint. In fact, human beings at present are actually more free to form their own personal opinions than most advanced technological races in the Greater Community are today. Shocking but true. This offers humanity one of its few but important advantages.

Developing a Greater Community perspective and understanding is the result of being able to see beyond your cultural and religious conditioning, to see beyond the prevailing attitudes and beliefs that have shaped your approach to life and your perspective, to rise beyond these, to see things in a bigger way from a higher vantage point.

You are still seeing with your own eyes. You are still relying upon your great human endowments. You have not become something else. You have become more of what you really are.

So what is developing a Greater Community perspective and understanding? First, it is the ability to look beyond the mass of conditioning that clouds your vision and that creates a wall around your experience. The ability to do this is the result of preparing in The Way of Knowledge. It is not something that you simply can will for yourself or hope to happen or expect to be given you by a Divine messenger. It is something you must build and cultivate within yourself, day in and day out, every day. This is how you build the foundation.

This is how you get up the mountain. You do not get up the mountain by sitting by the side of the road and dreaming and pondering how it must be and may be and could be for you. You pick yourself up and you start moving. You take the journey step by step. And you deal with everything you encounter along the way, which teaches you how to travel, teaches you what to take with you and helps refine your perception and your ability to move forward.

Here it is not simply that you have gotten to a higher vantage point and you can see more. You have actually gone through a real transformation in the journey itself.

So by the time that you reach the vantage point on the mountain from which you can see, your perception is refined, and your values are now more in harmony with your true nature. You have been able to let go of things that only burdened and confused you before. You are traveling light. You are swift of foot. You know now how to negotiate the difficult changes in the path itself. You know how to deal with danger and adversity and opposition, both within yourself and outside of you.

Then when you are finally in the clear and can see beyond the treetops from a higher vantage point, your vision has been refined, your abilities have been heightened, and your life has become light and focused. It is the journey, then, that prepares you for what you will see when you reach the vantage point.

Having a Greater Community perspective in many ways is like being able to stand outside your world and look in. It is being able to stand outside yourself and look in—not with alien eyes but with your own eyes.

As it stands now, people are within the world looking out. They are inside themselves looking out, looking through all the filters that have been created through their years and years of social conditioning. And they only see very little of what is happening. They see what they prefer to see or what they have been taught to see. And often they do not even see with their own eyes, but with the eyes that have been given to them.

If you could be outside your world looking in from a Greater Community perspective, you would see things now that are so obvious that you could not see before. You would see how small and fragile your world is, how vulnerable it is to outside intervention. You would see humanity living on the surface, visible to the discerning eye. You would see how humanity's endeavors, priorities and conflicts are all in full display for the discreet observer. You would see that your mind is unprotected from unwarranted intervention. You would see that humanity is swayed like the wind sways the grass by forces that humanity is not even aware of.

You would look into the world and you would see such tremendous promise in humanity and yet such grave vulnerability and irresponsibility. And you would see that humanity's future cannot simply be based upon the saintly endeavors of a few inspired individuals, but must rely upon a greater education being furthered here and preparation for a new life and a new existence.

If you could stand outside your world looking in, you would see how fragile the environment is, and you would see the enormous effects of its degradation. And you would see that there is very little left for humanity to exploit. You would see the enormity of the problem in all of its manifestations.

But from the inside looking out, do you see these things? You do not see these things. From the inside looking out, you do not know these things. You only hear and see what is told to you or what you might find yourself firsthand. You cannot see the bigger picture until you have the eyes to see and the heart to feel them.

Remember, you are not here for yourself alone. You are here for all of life. And for this, you must have an experience of this—an experience that you can relate to and that you can utilize to give yourself greater strength and motivation.

If you could stand outside your world looking in, you would see that you are being scrutinized by several different groups of visitors and that many establishments have been made in the world already and that humanity, as it goes about its daily affairs, is unaware of these greater events, is day by day losing ground and losing its own influence and self-determination. Subtle yet pervasive is this influence.

If you could stand outside your world looking in, you would see that it is a tiny place within a far greater community, a Greater Community where life exists and has evolved and represents life in all of its manifestations. You would see that your planet is a garden planet, a relative paradise compared to other inhabited worlds. And you would see that you are living with riches beyond compare but without any real appreciation of how valuable they really are.

If you could travel to other worlds that are inhabited, you would see how desolate many of them are, and you would see how many of their natural environments have been destroyed. For most worlds in the Greater Community that are inhabited have been colonized.

Then you would return to your world, and you would see it is a gem in the universe. You would say, "My God! What a precious place! We must care for this. Others in the Greater Community will want this for themselves. And if they see that we are neglecting its preservation, they will feel emboldened and privileged to take it for themselves."

If you could stand outside your world looking in, you would see that life is very different from what people believe in. You would see that the Creator is at work everywhere in the universe and is not preoccupied with human affairs and aspirations. You would see that your world is but another of many, many evolving worlds. It is in fact one of many worlds that are now in the process of emerging into the Greater Community. You would see the greater risks involved, and you would see that the human population is ignorant of its condition. And you would feel compelled to act, to educate people and to provide the perception that you have and the understanding that you have gained.

If you could stand outside yourself and look in, you would be able to take an honest and fair appraisal of your strengths and weaknesses. And you would see how much you need to become strong with Knowledge, how much you need to find Knowledge and discern it from the other prevailing motivations in your mind. You would see how you would need to define and develop your own mental environment and clarify your relationships with others and devote yourself only to those people with whom you share a greater purpose and meaning in life.

If you could stand outside yourself, you would see that Knowledge lives within you and is waiting to emerge and that you are struggling to allow this emergence to occur.

If you could stand outside yourself looking in, really, not as you look as another person, but as you yourself from the outside looking at you, you would see how much your thoughts and your activities are influenced by the prevailing attitudes, beliefs and manipulations of others. You would see how rare it is when you have original thoughts and how difficult it is to achieve a state of clarity within a sea of influence in the mental environment.

Gaining a Greater Community perspective and understanding is like standing outside the world and looking in, and it is like standing outside yourself and looking in—not critically, not fearfully, not hopefully, but with clear eyes, real discernment, with the strength of Knowledge, which can see clearly and know what is real from what is not, and can tell what is genuine from what is not, and can separate what is valuable from what is not.

Enough people in the world need to cultivate this perspective. It will be the result of their preparation in The Greater Community Way of Knowledge. It will be the result of their having the courage and the integrity to learn about life beyond their personal sphere and to gain a greater understanding about the course and destiny of human life. It will be the result of their Greater Community education. It will be the result of taking the Steps to Knowledge.

You may think that anyone who lives in the Greater Community has a Greater Community perspective. This, of course, is not true because many races are as isolated as you are. But even amongst those who are involved in trade and commerce, who travel, for instance, they are aware that intelligent life exists [beyond them] and that they are not the center of the universe. They have been able to outgrow their tribal mentality sufficiently to be able to deal with other races in a productive way.

But they do not have a Greater Community perspective in the sense that they are not yet strong with Knowledge. If they are not yet strong with Knowledge, they will not have this comprehension that We are speaking of. They will be dominated by their own concerns and interests. And if they are a highly unified and structured society, these individuals will not be able to think freely for themselves.

As We have said, human beings enjoy a greater personal privilege—freedom—in the world today overall than you would find in most places in the Greater Community. Humanity is not unified, and that is a great problem. But despite the many problems that this does generate, there is still relative freedom to think and to perceive.

DEVELOPING A GREATER COMMUNITY PERSPECTIVE AND UNDERSTANDING

Though your education does condition you and guide you, though influences do wall you in and prevent your full perception of your situation and your abilities, the opportunities are still there.

Here you come to understand a very important thing—that those individuals in communities in the Greater Community who have been able to learn The Way of Knowledge, to develop skill in Knowledge and are living life according to Knowledge, have had to do so under far greater duress than most people in the world face today. That is why your opportunity is so great. We may emphasize the great need of the time, but We must also emphasize your great freedom and opportunity to seize this need, to meet this need and to prepare accordingly.

In other worlds, races have had to prepare in The Way of Knowledge under tremendous oppression, under grave difficulties. They do not have the freedom of expression that you have today. In societies where there is skill in leading and manipulating the mental environment, this challenge becomes even more difficult, for the skill required to be a Being of Knowledge is even greater, and the skill it takes to create insulation for yourself and to have the freedom to create your own mental environment is far greater than what you as a human being face today.

Though life may seem hard in the world and problematic, it is still relatively easy compared to life in other worlds. Look at your environment. You have almost a luxurious environment compared to environments that exist in other worlds. This is what in part makes your world so attractive. You are sitting on a little piece of luxurious living, and you do not even know what you have.

While it is hoped within human culture that life in other worlds will be far better than it is in your world, the truth is that this is not the case. There are other worlds as beautiful as yours, but they are rare. It is technology that has enabled races in the Greater Community to establish settlements in many worlds under adverse conditions, but environments as beautiful as yours are very rare.

Gaining this greater vantage point and taking the journey that enables you to see and to know is the great opportunity that is placed before you now. You need this perception for yourself, and you need it for your world.

If you are not content with the little things of life—the little preoccupations, the little concerns—if you are not content to think the way everyone else is conditioned to think, if you are willing to go beyond the illusion of security that these preoccupations seem to create, then you need this Greater Community perspective and understanding because this represents the true context for coming to terms with your life and for expressing yourself wholeheartedly.

How do you develop such a perspective and understanding? It is the result of learning Greater Community Spirituality. It is the result of taking the Steps to Knowledge. It is the result of developing your own mental environment. It is the result of developing strong relationships that can express the reality and purpose of Knowledge.

These are the fundamental areas of study. These are the fundamental areas of development. And a preparation for achieving them is provided in the great book, Steps to Knowledge, which is part of the Teaching in The Greater Community Way of Knowledge.

Here you develop slowly and carefully the ability to see without preference, the ability to distinguish the presence of Knowledge within you. Here you cultivate stillness of mind so that the mind becomes more of a window rather than a door. You develop a penetrating insight and highly skillful scrutiny.

Here you learn to see yourself honestly and fairly, assessing your weaknesses and your strengths, correcting the former and embellishing the latter. You do this without a great set of formal beliefs, without heroes, without gods, without goddesses, without heavens, without hells, without a quest for mastery, without personal ambition. You simply take the Steps to Knowledge to enable you to do such a task, which has been achieved so rarely in human life before. A preparation is provided to provide the Steps to Knowledge and to take you up the mountain of life.

Along the way, you will have to re-evaluate your relationships and in the process of doing this will create a whole new foundation for how to relate to other people. Here you will look for the evidence of Knowledge, meaning and purpose in others. Rather than being charmed by their appearance or their behavior, rather than seek to have their resources or their assets, you will seek for a deeper resonance and a deeper compatibility.

For truly, in The Way of Knowledge, people who are very dissimilar, who could never really get along on a personal basis alone, can find a foundation substantial enough to commit themselves with each other and to each other to achieve a greater purpose in life. Such is the power and the grace of Knowledge.

Here you find a way to transcend many of the problems that circumscribe you today. And though you will have personal problems in the future, they will no longer be strong enough to prevent you from moving forward. For your personal mind, the mind that was developed and conditioned in the world, will always have difficulties in comprehending greater things. But as the knowing Mind within you, the Mind of Knowledge, emerges and takes its rightful place in your awareness, you will be able to deal with yourself compassionately. You will not allow small disabilities to thwart you from undertaking your greater endeavors.

Gaining this greater vantage point means you have to leave where you are now in terms of your consciousness and in terms of your beliefs. You cannot take them all with you. If you try to take them all with you, you stay right where you are.

Just like you cannot take the place [you are in] with you if you are going to journey up the mountain. You have to leave it behind even if it is a beautiful place, even if you have found an idyllic resting place on the mountain, and you wish, "Oh, this is so beautiful! I could stay here forever. This is so much better than any place I have ever been." Even if you have this experience, to progress you must move on.

Here you gain the strength and the understanding not to allow anything in life to thwart your greater purpose and endeavor. And here you find that you will not journey alone. The essence of the teachings in The Way of Knowledge is that they teach you that you are not alone. They teach you that you are already part of community and give you the basis and the foundation for establishing this primary relationship in community with others.

Then when you marry, you marry completely, and your marriage is deep and resonating. Then when you join with others in your work, you join with a greater sense of purpose and commitment, unwilling to let personal issues destroy the union that you are now setting out to build together.

The higher you go on the mountain, the more you realize you are not alone. This enables you to think with a bigger mind and to have a bigger perspective. And you learn as you go what constitutes a foundation for real relationship. And you see that it is not romance. It is not beauty. It is not money. It is not charm. It is not recreation.

These things are alluring in their own right, but they do not provide the foundation for real relationship. Here you find that foundation because you are building it within yourself. As Knowledge is growing within you, it becomes the basis upon [which you build] your relationships with others. This gives you the power to overcome personal differences and to deal with issues and problems as they arise. Then when you reach a vantage point from which you can see more, you will have a greater understanding about the meaning of life and the fundamental nature of relationships.

As We have said, the Greater Community is not made up of magnificent and varied individuals. It is made up of communities and groups. Within the Greater Community, the important thing is what group you are a part of, what relationships you establish.

In the world at this time there is still a tremendous emphasis on the individual. Individuals are admired and they are deified. There is hero worship here. That marks an important difference between life in the Greater Community and life within your world.

If you can establish and become part of a community of Knowledge in your relationships, then you have set out to begin the most important establishment in life. It is from this establishment that great gifts will be given into the world, that the world's difficulties will be addressed, that the grievous errors in human life will be rectified and that a new foundation can be built over time.

This is all the result of reaching this greater vantage point. This is all the result of building a Greater Community perspective and understanding. This is the result of going beyond yourself to see yourself and going beyond the limits of human consciousness and awareness to see the real condition of humanity.

Is it possible to do this, given all of the influences that prevail upon humanity today? Is it possible for you to do this, given your current circumstances and condition? The answer is a resounding yes. It is not only possible; it is necessary; it is vital; it is needed. It is not merely a wish or a preference; it is a must in life.

This is what is awaiting you. This is what you want and what you need. This is what your heart yearns for, even if you are uncertain and afraid.

Knowledge will bring you here, for only Knowledge can take you to Knowledge. That is why Knowledge becomes strong as you travel in The Way of Knowledge and take the Steps to Knowledge. Only Knowledge can take you to this greater vantage point, which is why by the time you arrive, you will become much stronger in Knowledge than you ever were before.

Personal ambition will not take you there; personal will will not take you there; the desire for riches and rewards will not take you there. Only Knowledge will take you there. And only relationships that are capable of embodying and expressing Knowledge will be able to travel with you as you journey up the mountain of life and begin to leave the confinement of the forest below.

It is time to begin your Greater Community preparation. This is your fundamental spiritual education and development. It encompasses the great truths that humanity has discovered on its own, but it goes beyond them to embrace life in the Greater Community and to embrace the tradition of spiritual development and the reclamation of Knowledge that represents the fundamental work of the Creator within life on a large scale.

The way is being provided, and you can begin. You begin with what you know today, and you build upon that. You begin with what you see today, and you build upon that. And you build each day. You do not take great leaps and bounds. You do not leap and bound up the mountain but take careful and determined steps.

The mountain is difficult. You are climbing. You can lose your way. You can lose your footing. You can become allured by things you see and experience along the way. You can become disheartened. That is why as you take each step, you become stronger. You become more focused. You become more determined. You become more forgiving and more compassionate, for you must proceed.

Developing a Greater Community perspective and understanding will give you the vantage point from which to understand and to discern the activities of Greater Community presences in the world today. From a purely human viewpoint, you will not be able to understand these things, and you will not see them clearly. You must gain greater eyes and a greater discernment.

Humanity has this capability, and it has this great need. You can do this. It can be done, and it must be done. And you will find that your discernment will not be carried out by you alone, but will be the result of many people pooling their intelligence to create a group mind focus. This creates a strength in the mental environment that an individual alone could not produce and direct.

It is said in The Way of Knowledge that there are no great individuals; there are only great relationships. How true this is, and how important this will be for you in cultivating a greater intelligence and awareness within yourself.

For it is known that anyone can make an error at any time and that the greatest prevention against making such errors is to have another set of eyes, another intelligence, looking with you to share in the looking, to join in the looking, to develop the discernment together, to develop the strength together, to experience the Grace together.

That is why The Way of Knowledge is The Way of Relationship. It is the path of joining. Here you give up your ambitions for personal enlightenment and instead begin the real spiritual work of beginning the reclamation of Knowledge within yourself, and developing the essential aspects of wisdom that will enable you to be in relationship completely and to build the group mind in Knowledge that We are speaking of.

Ultimately, what will enable humanity to establish itself in the Greater Community and to maintain its self-determination within this larger mental and physical environment, is to develop a group mind experience not based upon political persuasion, not based upon religious ideology, not based on the machinations of government, but upon the essential nature of Knowledge within each person.

Here the group mind experience is not produced by millions of beings but by small groups who are able to look for everyone. They are the watchtowers. They are the telescopes. They are the microscopes. They are the magnifiers of experience.

Here humanity can gain not only a position of survival but a position of advantage. For your visitors, though highly technically skilled and with great social cohesion, cannot offset the effects of Knowledge itself. Indeed, ultimately you may be able to influence them for the good. But until that time, you must be able to counter the effects of their presence and learn what it means in terms of the priorities of your life and the conditions that it will establish for the future.

There is great promise for humanity despite the grave risks it is facing now. But do not let this take from your attention that the need for preparation is vital. Let this not dissuade you from what you must do. Let this not give you false confidence. Greatness is achieved through great activity and through great relationships. It is the great activity and the great relationships that must be emphasized now.

CHAPTER 9

FINDING KNOWLEDGE

Gaining a Greater Community understanding and perspective is
certainly quite essential in preparing for the Greater Community
itself, but alone this would not be enough. Here you could not rely
simply upon the power of your intelligence or your will in order to
gain the discernment that you would need in order to function
within a more complicated mental environment. You would need
more than mental power or will power in order to function
successfully in this environment. For no matter how powerful you
might become as an individual, your power will be insignificant
compared to the power of the group mind that represents the real
dynamics of interaction in the mental environment within the
Greater Community itself.

Therefore, here you must call upon a greater power, a greater
intelligence, a greater strength within yourself. We call this
Knowledge. It is represented by your ability to know. When We use
this word Knowledge, We are not speaking of a body of information
or a set of ideas or something you would learn in a university. We
are talking about the potency of your spiritual Mind.

Very few people understand what this is, really. Perhaps they
accept that they have a spiritual nature; perhaps they can accept
theoretically that they are spiritual beings, that there is something
eternal about them and that this connects them with the Divine.

But in order for this to be truly relevant here and for your spirituality
to be truly comprehended, you must recognize that your spirituality
represents a Mind within you—a greater Mind, a Mind beyond the

personal mind with which you think and calculate. We call this Mind Knowledge. It is the knowing Mind within you. And its importance in understanding your ability to function in the mental environment is critical.

Knowledge possesses for you your true mission and purpose in life. It has maintained for you the greater understanding of why you have come into the world, who you must meet here and what you must accomplish.

That is not to say that everything that will happen is preordained, but that you have certain things to accomplish and certain relationships to establish within the context of this individual life. This represents your destiny within the world, and the Knowledge of this destiny and the power to discover it and to fulfill it reside within Knowledge within you.

Now some people will ask, "Well, is this the subconscious mind?" And I say, no, it is not the subconscious mind. The subconscious mind is still part of your personal mind, the mind that is directly connected to your physical existence.

Knowledge represents your eternal Mind, your spiritual Mind, but it is not simply a being. It is a Mind that thinks. It is a Mind that has a purpose and a mission and a direction in life.

When you begin to come close to Knowledge, when you take the Steps to Knowledge, you begin to experience and to receive the great purpose that Knowledge has for you. And in time you will come to fully realize that this purpose is your own and that it represents your true desire and your true will in life.

The reclamation of Knowledge represents the essence of spiritual discovery and spiritual development. Knowledge is waiting to be discovered and reclaimed. Should you become a student of Knowledge and travel The Way of Knowledge and learn to live The Way of Knowledge, then eventually your personal mind and the greater Mind within you will unite and become one. Here you will become fully integrated, and your power and meaning and potency as an individual will become fully demonstrated in the world.

Knowledge is calling for you even at this moment to come to it, to receive it—to receive its wisdom, to receive its counsel and to receive its direction as your own. This is the great spiritual calling within you, and it is occurring at this moment.

For the world is emerging into the Greater Community, and there is a great spiritual calling in the world that will enable people to realize this and to prepare for it accordingly. Knowledge within you knows what this means. It knows how important it is. It knows what role you will play. And it knows exactly where you must go and whom you must meet in order to achieve this.

How can any of these things be realized through reasoning or deduction? How can you use your thinking mind to find the will of the greater Mind in life and to express it fully? You may attempt to comprehend or idealize what spirituality means and how it functions in the world. You may attempt to understand or idealize the activity of the Divine within human affairs. But ultimately these things can only be known.

The meaning, the existence and the Will of your Creator can only be known. Your true purpose, meaning and direction in life can only be known. Your true relationships—those that you are destined to develop, to participate in—they can only be known. Your true nature, meaning and value can only be known.

Therefore, We turn to Knowledge as the great journey and pathway to find the true meaning and purpose of your life and to find the true foundation for real relationship, which you are destined to have while you are here. Knowledge within you holds all of this for you. Without Knowledge, you cannot find it. No matter how great your ideas, no matter how sophisticated your thinking processes, no matter how universal your beliefs, they cannot contain and possess what Knowledge holds for you.

Here you come to understand a fundamental truth: that your thinking mind has an important function to serve in your life in enabling you to express the greater reality that you possess and to negotiate the difficulties and the vicissitudes of life. But your thinking mind ultimately can only serve Knowledge. Yet without this service, it will act as if it were the thing to be served and will become a dominant and destructive force in your life. If your thinking mind then becomes the essential focus, you will not understand the greater reality that you possess and its essential role in enabling you to find and to fulfill your purpose in life.

There are many people in the world today who try to rely upon their intellectual understanding or upon their beliefs and associations in order to give them the foundation for comprehending their true nature and its purpose here. But this always leads to failure and disappointment, for your thinking mind can only serve the greater Mind in doing this. It alone cannot provide this foundation. It alone cannot yield the greater understanding, the greater experience, that you will need.

This then frees you to turn to Knowledge itself and to learn to take the Steps to Knowledge. This, in essence, is the true spiritual path. All religious traditions in the world are genuine insofar as they support this fundamental discovery and expression.

Yet if you look at spirituality and you take away history, culture and convention; if you take away all of the physical trappings of religion, what you have is the essence of spirituality. In the Greater Community, this is called Knowledge. It is demonstrated through your ability to know. It is experienced through profound realization within yourself and within the context of your relationships. It always focuses you upon truly productive activities in the world and leads you step by step, point to point, in realizing, expressing and fulfilling your unique calling and purpose in life.

As We have said before, within a Greater Community context, you must come to discover the real essence of spirituality. Beliefs, traditions, rituals, culture are only for humanity. You cannot bridge yourself beyond humanity, even to the plant and animal kingdoms in the world, unless you can find the real essence of spirituality and experience it for yourself.

Religion is important. It plays a fundamental role in giving people the opportunity to experience their true spiritual nature and its purpose in life. But it can only serve, just like your thinking mind, a greater reality. It alone is not the greater reality. Within you, the greater reality is demonstrated and embodied within Knowledge.

Here again We are not talking about ideas or beliefs. We are talking about the profound experience of knowing. This demonstrates and confirms your relationship with the Divine and your intrinsic relationship with all life.

Yet Knowledge has a specific purpose in the world for you. It remembers why you came into the world. It remembers the agreement you made with your Spiritual Family before you came here. It remembers your desire to re-enter physical life in order to provide a real contribution, which you must provide.

Knowledge has not forgotten, but you have. You have forgotten because you needed to forget in order to develop as a human being, in order to enter human society and to be able to function there. If your memory of your Ancient Home and your greater purpose were fully established in your mind as a child, you would not want to face the difficulties of living in the world. You would simply want to go Home, to your Ancient Home from which you have come and to which you will eventually return.

Therefore, you enter a period of amnesia when you enter the world in order to become a functional human being here. But once this is achieved sufficiently, then you must turn to Knowledge. You must find Knowledge and take the Steps to Knowledge.

What does this have to do with the Greater Community? Why is this the essential element in understanding and experiencing Greater Community Spirituality? Why is this fundamental in order to enable you to prepare for your encounter with other forms of intelligent life?

As We have said, Knowledge is the essence of your spirituality and your spiritual nature. It is also the essence of the spirituality and spiritual nature of all intelligent life in the universe.

While you do not hold in common the same history, the same culture, the same rituals, the same conventions or even the same beliefs or ideals, at the level of Knowledge you are one. You can comprehend each other. You can communicate Being to Being, essence to essence. Together you can transcend all of the boundaries of race, culture, identity, belief and association. This is your fundamental link with all intelligent life. It is the greater spirituality that you share with them. This is why it is the essence of Greater Community Spirituality.

Knowledge, however, is fundamental in enabling you to deal effectively with intelligent races from beyond the world and within the context of humanity itself. This is fundamentally true because Knowledge is the only part of you that cannot be influenced in the mental environment.

Let Us clarify this. Your thoughts, your wishes, your feelings, your emotions, your tendencies and your beliefs all are subject to influence and, in fact, are the result of years of influence. You will find if you examine your mind carefully that you are not the originator of most of the thoughts that you rely upon to give you certainty and stability. They have simply been absorbed from your environment. They are the product of conditioning. As We have said before, there is very little original thinking in the world.

One of the tasks of students of Knowledge is to fully come to terms with the extent of their own conditioning and to recognize the primary elements and forces that continue to fortify this conditioning. Though this produces social uniformity within a culture, it creates great restraints for the individual, restraints which a student of Knowledge must learn to recognize and overcome.

In order to find Knowledge, you must recognize everything that prevents you from discovering it. In order to follow Knowledge, you must recognize and overcome those obstacles that prevent you from doing so. Here you come face to face with those forces in the mental environment which in the past have directed and conditioned your thinking and those forces which continue to do so. Here you will find that most of your beliefs are not your own, that most of your thoughts are not your own, that many of your impulses are not your own. They have been conditioned into you over years and years of exposure.

It is for this reason that We do not recommend that the student of Knowledge listen to a great deal of television or read the newspaper a great deal unless there is a specific purpose or focus to learn about a world event or a certain aspect of the human condition. These forms of media simply reinforce old ideas to keep everyone thinking in a similar or same way with very little diversity from person to person. This kind of conditioning is both intentional and inadvertent. It is giving everyone the same information in the same way without a great deal of variation.

Yet Knowledge within you cannot be persuaded. It only responds to Knowledge in another and to Knowledge in the universe, which is the Mind of the Creator. It is not persuaded, it is not convinced, it is not even confused by all the manifestations of life, both within the physical and the mental environment. It knows what is true and what is not true. It is not affected by the false. It is not swayed by the false. It is not overcome by the false.

This is why it is the great strength and power within you. Its understanding of life is not dictated by personal viewpoint or by cultural conditioning. That is why it represents your freedom in the world.

Come close to Knowledge and you will have the freedom of Knowledge and the strength of Knowledge and the determination of Knowledge. Within the Greater Community, this is a critical element. This is the one thing that makes all the difference between whether you will be free or whether you will be persuaded and ultimately dominated.

As you learn to take the Steps to Knowledge, you will come to see the power of social conditioning and how immensely it has influenced your thinking and your behavior. Yet within a Greater Community context, the forces of persuasion are far more powerful and consciously directed.

As We have said, human beliefs, human ideals, even human religions, will be taken advantage of in the mental environment by all those visitors who seek to gain influence and power here within the world. Everything that people want, everything that people are afraid of, everything that people believe in, unconsciously, represent all of the elements that your visitors can use to guide and direct human thought and human behavior. This represents skill in the mental environment. It is an invisible form of manipulation, and yet its manifestations are very visible.

What you read, what you are told, what you listen to and how you are taught to see things all have tremendous manifestations in life. Here there are very few freethinking people because as yet within the world there are very few individuals who are strong with Knowledge.

If you consider this seriously, without preference and without grave anxiety, you will begin to gain a greater understanding of the human condition and why, within a Greater Community context, humanity is so very vulnerable.

Here you must go beyond your ideas of good and evil simply to understand the dynamics and the interactions of life. As We have said, your visitors are not evil; they simply have their own needs that compel them. And in most cases, they are not strong with Knowledge either, for they have been conditioned and programmed to think in a certain way and to carry out certain activities without any personal discernment at all.

If you are following what I am telling you so far, you will come to see that humanity needs Knowledge. It is not simply a spiritual quest now. It is essential for survival and self-determination. And, beyond this, perhaps you will begin to see that humanity even has an advantage in the Greater Community because humanity, given its complex social development and its rich spiritual heritages, has the capacity for Knowledge, a far greater capacity and opportunity for Knowledge than, say, your visitors have at this moment.

Whoever can become strong with Knowledge will be free within the mental environment and will be able to cast a positive and constructive influence there. Yet without Knowledge, you could not do this. It would not be possible. Your thoughts would simply be swayed by more powerful thoughts because in the Greater Community, you are dealing with group mind, not with a bunch of freethinking individuals. And within the mental environment, group mind is tremendously powerful.

Your visitors all practice group mind and demonstrate this. That is what gives them their skill in influencing human perception, human memory and human behavior in all of the direct encounters that they have had with human beings within the world. The evidence of this will certainly bear witness to all that I am saying.

If afterwards people thinking that it was a positive experience or negative experience does not belie the fact that they could not control their experience when in the presence of the visitors. You may call it good in order to reassure yourself or you may call it bad. But if you cannot determine your own will, if you cannot focus your own mind, if you cannot express your inner truth or nature within a direct interaction with a Greater Community presence, then you have been overcome in the mental environment. If this continues, you eventually will lose your will and will not be able to think freely.

Here the possibility of your gaining a foundation in Knowledge becomes increasingly remote. You will lose ground. You will become simply the effect of their group mind. And because they do not support the reclamation of Knowledge within the world, they will thwart your attempts to find your true nature and its message and purpose for you.

Perhaps you are thinking, "How is this possible? How could this happen within the world?" Yet I can assure you that it is happening at this moment and has been happening for decades and will become increasingly prevalent. For the Greater Community is here, and it is establishing its net of influence already. And this influence is far more pervasive than you at this moment may realize. That is why the need for Knowledge, the need for learning a Greater Community understanding and perspective, are so crucial at this time.

Humanity is losing ground. It was never strong to begin with in terms of the mental environment, but it is losing ground seriously. That is why there is an intense and urgent spiritual calling within the world. It is more urgent than people realize. They think perhaps, "Well, it is just an opportunity to become enlightened." No. It is a need to preserve the integrity and the self-determination of humanity itself.

Even if humanity did not have its grave environmental and social problems, the presence of the Greater Community would create an urgent calling in the world. Yet people are largely unaware of the greater forces that are shaping their experience now and that are determining their future and destiny.

Yet if you read human history, even here you can see that most people were not aware of the greater social and political forces that were shaping their future and their destiny. This has been demonstrated throughout human history, and yet the situation now has reached a whole other level, a whole other dimension.

Therefore, the calling for Knowledge, which is fundamentally a spiritual calling, is being sounded within the world with great intensity and urgency. That is why you cannot perhaps be satisfied with little personal comforts or personal pleasures. That is why something is driving you forward.

Perhaps you cannot understand it. Perhaps you do not know what it means. Perhaps it irritates you and prevents you from simply relying upon the few comforts that you have been able to establish along the way. Yet this represents the movement of Knowledge within you, and it represents the great and urgent calling that We are speaking of here.

In order for humanity to be able to emerge successfully into the Greater Community and to take a place there, a place where it can preserve and maintain its freedom and can establish its abilities, the development of Knowledge, individually and collectively, must become far greater than it is at this moment.

This will not be the result of government programs. This will not be the result of your education system. This will be the result of individuals, men and women like you, having the courage and the inner calling to follow The Way of Knowledge, and to become strong in Knowledge, and to claim their responsibility and to receive their inheritance while they are here in the world.

Men and women of Knowledge have always furthered the human race. They have always been the source of discovery, invention and social rejuvenation. They have always been the source of keeping religion alive by infusing the essence of spirituality there. And yet now We are at a great turning point where the requirement for this is even greater than it has ever been before.

Knowledge within you knows that humanity is emerging within the Greater Community. It knows this is why you came into the world. It knows that this is an overriding need and reality. And yet it knows exactly where you stand at this moment, what you believe, what you think, what you value, where your feelings reside and what influences them.

It knows that you must become free. It knows that you must become whole and powerful. It knows that you must find the great equanimity of Knowledge and the great strength of Knowledge. And it will move you towards this relentlessly. There will be no rest. There will be no reprieve until you can find this, for this represents the searching and the yearning of your very Being.

In the Greater Community, individuals in small groups have been able to establish Knowledge, to experience Knowledge and to express Knowledge. And yet this occurs usually under far graver and more difficult circumstances than you now face within your world. For in highly regimented and developed societies, the emergence of Knowledge within the individual is seen as a great threat, and it is often suppressed brutally.

Here citizens' minds, attitudes and priorities are highly controlled through the mental environment and through social conditioning. Therefore, the individual of Knowledge faces a much greater difficulty under these circumstances. To gain their freedom and to maintain it within their social setting and their mental environment represents a formidable task. Yet they are not alone.

And here We come to a very important part of your understanding and preparation for the Greater Community. Every individual that makes a conscious decision to become strong with Knowledge and to respond to the great calling that is occurring within the world will have tremendous assistance and will open themselves to a greater association of life, both within the world and beyond.

Overseeing human development are great Spiritual Forces. We call these the Unseen Ones, or at least this is how they are called in many cultures in the Greater Community. Like gardeners, they oversee the development of human intelligence and human Spirit as they oversee intelligence and Spirit within all worlds where intelligent life resides.

Here human societies represent a great fertility, and yet they are in tremendous disarray. Here it is possible for individuals to respond to Knowledge and to take the Steps to Knowledge, but it is very difficult for them to influence the direction of humanity itself because their numbers are so few and because their experience and their development is so much in contrast to the conventions and the traditions in human societies.

They stand out as remarkable people, and yet they must remain hidden in order not to face extreme adversity, persecution or misunderstanding. Yet they have a greater association with the Unseen Ones, a greater spiritual association, which becomes stronger and stronger as they advance and progress.

This, then, gives you a clear idea of what humanity's real Allies in the Greater Community are like and why they are concerned about human development and the preservation of human integrity. Your true Allies in the Greater Community represent a community of Knowledge. They are not great military or political forces. For the most part, they remain hidden in the Greater Community. Yet they can communicate through the Unseen Ones to you even while you are here, for it is a greater spiritual association and network into which you emerge as you advance in The Way of Knowledge.

Here you will see that while there is a great and complex development of interactions within the physical world, there is, in a sense, behind the scenes, a great network of communication that extends beyond the physical realm. Because this is at the level of Knowledge, it demonstrates Knowledge and reflects Knowledge. It is not a psychic environment in the sense that any kind of force can reside there. The mental environment is a psychic environment, but the environment of Knowledge is not a psychic environment in the same way.

Here you begin to realize that you have Allies in the Greater Community. They support the reclamation of Knowledge in the world, and they are connected to the Unseen Ones, just like you are learning to be connected to the Unseen Ones. They wish to fortify Knowledge within the entire universe. They wish to keep Knowledge alive within the complex mental and social environments that exist within the Greater Community. Their mission in life is to express Knowledge, to demonstrate Knowledge and to keep Knowledge alive in the minds and hearts of individuals, both within their respective worlds and throughout the Greater Community itself.

Though you will never meet them face to face, these represent your greatest Allies and your most potent relationships. Only if you advance in The Way of Knowledge, only if you pass through the great thresholds in realization will you come to be able to experience them directly, and the power of their intention, and the graciousness of their will.

Yet at this point, it is important that you know that they exist, or you will feel that humanity has absolutely no chance in the Greater Community and that everything that I am presenting here will seem absolutely overwhelming, and this will discourage you. But do not become discouraged, for the power of the Creator, the power of the Unseen Ones and the power of the great communities of Knowledge as they exist throughout the Greater Community abide with you and support you in your difficult task of overcoming your social conditioning, of gaining freedom in your mental environment and of finding the way to Knowledge.

Take heart also because in the world today there is a great Teaching that the Creator has willed to come into existence here. It represents the desire and the will of your true Allies to enable you to find your freedom and to express it constructively in service to the world.

A great Teaching called The Greater Community Way of Knowledge is being given to humanity. Its purpose is to prepare humanity for the Greater Community and to provide the fundamental and essential teaching in learning, living and expressing The Way of Knowledge. It provides a unique method of study called Steps to Knowledge.

It is meant for everyone in the world and anyone who can feel the great calling within themselves at this moment. It lays the foundation for spiritual reclamation, which We call the reclamation of Knowledge. It lays the foundation for gaining a Greater Community perspective and understanding. It enables you to build a foundation for recognizing and establishing true and purposeful relationships with others. It brings the reality and the experience of Knowledge into daily life, into all aspects of your activities within the world. And lastly, it prepares you for the Greater Community by engaging you with your true power and ability, by providing the foundation for freedom and by teaching you the dynamics of intelligent interaction within a greater mental environment into which you are now emerging as a race.

It responds to your destiny; it emphasizes your destiny. It responds to your true spiritual nature; it emphasizes your true spiritual nature. This Teaching is being presented through one person, but it is not the product of this one person's education alone, for there is no individual in the world who could create such a Teaching.

Take heart, then, for you have great assistance. The method of preparation is being given to you. It is available to you at this moment. This book is a demonstration of its reality and existence in the world.

Take heart because the Unseen Ones are with you and will guide you and bless you as you proceed and as you advance in The Way of Knowledge.

Take heart because you have strong Allies in the Greater Community who, through great difficulty and sacrifice, have established the reality of Knowledge and have advanced The Way of Knowledge within their own worlds. Their accomplishments are made available to you through the study of a Greater Community Way of Knowledge. And their awareness and the greatness of their Spirit can be experienced directly as you learn to communicate with others at the level of Knowledge and enter this greater spiritual panorama of life.

Here you enter without fantastic beliefs, without complicated metaphysical belief systems, without high ideals, without unrealistic associations. Instead, you will enter with a pureness of spirit and with a wholeness of mind that alone will enable a person or a being anywhere in the Greater Community to enter this greater association of life that We call Knowledge.

Your preparation for the Greater Community, therefore, is a spiritual preparation. It is a fundamental preparation in reclaiming your spiritual power and intelligence. It is expressed by following The Way of Knowledge and by taking the Steps to Knowledge. Here you transcend the limits of religion and enter into the greater panorama of spirituality as it truly functions and exists within the physical reality of your daily life and within the reality of the Greater Community.

CHAPTER 10

GAINING STRENGTH AND INFLUENCE IN THE MENTAL ENVIRONMENT

As you have a physical proximity in which you live and function, you also have a mental environment in which you learn to think. Yet it takes a long time to learn how to develop discernment and ability within this mental environment. In fact, for humanity at this point, the mental environment represents a great frontier, a whole new area to explore and within which to gain strength and ability.

It is important for you to know, however, that there is an environment in which you think. This environment is filled with many forces, very few of which have anything to do with you personally. You could go into any home on any avenue, on any street, in any city, and each home would have its own mental environment. And the individuals living in those environments represent the chief forces within those mental environments.

Your experience of the mental environment has been part of your life since you were born. There are so many examples if you begin to think about it. Every place you go has its own mental environment. Every home you enter has its unique mental environment. Every person around whom you spend any amount of time, you create a mental environment together.

Within your own mental environment, you have the possibility or the potential to be the greatest influence, and this is encouraged here. But as We have said, your mental environment is filled with other forces and influences as well, most of which have very little to do with you. That is because you cannot isolate yourself in the world. And within the mental environment, there are no borders or boundaries unless you learn to establish them yourself.

Into even the sanctity of your own home, the influences of the world find expression through the media, through the written word and through your interactions with people. It is necessary in becoming a student of Knowledge to learn to become responsible and effective in your own mental environment, for you cannot hope to advance in The Way of Knowledge, you cannot hope to gain greater clarity or ability if the things that are influencing your life are not addressed and recognized. Here you must learn what is affecting you, and then you must select who and what are beneficial and who and what are not beneficial.

Within this process, you come to realize that there are no neutral influences in the mental environment. Everything and everyone with whom you come into contact in any kind of meaningful way is either helping or hindering you in your advancement. However, as a student of Knowledge, you learn to utilize all influences that you encounter for your own benefit and for the benefit of others.

Yet this represents a more advanced skill. And in the interim, for your own well-being and to enable you to proceed, you must learn to limit or offset those influences that hinder you and emphasize and encourage those influences that actually help you along the way. If this is not done, your progress will be thwarted and will be very slow and difficult.

This is a natural part of gaining inner authority. This is a natural part of claiming responsibility for your life and learning how to direct it according to the wisdom and the grace of Knowledge within you.

Surely, you must encounter those influences and those relationships
that stand in the way of this. And you will encounter them even at
the outset, for as your studenthood in The Way of Knowledge
becomes stronger, you will come to realize, for example, who in your
life really supports this within you and who does not, who can really
encourage it and who is afraid of it, who really trusts it and who does
not.

Many people when they begin their true spiritual journey discover
with great shock that many of their longstanding relationships stand
in contrast to their primary aim and purpose now. And they are
surprised, for even long-term friendships can be seen to be
counterproductive.

Often this is very difficult for the person starting out because they
have a natural allegiance to their friends and to their loved ones. But
gaining a greater allegiance to Knowledge sometimes brings conflict.
For those relationships to which they hold allegiance often thwart or
interfere with their ability to gain trust and integrity within
themselves.

For many people, this is the first great hurdle to overcome. They must
overcome their allegiances to others to emphasize a greater allegiance
to Knowledge. In other words, instead of doing what other people
want them to do, they must gain the inner authority to do what they
know they must do. This can be quite challenging.

It is remarkable when you realize how great an influence your
relationships have upon you and how much you adapt yourself to
them. Accommodating yourself to other people may be a social
necessity under certain circumstances, but within the foundation of
your life, it will often impose very damaging effects.

The man and woman of Knowledge, if they have progressed far enough, will be able to make natural and strong commitments in their relationships, but they must have the inner authority to do this and to know how it can be done responsibly and effectively. Someone who does not have this authority cannot make real commitments to others. They are not in a position to direct or to determine their lives, and so they cannot give of themselves freely.

You must have yourself to give yourself. You must know yourself to direct your life. Otherwise, you will have other people and other forces direct your life. In fact, this is happening all around you.

Look about and you will see that people have given over the authority of their lives to their relationships with work, with people, with their habits, with their addictions, with their fears, with their interests, with their preoccupations and so forth. And the world encourages this because, in a sense, societies around the world want their populations to be compliant and to be uniform and to be obedient.

So people are weakened, and their delights and their phobias are emphasized. And they are encouraged to consume. And they are encouraged to believe certain things and to avoid thinking about other things. This greatly affects the physical environment in which you live, but it is predominantly felt at the level of thought and belief.

Now We enter into a new environment, an environment into which people have rarely ventured in a conscious way. Very few people in the world realize the effect of their thoughts upon others or the effect of others' thoughts upon them in any kind of objective way.

Yes, they feel good around certain people and not as good around others, but they do not understand the dynamics of why this is the case and how they can learn to deal with it effectively. Giving yourself to those whom you like and avoiding those whom you do not like does not constitute any degree of ability or effectiveness in the mental environment.

Here there are two great stages in learning. The first is to understand what your mental environment is at the moment and to learn how to redirect it, or to reconstitute it to become a supportive environment, an environment that supports the reclamation of Knowledge, that supports your quest for real integrity and ability. This first stage requires a tremendous amount of re-evaluation and the exertion of your own Knowledge as opposed to your will alone. For will is exerted to support ideas and beliefs, but Knowledge is exerted to support reality and relationship.

Here your allegiance must shift from your allegiance to your ideas, your allegiance to your relationships, and your allegiance to certain trends in society to a greater allegiance to Knowledge within yourself. If this can be established, then Knowledge will show you how to give yourself into the world, show you where to make commitments and help you to discern those relationships that deserve your commitment and that benefit from it in an effective and constructive way.

Yet how difficult this is. This is a struggle, in a certain respect, for you must fight for your freedom. And what you fight primarily are the ideas that have been imposed upon you and that you have accepted. Here the struggle is more internal than external though there can be conflicts with other people, particularly those individuals who, by their intention or by their ignorance, thwart the emergence of Knowledge within you.

Yet even if you were isolated and were out of contact with people, you would still see in your assessment of your own mental environment that there is a great deal of influence there that did not come from you. It came from your family; it came from your society; it came through your education. Some of it is beneficial; some of it is not. Some of it is helping you at this moment; some of it is not. Some of it enables you to see and know what you must see and know; some of it does not.

Here there is a great deal of sorting out and some confusion as well. For you are shifting your sense of certainty from your ideas to Knowledge itself. You are saying, "My foundation is not simply a set of ideas or beliefs or associations," and you are moving it to the real foundation within yourself, which is represented by the foundation of Knowledge.

The second great stage of learning regarding the mental environment has to do with learning how to cast influence within the mental environment. You cannot cast an influence within the mental environment in a conscious and effective way unless you have gained a certain amount of control over the mental environment in which you yourself function.

Developing this control requires focusing upon your own thinking and upon the relationships with which you have an immediate interaction and involvement. You cannot offset the mental environment of the whole world. You cannot offset the mental environment of the city in which you live. And perhaps you cannot even offset the mental environment of your family or your close group of relationships. But you can establish your own mental environment within it, and you are encouraged to take this responsibility and to become empowered to do so.

Here you see an important difference between the teaching in Greater Community Spirituality and The Greater Community Way of Knowledge and many other spiritual teachings, which encourage you to give up this sense of authority, to give up this sense of responsibility over the management of your own mind and body. They encourage you to surrender—to surrender to ideas, to surrender to beliefs, to surrender to conventions or rituals, or to surrender to the Creator, or to the force and spirit of the Creator.

This difference creates considerable confusion, for people are not certain what their responsibility is. They are not certain what they are to give themselves to and from what they should hold themselves back. Let Us clarify this.

In order to become a man or a woman of Knowledge, in order to become a spiritually realized Being within physical life, you must claim authority over your own affairs. The Creator will not do this for you, for the Creator has given you Knowledge to enable you to do this yourself.

Here you must be the captain of your own ship. You cannot let the winds and the currents determine how you sail, and if you sail, and what you carry on board. Yes, you use the winds and the currents, but you must gain authority over your own ship in order to learn to do this. The captain of the ship does not simply let the winds and the currents take his or her ship wherever they may. Instead, he or she must learn how to control these forces and use them to gain direction and to move within the world.

Here there is a practical form of mastery, but here you do not claim to be the master, for Knowledge is the master, and the Creator is the master. But they can only work through you if you have developed strength and capability. If you are reckless or irresponsible regarding your physical interactions or mental interactions, Knowledge will not emerge within you, for you will not be ready.

The Creator will not call you into service, for you will not be ready. You will not be given greater insight, greater ability, greater skills because you will not be ready. Therefore, the student of Knowledge becomes ready by gaining ability in their affairs with others, in their involvements in the world, and in developing their own mental environment.

Now when I say developing your own mental environment, what does this really mean? Does this mean you put pretty pictures on your walls and play beautiful music all day long? Does this mean you burn incense and only have pleasant things to sense and smell and experience? No, it does not mean this.

It means you learn to clear the way for Knowledge. It means you create a conducive environment mentally within yourself and in your immediate circumstances for Knowledge to emerge within you and to express itself through your life.

Here you must open things up, clear things away, learn to recognize and offset negative influences, learn to recognize the degree to which you have been conditioned and affected by society and by your relationships, and to adjust them accordingly so that you have the freedom and the opportunity to find this greater Intelligence within you and allow it to emerge within your mind and within your life.

GAINING STRENGTH AND INFLUENCE IN THE MENTAL ENVIRONMENT

Within this short chapter, We will not attempt to describe all the dynamics of developing skill in the mental environment, for that is a very great subject and will require a much longer presentation. Yet it is important here for you to realize that you have a responsibility in terms of what you think and what you do, and you are held accountable for this.

The fact that you may feel swayed by forces greater than yourself, internal forces and external forces, does not deny the fact that you have a certain realm of responsibility. If you do not claim this responsibility, then other forces and powers will claim it for you. Let Us explain what We mean.

It is a fundamental truth in the universe, in the Greater Community in which you live and within the world in which you live, that if you do not claim authority over your life, then others will claim it for you. If you do not assume this responsibility, and if you do not garner the necessary wisdom, strength and skill that are required, then you will simply acquiesce to other forces. These other forces can be a dominating person in your life; they can be a dominating set of circumstances and relationships; they can be the predominating beliefs and ideals of your culture or your religion; and they can be forces from the Greater Community.

As governments around the world want to keep their populations compliant and obedient, so the Greater Community presences within the world today, those who are interacting in human affairs, want to sway the thinking of humanity, want to direct human interest and human energy.

However, when you have skill in the mental environment, you recognize that the mental environment provides the greatest opportunity to exert influence and to produce the results that you want to produce.

The Greater Community visitors in the world today who are interacting in human affairs do not want to destroy humanity, do not want to wipe humanity out, do not want to replace human beings with themselves, for that is not practical. Rather, they would have people respond to their ideas while hiding themselves as the sender of these influences so that human beings will in time learn to work according to how the visitors want them to work, to produce the resources and to produce the skills and to produce the biological and genetic materials that the visitors are seeking.

To make this possible, people must become compliant. They must [believe] in something that is at least conducive to the objectives that the visitors want to create for themselves. This becomes very subtle in its dynamics, but it is important for you to know that if you do not claim authority and ability in your own mental environment, if you do not learn to take responsibility for what goes on within your own mind and for your own behavior, then you will naturally acquiesce, not all at once but incrementally. You will simply be moved around by forces that you cannot possibly understand. And whether you acquiesce happily or whether you go along with great anger and resentment, you will be moved.

How do you start? You start by learning The Way of Knowledge. You start by gaining a foundation within this deep and mysterious part of yourself. You begin by realizing that you are not free and that you want to become free—not just free of external restraints but free spiritually, free mentally, free to think, free to direct your energy, not according to the dictates or the will of others, but according to the reality and authority of Knowledge within you.

GAINING STRENGTH AND INFLUENCE IN THE MENTAL ENVIRONMENT

You begin with this understanding. Here you realize you do not really understand the mental environment. You do not really understand what Knowledge is yet or what it can do for you and the world. But you are at least aware that they exist, and you have a certain starting understanding that will enable you to proceed. Within the scope of this chapter and this book, We wish to give you this beginning understanding.

Now many people might say, "Well, I already know about these things. I know that people influence me, and I am trying to stop it!" But if this is your response, this does not yet recognize the real picture. Becoming defiant and angry does not mean that you are really developing skill and responsibility within your own mental environment.

It is easy to be angry and to lash out against the forces that you can recognize that are influencing everyone around you, such as institutions and governments and religions or the financial powers within your culture. But this does not mean you are claiming ability and responsibility.

Becoming a rebel does not give you the power to create, and it is the power to create that We wish to emphasize here. For if you are to enter the second stage of development in gaining skill and ability in the mental environment, you must have the power to create, and what you will create will not be a product of your imagination. It will not be a product of your desires or your fantasies, but if truly understood and truly gained will be the creation of Knowledge within you. And here your greatest reality will begin to emanate through your life.

Now it is an amazing thing that individuals within your world who have gained these kinds of abilities are often hidden or withdrawn within their own societies. You might think that if you had this ability you would come forth and let your light shine for everyone, but that is not wise. That is not how Knowledge works.

Knowledge does not overtake you and dominate you. Knowledge calls for you. It is hidden within you. It does not make a great show. Only if your life is threatened or you are in grave danger will it fully exert itself and manifest itself within your mind to overtake your actions and to rescue you. But in all other circumstances, it seems to remain hidden, distant, mysterious and yet an ever-present force within you.

The man or woman of Knowledge becomes like this in the world—present, effective but hidden. Why is this the case? Because there is much adversity in the world. The institutions, the prevailing attitudes and all those who believe in them and whose minds are fixed by them will be afraid of Knowledge and may even actively oppose its expressions.

Throughout the Greater Community, except in those communities of Knowledge, freethinking individuals are recognized as a threat, as something to watch out for, as something to be suspicious of, for they are exercising a greater power than government, a greater power than the power of institutions. They have a power greater than the greatest individual rulers living within the Greater Community. Only in a community of Knowledge will their example be encouraged and able to shine freely, but even these communities are relatively hidden within the Greater Community as a whole.

GAINING STRENGTH AND INFLUENCE IN THE MENTAL ENVIRONMENT

As We said at the beginning of Our book, this may be disappointing to many people who thought that advanced races represented a sort of spiritual kingdom, a spiritual reality without conflict, without greed, without manipulation. But this is confusing your Ancient Home with physical reality. It is always a mistake when you do that.

The fact that the mental environment is so heavily used and manipulated within the Greater Community produces a greater requirement for you and for others who have real spiritual inclinations to develop skill within the mental environment.

However, at first you will do this for yourself. You will do this for yourself because you want to be free. You will do this for yourself because you want to be unencumbered. You will do this for yourself because you will want to know your own heart. You will do this for yourself because you want to have your own life. You do not want to simply be ruled mindlessly by forces that you cannot even recognize or understand.

Here you come to recognize there is great adversity. There are great obstacles in life to claiming this power and this ability. Though the Unseen Ones watch over you and encourage you, though you have great spiritual allies within the world and beyond, you still live in a world where Knowledge is not known, where Knowledge is not valued.

It is a world of law and conventions, of greed and power, yet it is also a world of goodness, a world of beauty and opportunity. But goodness, beauty and opportunity must contend with all the forces that oppose them and all the problems that these other forces have created for humanity as a whole.

Therefore, do not be a dreamer. Become potent. Gain this ability to objectively review your own thoughts and inclinations and see if they come from Knowledge or are merely the product of your exposure to culture and to conventions.

How will you be able to do this? You will be able to do this by learning the Steps to Knowledge. You cannot simply make this happen overnight. How can you undo all your years of existence by a few simple techniques or by simply wanting to do it? You must have the methodology. You must have the right understanding. You must have the correct approach.

Your study of The Way of Knowledge will give all of these to you. It will give you your inner authority. And it will give you all the responsibilities and all the challenges that go along with it. It will teach you about the mental environment because it will bring you to Knowledge.

Here you will see that within your mental environment and within the mental environments of wherever you go that you might be exposed to, there are forces that encourage the expression of Knowledge and there are forces that oppose it. As We have said, there are no neutral forces within the mental environment. Everything either helps or hinders your expression and your experience of this.

Of those forces that oppose the emergence of Knowledge within you, very little of this is truly evil. Many people oppose the expression of Knowledge simply because they do not know Knowledge exists, and they are afraid of their own inner inclinations. They are afraid to rock the boat. They are afraid to challenge their allegiances to people and to organizations and to beliefs. They are afraid to become free. They are afraid of the risks. They are afraid of what they believe they will lose.

And yet there are forces that are determined to keep humanity obedient, weak and indulgent. There are individuals committed to this. There are organizations committed to this. They cast a very great influence upon the mental environment of whole nations, upon the thought of whole populations. They seek to manipulate human weakness and inclinations for their own benefit.

This manipulation of the mental environment has been going on within human societies throughout your history, and yet there are greater forces within the world now who have greater powers and skill within the mental environment. As We have said, they will focus their attention upon the governments and institutions that have the greatest effect upon the human population. And they will focus their intent and their interaction upon individuals everywhere who are vulnerable and who have certain gifts and sensitivities that they are seeking for themselves.

At this point, you might be thinking, "Oh, my, this is too much for me! I don't think I can think of all these things. This is overwhelming!" But listen. It is not overwhelming. It is part of your experience right now.

We are giving you the power, the authority and the purpose to gain the abilities that you need, to gain the understanding that you must have to become and to do and to express what you came here to become, to do and to express—to be your true Self, to find your great inner harmony, to make a positive contribution to the world, and to realize your inherent nature and your association with your Spiritual Family.

Knowledge represents your greatest desire and your greatest need. The fact that you do not experience it today gives evidence in and of itself that you live in an environment that thwarts this discovery and does not support it, that you in the past have engaged in relationships that cannot support the emergence of Knowledge and would actively oppose it should you seek to become a student yourself.

We are giving you power to deal with the influences in your life now and to understand these influences and to gain greater authority over your life and affairs. This is not too much for you. You have been conditioned to think that you are weak and ineffective. You have been conditioned to think that you can do very little and that you must simply go along with things as they are. You have been conditioned to think that you have very little inner authority and that the best thing you can do is try to be comfortable and avoid trouble.

But you must outgrow this conditioning. You must break away from it. It is pervasive in the world today, and it will become increasingly so in the future as the Greater Community presences in the world seek to pacify humanity and to make it even more compliant and obedient, to make it even more vulnerable to control and manipulation within the mental environment.

This is a call for you to awaken. This book is a call to awaken. Your awakening is what you must do to accomplish what you came here to accomplish. You live within both a physical and a mental environment. There are forces within both of these environments that affect you, and yet you can become effective in both of these environments as well.

Engage with Knowledge. Clear the way for Knowledge to emerge within your life. Adjust your thinking and involvements with other people to make this possible, and you will speak with an authority that is greater than the world. You will have an authority that is more substantial and more complete and universal than any power, than any institution, than any government that you might encounter within the world or within the Greater Community.

The Creator has given you this authority, but it is up to you to receive it and to learn what it means and to take the steps towards its reclamation and expression. The Creator cannot do that for you. The Unseen Ones who watch over you cannot do this for you. Do not abdicate this responsibility. This is your responsibility.

This is what will make you strong. This is what will make you competent. This is what will enable you to develop discernment and discretion. This is what will refine your perception. This is what will teach you how to learn what is positive and helpful and what is not, both within your own mind and in the world around you.

You become a man and woman of Knowledge by taking the Steps to Knowledge. There are many steps. Each one is important. Each one prepares for the next. Like climbing a great mountain, you do not go from the bottom to the top in a few giant leaps. Likewise, the Creator does not come and elevate you up to the top. No.

You must make the journey. It is the journey that will make you strong. It is the journey that will make you wise. It is the journey that will give you what you really need and what you really want. And like journeying up a mountain, you will have to leave behind those people and those situations that cannot support your journey and that cannot enable it.

Here you claim authority within yourself, and here you become responsible, or able to respond, to your deeper inclinations. Here you are a student of Knowledge whether you know it or not. Here you are learning the essential steps whether you know it or not.

Yet sooner or later you will need a formal preparation, for there is only so much you can do for yourself. You cannot train yourself. You cannot take yourself where you have never gone. You cannot prepare yourself for a greater set of abilities to live in a greater reality.

For this you need assistance. You need a method of study. You need a spiritual practice. And you need true relationships that can support you and assist you.

The Greater Community Way of Knowledge has been given to enable you to do this. It is not possible to become a man or woman of Knowledge and not learn about the mental environment and not gain authority and competence there. This will happen for you, but you must take the steps. This is your responsibility.

There are great needs in the world today, greater than you realize. There are great forces in the mental environment who will seek domination over humanity and are doing so at this moment. There is a great need for men and women of Knowledge to keep Knowledge alive and to empower others so that humanity may maintain its integrity and its self-determination as it emerges into a greater and more complicated universe.

There is a great calling in the world today. You can feel it within yourself. It is not calling for someone else. It is calling for you. Do not look over your shoulder and say, "Well, someone had better respond to this!" It is you.

GAINING STRENGTH AND INFLUENCE IN THE MENTAL ENVIRONMENT

You are the one responding to the call for Knowledge. You are the one responding to the world's emergence into the Greater Community. This represents a deeper receptivity and a greater responsibility within you. Honor this. Support it. It is of the greatest importance.

CHAPTER 11

DEVELOPING CLARITY AND DISCERNMENT

Certainly, becoming aware of what you think and why you think what you think is directly connected to how you see what you see and what you value. If you are taught to think in a certain way, then you will only see certain things that are associated with that, and this will help determine what you value.

Much of your prior education was devoted to this, but We are beginning now a new education, a fundamental education. This represents your second great education in life. Your first education was to learn to become a functional human being so you could participate within the world. But this is only a first stage. The second great stage in education is the reclamation and the expression of Knowledge, the great knowing Mind that lives within you. Each of these forms of education is very complete, but they are only indirectly related.

Your first education to become a functional human being, to become socially integrated, to become socially determined and to become socially interactive is not aimed at you becoming a man or a woman of Knowledge. Instead, it is aimed at you becoming a productive member of society. Everything you have learned about the history and the meaning of human existence primarily has been aimed to produce this result. This is an education you have gained living in isolation in the world, and as a result your education has mostly been focused upon human interests, human activities, human history and human ideals.

Yet your second great education in life is the reclamation and the expression of Knowledge. This is when your spiritual emergence begins. This is what it really means to become reborn. It is like a new beginning. And just like when you began life as a small child, you start out very uncertain, very shaky in your foundation, and you enter a brave new world with new influences and new things to consider. You are not leaving your life. You are not going anywhere. But you are penetrating the whole other part of life, which you are not encouraged to learn about in your prior education.

Part of your second great education is learning a greater discernment and a greater perception. To develop this discernment and perception, you must become aware of things that you were not aware of before. You must become responsive to things within yourself and in your environment that you were not encouraged to see or interact with previously.

While your first great stage of education did not hold as a goal for you to become a man or a woman of Knowledge, it is true that your second stage of education does require that you have become socially integrated and developed, but only to a certain degree. For if you could not function in the world, then Knowledge could not work through you. If you do not know how to get along with people at all, then Knowledge could not exert its beneficial presence within your relationships. If you could not accomplish anything in human society, then how could Knowledge contribute through you within that society?

In other words, you need a certain foundation in order to begin the great study and reclamation of Knowledge. You need a certain foundation to have a spiritual emergence occur within your life. This does not mean that you are totally socially integrated or that you accept all social mandates or that you get along with everyone wonderfully or that you believe in all of the great ideals of your society. Not at all. But it does mean that you are capable of participating, that you are able to participate and that you are competent to communicate and interact with others.

Within yourself, you may be a great rebel against the very fabric of society as it is manifested today, but it is important as far as Knowledge is concerned that you are able to participate within that society. If you were completely alienated, if you could not express yourself, then the possibility for the great Spirit to work through you would be very limited.

Here Knowledge uses all things you have learned before to focus your life in a new direction. Here Knowledge does not destroy what you have learned but gives it a greater employment and a greater focus. This demonstrates one of the great laws of life—that the Creator does not destroy, but instead re-employs.

The whole idea that the Creator would punish you for your sins is utterly ridiculous and has no validity in reality. That is the creation of religious institutions in order to engender obedience and conformity in its followers. The Creator re-employs; the Creator does not destroy. Whatever you have created in life, however full of error, however misapplied your efforts may have been, Knowledge will show you a way to use what you have learned in a new and constructive way.

Therefore, Knowledge will take what you have learned in terms of discernment, in terms of perception, and build upon that. It will build upon your accomplishments rather than deny them. It will validate what you have achieved thus far rather than discourage you.

Though you may need to take an entirely different tack in life, though you will be venturing into an entirely new kind of living, you will use what you have gained thus far, for nothing will be wasted.

Here your life becomes really validated as it finds a greater application and a greater meaning. Here your past will be used to create a future of greater proportions and greater benefit. Here the shadows that have hung over you will be cast aside as the real content of your life finds new expression, meaning and value. Here you will begin to see the world in a new way. Here you will gain a greater discernment of what you are looking at and what you are interacting with.

The man or the woman of Knowledge is always looking. Whereas everyone else is always judging, the man or woman of Knowledge is always looking. They want to see because real seeing is connected with real Knowing. You will more often see and then know rather than know and then see, but they do both go together.

To really know the meaning and purpose of your life, you must get high enough up the mountain so that you can see the panorama of your experience. Otherwise, you will just have beliefs, and beliefs are removed from reality. The best thing a belief can do is help you to interpret reality, but the belief is not reality itself.

Many people have never gone beyond their beliefs. They have never found Knowledge in a real and substantial way, and so they do not see that there is life beyond their beliefs. There are even people who think that life is belief—whatever you believe is what you will live and experience. But this is only valid at the level of perception.

There is actually a reality beyond your beliefs. It is this reality that you must find and become engaged with. Here beliefs are like the glasses that you wear. They either help you see or they do not. They are either the right prescription for you or they are not. And over time, your perception will change.

Therefore, your ideas and beliefs need to be flexible and adaptable. They are only temporary expediencies to help you see and to help you know. You cannot live without belief because you have a mind that thinks, that needs beliefs to organize its thoughts and to become stable. But belief, when it is directed by Knowledge, is very different from belief that is directed only by the mind.

For example, you can believe in something very firmly and be very identified with your belief, but your Being may have nothing to do with it. For example, people will become married to another person because of what they believe about that person, but their Being is not getting married. People walk down the aisle and make their vows and commit all of their resources to a relationship in which their Being has absolutely no involvement whatsoever. Though this sounds crazy, it happens all the time.

That is just trying to live life without Knowledge. That is trying to make commitments without Knowledge. That is trying to govern what you believe without Knowledge.

But with Knowledge as the foundation, belief becomes then a tool of perception, a means of greater discernment. Here your ideas change, not simply because change is important but because you need to be able to see—you need to be able to use your ideas and your beliefs to see more clearly, to know more clearly, to be able to discern what you are dealing with in the world.

It could be said that all human error is the result of poor discernment. And poor discernment is the result of not being engaged with Knowledge sufficiently. For Knowledge will reorganize your ideas and will redirect your perception. As I have said, it will not destroy what you have learned but will give it a new focus and a new relevancy.

Here it seems like you are starting out for the first time. You will feel like a rank beginner, but at the same time you will be drawing upon everything you have learned thus far. But it will be different. You will feel different. The experience will be different. What you see will be different. What you will sense, what you will know will be different.

The first great stage of your education taught you what to see and what to look for and what to value. But in the second great stage of your education, in the reclamation of Knowledge, you will learn to see and value something entirely new and something far more meaningful. But the fact that you have learned how to see, that you are capable of seeing, is the result of the first stage of your education. This now is being brought into a greater arena of life and given a greater employment.

It is a remarkable thing how little people see. You will find this in your own experience as you come to realize how little you have seen. People are literally unaware of great things happening in their lives. They are unaware that they are making critical mistakes. They are unaware of great opportunities. They are unaware that there are important alternatives to what they are seeing and what they are believing. They are unaware that they are violating Knowledge in many of their engagements and associations, and yet they feel all the discomforts that are the result of this. And rather than going to the source of the discomfort, they seek for more pleasure, or they take pills, or they try to reinforce old ideas, or they try to lose themselves in constant outer activity.

It is remarkable that people do not see, but it is also tragic. Human suffering in all of its manifestations that you see throughout the world, much of it is the result of not seeing and not knowing and not being able to respond appropriately to what is happening in life.

Certainly, there is suffering that is the result of a lack of food, a lack of medicine, a lack of the basic necessities of life. But beyond this, the great psychological suffering that you see is the result of a lack of discernment, which in turn is the result of a lack of Knowledge. Knowledge has not been allowed to emerge sufficiently within these individuals, as they have not been able to adapt to the changing circumstances of their lives.

What is real seeing? Real seeing is seeing what is there. It is not just seeing what you want to see. It is not just seeing what you like. It is not just seeing what you are afraid of. It is not just seeing according to the prevailing attitudes and beliefs in your mind. It is being able to see through the mind. Here the mind is either a window or a wall. It is either a maze that is impenetrable or it becomes a refined telescope.

It is possible for you to see what is really there, to have a direct experience. We call this direct experience when you see what is really there. For a moment you are clicked out of your own thoughts and preoccupations long enough to have a direct experience of something outside yourself. This is very important. This reconnects you with the world. It reconnects you with other people. And it reconnects you with the changing circumstances of your life and gives you an opportunity to gain a different vantage point from which to see and to act.

The most effective way of developing direct experience, and as a result gaining a new perspective and greater discernment, is becoming a student of Knowledge. Why? Because when you engage with Knowledge, you engage in life as it is actually happening at this moment within you. You engage with the Source of the life force within yourself, which is directly engaged or connected to the larger events that are happening in the world.

This takes you out of your self-preoccupation. This takes you out of your obsessions with yourself and your particular interests. This frees you from the restraints in your own mental environment and from the mental environment of your culture as a whole. This brings you out of yourself, out of your mind, and into life as it is really happening.

Now life itself will sometimes dump cold water on you, and you will find yourself in a situation to which you will have to respond. These situations are almost always redemptive, but they can be very difficult and very costly. Why become aware and awake only under great adversity when the opportunity is there for you every day? Why wait until your problems become so severe and so demanding that you must respond to them in a state of emergency, usually at great cost to yourself? Why wait until catastrophe comes when it could have been avoided at the outset?

Real seeing and real knowing go together. One can follow the other, but they always go together. Out of this comes effective action, dynamic action. Out of this comes revitalization of your body and greater health as a result.

DEVELOPING CLARITY AND DISCERNMENT

Knowledge only sees what is important to see. As you learn to see with Knowledge, you learn to penetrate the surface of things, the manifestations of things. You learn to penetrate the prevailing attitudes and beliefs under which you have labored all these years, and you gain discernment. What is discernment again but seeing what is really there, discerning what is important to discern?

Perception, then, can either simply be a mechanism for projecting the prevailing attitudes in your mind and using them to attempt to understand life around you, or perception can become a means of engaging with life as it really is. The former promotes and deepens self-obsession and self-absorption. The latter brings you into life, into a dynamic engagement.

You have already suffered self-obsession and all of its debilitating effects. If that is not enough to convince you, simply look at life around you. Human beings, so gifted and so intelligent, are living under such dismal psychological and physical conditions.

You can blame life. You can blame the government. You can blame your parents. You can blame whatever you want to blame. But the responsibility is yours ultimately, for you are the one who can change what you see. You are the one who can find out what you know. You cannot change what you know because you cannot change Knowledge, but you can enable Knowledge to reveal itself to you and to show you how to engage with life in a truly effective and meaningful way. Let Us talk about this.

In looking with Knowledge, there is no right and no wrong. There is instead yes or no. Knowledge is not constantly involved in judging and evaluating people and situations. It is simply trying to get you where you need to go and help you find those people you need to find to get where you need to go. Knowledge is on a mission in life. It is trying to bring you into the mission that has brought you into the world, for only here will you find fulfillment and real happiness.

It is not just sitting by the side of the road, judging everything that comes along. It is not a spectator in life. It is an active participant. And it is the catalyst for change and redemption.

Many people look at Spirit in a very passive way as if it were something out there floating around in space. It is something that is just being, like a lightbulb in the ceiling, just sending out light everywhere. It is noninvolved. It is totally detached. If things go well, if things do not go well, what does it matter? It is like the sun above the clouds. It shines regardless of the conditions below.

But this perception of Spirit is really not correct. Only if you are trying to get out of life would you foster such a perception. But Knowledge is trying to bring you into life. It may have to get you out of life temporarily in order to give you a different vantage point, in order to enable you to re-evaluate your ideas and your priorities, but its intention is to bring you into life, to engage you with life, because that is why you have come.

You did not go through all the trouble to get here simply to become a bystander, simply to watch the parade. You came here to make things happen. You came here to accomplish things, not only for yourself but for the whole world. Your gift and contribution is primarily for others.

So when Knowledge looks in the world, it does not say, "That is good and that is bad." No, it says, "yes," and "no," yes meaning this is helpful for the discovery and expression of your purpose or no, this is not helpful. As a result, Knowledge does not condemn. It does not judge and cast people into Hell.

This whole notion of God judging and the Final Judgment and you being cast into purgatory is completely a fabrication of the mind. Its only connection to reality is that if you are not connected with Knowledge, you are sort of living in a purgatory every day. You are living without certainty. You are living without a greater conscience. You are living without direction. You are living without wisdom. You are like a car careening down the mountainside without any brakes, out of control. This is Hell enough.

God is re-employing. God is emphasizing a greater purpose. God is speaking through Knowledge to you. That is your connection with God. God does not appear at the foot of your bed. That only happens in movies. God is speaking through Knowledge to you, reminding you that you came here for a purpose, reminding you that you want to accomplish something here, reminding, reminding, reminding you of your true nature and mission.

God is not trying to take you out of the world. God is trying to get you into the world to do something for life. This is what redeems you. This is what restores your value. This is what turns your past from a painful record, a failure and disassociation into a real meaningful engagement with life. This is what transforms everything that has been created in the world into something good and beneficial. A great part of this transformation is the transformation of perception.

Looking with Knowledge, then, you are able to see beyond appearances. You are able to see beyond your own ideas even. You are able to see things that your previous beliefs would not let you see.

You are able to entertain alternatives. You are able to see elements within your mental and physical environment that you simply could not interact with before.

Knowledge will teach you how to see, what to see and how to engage with things in a productive and effective way. This will be very different from your obsessions, your beliefs and your attitudes and your compulsions—fundamentally different. For you will be seeing from a greater vantage point within yourself, and as you learn to see in this way, you will develop new eyes and a new consciousness.

Knowledge within you knows that the world is emerging into the Greater Community. This may be very different from your beliefs, but Knowledge is not affected by your beliefs. It knows that it knows. That is why it is Knowledge. It cannot be swayed. It cannot be corrupted. It cannot be disengaged from itself.

This is why it represents a source of power and integrity within you, for as you become close to Knowledge, as you begin to feel the effects of Knowledge more and more, both within the mundane activities of your life and within your greater understanding of where you are going and what you are doing, you will begin to share its attributes. Your sense of invulnerability will grow, and with it your discernment of the world will grow as well.

Here you will not be preoccupied with all kinds of meaningless things. Instead, your mind will become quiet and still. Your vision will become penetrating. Instead of answering your own questions, you will look for the answer in life. While Knowledge is trying to bring you into the world in a real way, it does not encourage you to try to find all your answers within yourself because most of your answers will be found in the world.

Though the answer already lives within you, it must be connected to the real events in which it can be expressed and become relevant. This brings you back into the world. This frees you from self-obsession, which is the source of all mental illness.

In studying Steps to Knowledge, the method of study in learning a Greater Community Way of Knowledge, your mind is taught how to become still. This is a fundamental skill. It is a skill that is taught in many of the world's traditions. [Stillness] is necessary to gain discernment, for if your mind is racing or caught up with its own ideas, how can you see anything?

People look. They do not see. Why? Because they are not being present. Why are they not present? Because they are caught up in their own thinking. It is like the television is running in their mind all the time, and they cannot seem to break away from it. So how can they see anything? How can they feel anything? They are disassociated from the world, and as a result can easily become manipulated.

It is easy to manipulate someone who is obsessed. It is difficult to influence someone who is present. It is easy to manipulate someone who is dominated by their own ideas. It is difficult to influence someone who is looking beyond themselves.

This is why those visitors from the Greater Community who are interacting in human affairs do not support the reclamation of Knowledge. They do not want human beings to become powerful and observant because [then human beings] cannot be used; they cannot be influenced. They become a far greater adversary here.

Here you may have a greater calling than even your visitors. If you can reclaim Knowledge and with it discernment and perception, then you have something to teach them, if they are able to learn. And all their great technology and even all of their ability to influence the mental environment will not be comparable to the cultivation of Knowledge within the human mind. This is humanity's only defense and your most important asset in both gaining a real practical mastery within your own life and in preparing for the Greater Community itself.

Knowledge within you looks at your visitors and comprehends their intent, sees their strengths, sees their weaknesses, understands the elements that are governing their mental environment, comprehends their lack of freedom, comprehends their skill and reads everything objectively, just as it is.

But people in the world, if they are aware of this at all, think, "Oh, they are angels! They are spiritually enlightened and coming to rescue us and to teach us the ways of enlightenment. This will be the end of war and conflict forever." Or they think, "Oh, they are coming here to devour us! They are going to destroy us! They are going to have us for dinner! They are going to overtake us!" This is not seeing. This is only projecting one's own beliefs and attitudes upon a situation that one cannot discern clearly.

In the mind of the believer, visitors from the Greater Community must either be angels or demons because any power from the skies must either be angelic or demonic. And so the visitors are conceptualized as either angelic or demonic forms. But this is not seeing. This is not having discernment. This is simply projecting one's prevailing ideas and beliefs. This is not looking to see what is really there. This is only projecting what one believes to give one a sense of stability and security in light of a whole new experience. Knowledge sees what is there. Belief only sees itself.

As you come to feel the great need for Knowledge within your life—the need for certainty, the need for clarity, the need for a sense of real purpose and mission in life—you also come to recognize how much you need to be able to see clearly and be present to what is happening around you.

Most of the mistakes you have ever made in life were the result of not being present and not being discerning. You were somewhere else in your mind when something happened. You did not see it coming. And perhaps afterwards you felt, "Oh, life is so hard on me! I had such bad luck today," but you did not see it coming.

People do not end up where they are simply by chance. They end up there either because they intended to be there in a conscious way or they were not present while other things were setting their course for them.

How many people make pivotal decisions in life without being really aware of what they are doing? And how can you not be aware of what you are doing unless you are preoccupied in your own thoughts and are not engaged with what is really happening around you?

People get married every day, not realizing who they are marrying, what they are getting themselves into, what the responsibilities are. But they are willing to sacrifice so much. And others say, "Well, you have to take your chances in life!"

But the more intelligent you are, which means the closer you are to Knowledge and the more discerning you are, you realize you take fewer chances, but you also realize the chances are more significant. It becomes more important not to make critical mistakes, especially repeat ones you have made before. You do not take such a casual attitude towards things that have such grave consequences.

Developing discernment and clear perception, then, begins with being still. To be still you have to be present, and you have to learn how to disengage from your own mind. This is a great training in and of itself. This is not easy, but every little step of advancement you make here yields so much to you.

Every little accomplishment gives you a sense of discernment, a sense of awareness, a sense of capability that simply was not there before. And, yes, your mind will keep on judging and evaluating because your mind works like a machine. Until it can gain service to the greater power within you, it seems to be like a runaway train.

But more and more, you are able to step aside from it. More and more, you are able to see over its manifestations. More and more, you are able to take a second look. You step back. You look. You do not answer your own questions. You look. You wait. You become still.

The animals do this every day. They watch. They become still. They watch. They give their full awareness to what they are seeing. But for human beings, this is very difficult, for their minds are overactive. Their imaginations have no context, so they are creating scenarios constantly until people end up living more in the world of imagination than in the world of reality. They cannot distinguish what they are thinking from what is actually happening.

This is a grave disability and one that is very serious, particularly in terms of the Greater Community presences in the world and humanity's emergence into a Greater Community of life. But you experience this disability every day.

As We have said, you will begin the reclamation of Knowledge and the development of real discernment primarily for yourself at first. And then you will realize over time that you really are not just doing this for yourself, that if you did it for yourself, you would not exert the energy and the effort required. But instead you are doing this for the world, for something greater. This solidifies your commitment to the truth and gives you greater skill in discerning the truth.

When you look at things in the world in a conscious way, ask yourself, "What am I seeing? Is this beneficial? Should I become engaged with this? Should I say anything? Is this important?"

Now you will notice that all of these questions call for either a yes or a no answer. This is a very good way of questioning because this tends to bypass the mind, which has great difficulty in dealing with questions like this, and goes to Knowledge, which simply knows.

The mind takes a basic question and turns it into a complex series of considerations, which may have little to do with what you are dealing with directly. So while the mind goes on and on and on, trying to use all of its criteria, Knowledge knows.

Sometimes the mind's criteria are important; often they are not. But to develop a new kind of seeing, you must learn to go beyond the mind, at least temporarily. In the future, you will need to use the mind, but right now you do not have the strength to use the mind, for you are used to having it use you. So to gain a greater sense of authority and ability, you must learn to bypass the thinking mind.

This is only part of the training, for there are many ways to find what you know. Sometimes you find this by bypassing the mind. Sometimes you find this by going through the mind and the mental processes of which you are aware. But the answer is always beyond the mind.

As you learn to become still, this will quiet your mind and teach you how to see beyond it and to see through it. As you learn to do this, you will be able to see and engage more clearly and directly with what is happening around you. Here your beliefs are secondary. You are trying to see what is there. And if you are patient and do not try to answer your own questions, you will go through a series of real breakthroughs in your perception. This will have an immense effect on all aspects of your life.

Ultimately, this will prepare you to engage with the Greater Community because you will be able to see with Knowledge, and will not be fooled by the appearances of things, and will not be governed by your preferences. This gives you power and certainty within the mental environment, for just like in your physical environment, Knowledge is not fooled by the appearance of things.

The closer you are to Knowledge, the stronger you are with Knowledge, the more Knowledge is directing you, the more you will have this great clarity, this great perception and the more discerning you will become. As a result of this, you will become a great benefactor to others. You will teach them how to see, how to know, how to become still, how to become discerning. You will teach this through demonstration, and you will teach this through all the things that you advocate and that you support in life.

Humanity is emerging into a Greater Community of life. The need for discernment, the need for clear perception now is greater than it has ever been. The failure to develop these essential qualities within yourself will not simply be a personal tragedy for you but will engender a greater tragedy for humanity as a whole.

When you look with Knowledge, you look without fear, and you look without preference. As a result, you do not promote fear and preference within yourself. This is the beginning of true objectivity, something that is very, very difficult to achieve in life. And yet the possibility for achieving this is so much greater now because of the presence of The Greater Community Way of Knowledge.

Finally, there is a Teaching that enables you to see and to know. This is its foundation. It teaches you how to become still and observant. It teaches you how to connect with things on the outside without being swept up by your own thoughts and beliefs. And yet even beyond this, it teaches you how to see with a greater vision, the greater vision that one would have as a result of living in a Greater Community of life. It teaches you how to see beyond your isolation as a human being within the world. It teaches you a Greater Community perception, awareness and understanding.

To participate in the Greater Community, you must have great discernment. You must develop some skill in the mental environment. And if you are to truly be a positive force in life, you must become a man or woman of Knowledge. There is only one preparation in the world today that can enable you to do all of these things. It is called The Greater Community Way of Knowledge. It is presented through the sacred texts, Steps to Knowledge and Wisdom from the Greater Community [and the other books of the New Message.]

The preparation is here. The need is great. Your need is great. You cannot afford to continue to stumble blindly forward in life, hoping that good things will happen for you, but disconnected and unaware of the greater events that are shaping your future, your experience and your destiny. How can you afford this when the means for gaining vision, gaining insight and developing discernment are now available to you?

Yet this preparation will take much patience. You cannot undo decades of habits and years and years of social conditioning in a day, a week or a month. The transformation of your vision and your awareness is something that happens in steps and stages. And yet the calling is in the world to undertake exactly this preparation.

There is no time now for ambivalence. There is no time now for self-obsession. There is no time now to indulge yourself in your small pleasures. There is only time now to develop your greatest abilities, to become the person you really are, to gain the rewards of Knowledge, the skills of Knowledge, and to help humanity learn to see its condition, its influences and its destiny.

Knowledge will give you this vision. Knowledge will become your eyes. Knowledge will teach you to become still and penetrating, open and compassionate. Knowledge will generate its own mental environment within your mind and within the sphere of your life. Then your life will become a contribution, for Knowledge will emanate from you and around you. And others will learn to see as a result of being in your presence.

Yet this can only happen if you undertake the Steps to Knowledge, if you prepare in The Way of Knowledge, if you take all the steps that are necessary to regain your vision, to refine your perception and to develop your discernment. This is what awaits you and this is what We offer.

CHAPTER 12

GOING BEYOND THE LIMITS OF HUMAN RELIGION AND BELIEF

The religious traditions of the world have a rich heritage, and from a Greater Community perspective, they have kept Knowledge alive in the world despite their manipulation by world governments, societies and so forth. They have kept the glow of spirituality alive for many, many people.

Yet because humanity has evolved in a state of relative isolation and has not had the challenge and the benefit of encounters with other forms of intelligent life in the Greater Community, in any kind of large scale way, the traditions within this world have certain fundamental limitations. These limitations are understandable given humanity's isolation, and they must be understood as the result, in large part, of this isolation.

For the student of Knowledge, there are certain things that must be reconciled. These emanate out of the cultures and religious traditions in which most people in the world have been reared. They represent both the aspirations of humanity and the limits of humanity's awareness and understanding.

Whether you come out of a strict religious background or not, you are affected by this conditioning, for these are the undercurrents of your cultural conditioning overall. And whether you are aware of them or not, they do condition your viewpoint.

Let Us address these now so that you have a clearer understanding of what a spiritual calling means within the world, and how the circumstances of the world have changed and what this requires now.

There are certain conventions of belief in the world that are prevalent throughout the world, both in religious traditions that encompass many nations and within tribal traditions as well. The root of these traditions is an attempt to negotiate the difficulties of life and to maintain confidence in a larger or greater power, in a Divine power, that can protect and guide human activity.

Though religions have become many other things in their cultural and political associations, the essence of their practice is to keep spiritual experience alive, to enable people to have a direct experience of divinity and to bring a higher consciousness into the world, a set of ethics that are greater than what the marketplace can dictate and what mundane life itself stimulates in people.

Yet there are also certain problems. These problems provide a great hindrance to understanding the Greater Community and the meaning of spirituality in the Greater Community. It is for this reason that the religious institutions today stand largely in the way of understanding the meaning of the Greater Community or what is required for people to prepare adequately for the Greater Community.

Intrinsic in this is the fact that their basic understanding of humanity and its relationship with nature and the Divine will be severely challenged by the reality that humanity is emerging into a Greater Community. Here they must realize that their most cherished ideals are not absolute. They are not universal, for the most part, and the requirements of spiritual life must now be reassessed. And the

202

parameters of life and the meaning of life must have a greater context in which to become meaningful.

We think this is a very healthy thing for all religious traditions in the world. They must grow and expand. If they do not grow and expand, they will contract and become basically reactionary and oppose the great changes that are occurring to humanity at this time. This will bring new life and new spirit into their traditions and new awareness that humanity so desperately needs now.

There are certain dichotomies within the present religious traditions in the world that must be addressed. We have already referred to many of these so far, but let Us take a closer look now.

First, let Us examine the whole idea of Heaven and Hell within the context of the Greater Community itself. Simply said, Heaven represents where you have come from and where you will return to, but in terms of today's experience, it has to do with your closeness to Knowledge, your allegiance to Knowledge and your identification with Knowledge.

Hell represents your inability to gain access to your true nature, which casts you into a world of grave uncertainty and doubt, anxiety and suffering. This is the purgatory. Purgatory is not the reward for bad behavior. Purgatory is not the place you go if Heaven does not want you. Heaven always wants you.

Purgatory is living without Knowledge. It is being cast apart. It is living a life of isolation and separation—separation from Knowledge within yourself and separation from the meaning of your true relationships in life.

In the Greater Community, there is no Heaven and Hell in the traditional sense. If you think about this, it will begin to make sense to you. For what is good behavior in a human environment would have to be changed in other civilizations and other environments. In many cases, other races have their own concoction of Heaven and Hell, their reward for good behavior, their punishment for bad behavior. They would seem as irrelevant to you as your rendition of Heaven and Hell might seem to them. There is nothing universal here. This is a local custom, a local tradition—in this case, local to your world.

In the Greater Community, there is no beginning and no end. There is no fantastic creation story. There is no imminent end to life in the universe. Learning, however, does have an end. And there will be an end to manifest life, but it is so far in the future as to be beyond the realm of your concern.

Likewise, the evolution of life within the physical reality is something that occurred far before the creation of your world. So the beginning is so long ago, and the end is so far in the future that these cannot be defining relevancies for your understanding of the meaning and nature of Divinity in your life.

Again, We must distinguish between the powers of persuasion used through your religious institutions and the meaning of living a truly religious life. Conformity and obedience mixed with political expediency have given rise to many of the ideals and precepts which seem to affect most people's thinking here.

It is as if to say that unless there is a great threat of punishment, unless there are absolutes in which people have to believe, they will wander aimlessly. Having no real incentive on their own, they must be governed, and so these things are created to govern effectively.

But the student of Knowledge must look beyond these dichotomies and see the real truth that exists there. Let Us look at the dichotomy between good and evil. This is a very difficult one because many people have very, very radical ideas concerning this.

Much of the idealism that exists is not so much the result of real serious consideration and contemplation but is more a social reaction. For example, people think because of the domination of the church in the past, they must reject the idea of evil. Have they really thought about this, or is it simply a reaction?

Clearly, there are those who are committed to good, and there are those who are committed to working against the good. They represent the opposite extremes. In the middle is everyone else, being swayed one way or the other.

There are forces of good and there are forces of dissonance. You may call them good and evil, but they are in essence more complex than this. The capability to do good and the capability to do evil are within each person. Which, then, becomes the predominant force in a person's life? In any person, one is either radically or even slightly more predominant than the other.

Within the context of the Greater Community and within Greater Community Spirituality, this can be seen in another way. Here We come back again to the essence of Knowledge. When you are connected to Knowledge, you do good. When you are not connected to Knowledge, you tend to work against the good even though you have inclinations for the good.

No one in life is entirely good, and no one in life is entirely evil. You cannot be entirely good because there is always the opportunity that you can be deceived or can make a mistake in your perception and judgment and so forth. Everyone is capable of making mistakes in physical life. This is as true in the world as it is throughout the Greater Community.

Likewise, no one can be entirely evil because you cannot eradicate Knowledge from the individual. You cannot destroy what God has put there. It can be denied; it can be thwarted; it can be completely avoided, but it cannot be eliminated.

Therefore, every individual, regardless of how detrimental their behavior may be, is capable and has the potentiality for doing good. Here you must outgrow a childish view of what is good and what is evil, outgrow a childish view of angels and demons, and come back to the reality of life.

The Creator knows when you come into the world that the world is full of difficulties and that you will make many mistakes and that you may not even be successful in finding your purpose and your way here. Clearly, that is understood.

In fact, very few people find their purpose and their mission here. Everyone else makes the attempt but somehow cannot succeed. This is because the world is so difficult and because to gain their first great stage of education, they must largely be ignorant of their true nature, their true origin and their true destiny.

Again, if you were so aware of your Ancient Home and your relationships there, you would not want to enter into the world. It would be too difficult. Your yearning to go Home would be so great that it would disable you from participating here fully. When you are with your Spiritual Family before you enter the world, the world does not look so hard. Being there, everything is so intact; everything is so complete; you are so totally understood. You come into the world, and that is all gone. It is a whole different reality.

Therefore, the Creator knows that you will make many mistakes here. That is why condemnation is out of the question. The important thing is that you find your true Self, that you find your purpose and your mission here. All the emphasis is on this.

The Creator gives you Knowledge to make this possible. Without Knowledge, you would be overtaken and overcome by the world. You would have no capacity to discern and to discover the truth. You would have no real conscience. Without Knowledge, you could become completely evil.

But most people in the world today do not realize that they possess Knowledge. It is not part of their religious education. They are taught to believe and to be obedient. They are taught to believe in ideas, in words, in books, in standards and in conventions. And they are threatened with terrible retribution if they fail to do so. There is no teaching in The Way of Knowledge. There is no method for reclaiming Knowledge. This is understandable in a primitive race, but humanity now is emerging out of its primitive state even though much of its behavior is still very primitive.

People need to know. Belief is not enough. Belief is weak and fallible and easily persuaded and influenced. That is not what is needed in the world today. Humanity does not need a better belief. It needs nothing less than Knowledge itself.

And yet what a revolution this will be in religious thought. People who have relied upon their ideologies and institutions to give them stability and identity will be greatly threatened by this idea, for they do not believe in the inherent goodness of humanity or in the reality and the meaning of Knowledge.

So the emphasis on Heaven and Hell, the emphasis on reward and punishment in the afterlife, the emphasis on good and evil—all are perpetrated in an environment where Knowledge is unknown and is not emphasized. This creates a very difficult environment for the man or woman of Knowledge to begin to travel the way that Knowledge provides. They must deal with these forces not only in their environment, but within themselves.

Some people's religious training has been so adamant and so forcefully placed upon them that they cannot seem to outgrow it. It is such a crushing weight. It weighs upon them. They feel so much guilt trying to shift their allegiance from an old set of ideas to the living reality within them.

Out of this dichotomy of good and evil, Heaven and Hell, comes a profound inability to discern a new experience. Things are judged according to a set of beliefs that in essence are really irrelevant to the new experience itself.

For example, the Greater Community is in the world. Those people who are aware of this tend to project these notions of good and evil. They say, "Are they good? Are they evil? Are they Divine? Are they satanic?" Even educated people who do not say this might actually feel it. They are concerned. These superstitions are so deeply established and are so much a part of culture and cultural identity that it is very difficult sometimes to recognize them and to outgrow them.

Without Knowledge, religion does become superstition. It becomes belief, and belief is easy to govern and to influence. Without Knowledge, people can believe all kinds of things, even if they are in direct contrast with their experience.

People can be taught that they are inherently evil and therefore must subjugate themselves to rigorous adherence to religious ideologies. And yet this betrays a natural experience of themselves. They can be taught that they are physically bad, that their bodies are bad, that physical experience is bad, that somehow being alive is a great misfortune and is a form of punishment in and of itself. Yet this is in complete contrast to the real experience of life itself and is a complete contradiction of the real nature of people's purpose and presence in the world, which is inherently to do good.

The Creator has sent everyone here to do good. But everyone must go through the world first. For many, this will be enough to deny their great opportunity and their greater expression.

Hero worship is another inherent part of human religions for the most part. It is emphasized in some traditions more than others. People need to have some kind of superhuman to believe in, someone who is greater, someone who does not seem to exhibit human fallibility, someone who is in a perfect state.

And yet can this be true in the Greater Community? Can one person be the means to God in the Greater Community? That would be like a visiting race coming here and saying to you, "Well, you cannot get into Heaven unless you completely believe and follow and obey our hero," who of course would not be human.

Though this may be meaningful within a human context to inspire greater works and a higher level of intelligence and consciousness in people, within the Greater Community, it does not hold.

There can be no superbeings in the Greater Community. There are only beings in physical life who are either strong or weak with Knowledge. Beyond this, there is the development of their social systems and their technology and their ethics.

But the critical factor is whether they are strong in Knowledge or not because, as We have seen within the world, good ethics without Knowledge lead to bad results. Many things that people begin start out as a good intention, but it does not end up in a positive way.

Therefore, the idea of hero worship in the Greater Community cannot be relevant. As great as Jesus is within the world, though he is still largely misunderstood, from a Greater Community standpoint, he is a local hero.

Great teachers have been sent into all communities of intelligent life. Many have suffered the same fate as Jesus, however. In some cases, religions have been built upon them, which hardly reflect their true nature and purpose.

In many religious traditions in the world, there is the idea that someone else must be the intermediary between you and the Creator: some Divine person, a person who holds a great office in a religious institution. If there were real wisdom in these institutions and they were governed by complete benevolence, this would be possible and beneficial. But everyone is fallible. So this leads to great misunderstanding and great abuse and misappropriation of office.

In the Greater Community, people are given much more responsibility. This responsibility requires a very developed form of self-honesty, which has not been highly cultivated yet within the world because if people learn The Way of Knowledge, they may call anything that they really want, anything that they are attached to, anything that they are craving for themselves as coming from Knowledge within them.

People will make these errors. They will think, "I want what I want and to hell with the rest!" They will call it Knowledge or whatever they think will give them the advantage in gaining what they want.

So you see the problem. But despite the great potential for error, The Way of Knowledge must be taught to humanity, for its superstitions, its lack of vision, its religious ideology, so blind [humanity] to the greater conditions that are shaping its destiny and its future, that there must be a great inroad in The Way of Knowledge. This will not replace the world's religions but will give them real promise and the possibility to exist and be meaningful within a Greater Community of life context.

So deeply ingrained are many spiritual ideas that they pose a serious problem for the student of Knowledge, both within themselves and within their relationships. The great saints in the history of humanity have always stood outside the prevailing traditions of their time. Even if they played a key role in the restoration of those traditions, even if they were key figures, they were always following a greater authority within themselves. As a result, they often suffered great tribulation and persecution from the religious authorities that they were there to serve.

Within the world today, there are many prevailing superstitions. They do not come from Knowledge. The belief that God is preeminently concerned with the welfare of [humanity] to the exclusion of everything else is a superstition. The idea that if you are a bad person, you go to live in Hell for eternity is a superstition. The idea that everyone must believe in one teacher in order to find Heaven is a superstition. The belief that any power from the heavens or any visitors from the stars must either be demonic or angelic is a superstition.

Though some of these seem incredible and you would think, "I don't believe in these things myself," you will find upon closer examination that they have been part of your conditioning because they are so prevalent in human societies. Even sophisticated people who would never claim such views for themselves publicly may feel them within themselves in private.

How many people are afraid of becoming evil or of falling in the clutches of an evil force? This will lead them to doubt their own deeper inclinations. How many people could be persuaded, based upon the ancient writings within a certain tradition, that their inclination to do good in the world would actually be a bad thing? Kings and royalty in the past gave themselves Divine appointment and convinced enough people to believe in it.

There is another problem here. Aside from keeping humanity in an infant state, in a state of ignorance and superstition, certain prevailing religious ideas also make humanity extremely vulnerable to manipulation from those in the Greater Community.

Humanity has been studied intensely for the past half century, not just human physiology but human culture and human religion, human ideology and human motivation, human psychology. Though people consider themselves to be marvelously complex, the truth is this is not the case. If you could see yourself from the outside and observe yourself, you would see that your behavior is not that complicated, and you would see your own vulnerabilities.

As We have said, in preparing for the Greater Community, human governments and human religious institutions will be the prime target of those seeking to influence humanity for their own aims. Both are vulnerable.

Governments seek power. Religious institutions seek power. But religious institutions gain their power through persuasion, through affecting the mental environment. Governments gain power in other ways, but they too must exert influence. So political and religious institutions then become the most influential in the world in affecting human behavior, human values, human ideals and human priorities.

It is an amazing thing, but the manipulation of human religion creates such a grave problem. Greater Community forces, as We have said, can create a projection of an image of a saint appearing before people. Though it is merely a projection within their minds, they will think it is real. If they are not strong in Knowledge and cannot make the discernment, they will believe in what they see.

This is not difficult for Greater Community forces to do. They can make people think that their presence here is part of a spiritual rejuvenation, or a spiritual threshold, or as a fulfillment of ancient prophecies, or constitutes the Second Coming of Christ. These kinds of projections can motivate large numbers of people to take action in violation of their own nature and Knowledge.

The very religious traditions whose real mandate is to empower and to uplift humanity have instead become one of humanity's great liabilities. This is because Knowledge is not yet strong within the human family. [Yet] the potential for Knowledge is great; the opportunity to learn The Way of Knowledge is remarkable, especially compared to other societies in the Greater Community.

People are not trained in natural knowing, in natural goodness, in natural inclinations. They are not taught to claim the great endowment of Knowledge that they have. They are taught to be obedient, to follow, to serve even if such activities betray their nature and their greater instincts.

At this point, you may say, "Well, it sounds like humanity is really bad!" But this is not the case, for this happens throughout the Greater Community. All races that develop in isolation have this problem. They feel that they are the center of the universe. They feel that their ideas of divinity and creation are preeminent and universal. They believe that their values must hold true for everyone and everything.

As We have said at the beginning of this discourse, this is largely the result of living in isolation. Contact with other forms of intelligence, trade, commerce and interactions with other intelligent races, temper these extreme positions and will require a reconsideration of many of society's values and most cherished ideals.

This brings Us to another critical thing to reconsider. Many people hope and some fervently believe that the Creator will rescue them, will save them. There is a certain vulnerability in life that is very genuine and very real. Your ancestors prayed for a good crop so that they could survive. People now pray for a good outcome for their endeavors, a good result for their marriages, a resolution to their problems with health, and they appeal to the Divine.

This is normal and natural for human beings to do this, but it creates a great problem in understanding the nature and activity of the Divine within the world. The coming of the Greater Community will stimulate this expectation, this desire and this demand for divine protection and intervention, but it will not seem to be there. "Where is God to protect us? Where is Jesus? Where is the Buddha? Where is the Muhammad to guide us now?"

For many, this will be a spiritual crisis. Their whole notion of the preeminence of humanity in God's eyes will be shattered. Their whole understanding of the cosmos and the nature of Divine activity within life will be so shaken and so altered that for many people it will be too much.

This will lead to a great denial of the presence and the reality of the Greater Community. People will not want to accept this new reality because they cannot even consider it and its implications. And yet, it is part of their life. It is part of their education. It is a required condition for their growth and development. It is the inevitable result of developing as a race within a world. For eventually all races in all worlds must come in contact with the Greater Community that represents their greater context. And in all cases, their own cherished ideals, beliefs and assumptions will be greatly challenged. For who could have a universal approach to life without a direct experience of the universe?

The Creator is actively involved in every person's life through Knowledge within them and through the activity of the Unseen Ones. But there are not many Unseen Ones, contrary to what people believe. People often give themselves confidence by saying, "Well, I have all these angels around me all the time!" But it is not like that.

Each Unseen One must [oversee] hundreds of individuals. So the need for individual responsibility, the development of Knowledge and the emergence of true self-motivation within the individual are crucial and are much more needed today than they ever have been before.

Old traditions are breaking down. Tribal identities and cultures are being assimilated by larger groups. Around the world, nations are being fused into each other through economic interdependence and environmental degradation. Isolation is very difficult to attain within the world now. And the world's isolation is now being cast away by the presence of the Greater Community.

These prevailing ideas have had certain benefits for humanity, but they have outgrown any usefulness they may have had in the distant past. Humanity must become stronger mentally. It must become more competent, more discerning, more able. The motivation to do good, to be a force for good, must come from individuals increasingly now.

The world is in a turbulent state of transition. It is in the process of becoming one community, not because people want it to become one community but because it must become one community to survive. People know this, but they cannot even tolerate the idea intellectually or emotionally.

There is a notion that life will only give you what you are ready to deal with. Many people think this now. It is one of the mythologies of this age. But the fact is that life will give you what life must give you whether you are ready or not, whether you can handle it or not, whether you can assimilate it or not.

It is no longer enough to believe in great things. You must become great, greater than you are now, as great as you can be. It is not enough to believe in your institutions or their ideals. You must find what God has put within you and allow it to emerge within you. It is not enough to believe in the work of the great saints who lived in the world long ago, for you are living in a different world now, under a different set of requirements.

There is no one person who will lead humanity out of the wilderness. There is no one individual who will save humanity from the Greater Community. There is only the cultivation of human responsibility, human ability and human cooperation.

These all are the results of Knowledge. These all are the results of the natural responsibility and wisdom and capability that the Creator has given to each person. These are the things that must be emphasized now.

The world is emerging into the Greater Community. There is a great calling in the world. It is a calling for Knowledge. It is the beginning of a new era, a difficult era, a great era. Humanity will be successful only if it can cultivate the abilities that We are describing here. This is its opportunity and the time is now.

CHAPTER 13

Human Responses to the Greater Community

It will take some time before people can become used to this idea of the Greater Community. It represents such a great threshold, such an enormous turning point for humanity. Some people will move towards it; some will move away from it; some will move against it. These are the three possible responses that any person can have to new ideas and to new experience. Within each of these three possible responses, there are several different manifestations. Let Us take a look now and see what each of these means, and where these responses come from within the person and within human society itself.

The first response to the Greater Community would be to go away from it. Human beings have a remarkable tendency to engage in denial—denying things that are ever present, denying things that are critical problems in the world, denying things that are chronic difficulties, acting like they are not there or pretending that they are in control of something when actually they are not at all.

Because the Greater Community represents a tremendous change in perception and understanding, because the Greater Community will require such a tremendous change in perception and understanding, there will be a great deal of denial. Many people will simply not want to think of it at all. And though the evidence is growing every day that there is a great deal of visitation going on in the world and that many of these visitors are interfering in human affairs, people act like nothing is happening at all. They will go about their own business, preoccupied with their own personal affairs. They simply will not allow this to come into their consciousness.

This kind of denial is endemic in the world. People do not want to know. Why is this? Where does this come from? Why does this tendency exist in people to such a great extent?

Within the human nature, there are protections against pain, and there is a certain necessity that people be able to gain some kind of sense of control over their affairs. This produces a stability for the individual. This keeps the individual's motivation to live and to be productive in a functional state. And yet the very mechanism that protects and preserves individuals also works against them, for it can deny the very circumstances and the very events that threaten people's well-being and that would undermine their real ability to exert control over their lives.

When you read human history, you see the evidence that people were in tremendous denial at times of challenge or change. They acted like nothing was happening, or if they had to admit that something was happening, that they were in fact in charge of it and it would work out fine.

In some cases, they would appeal to a greater power, saying, "God is in charge of this," and "God will take care of it," and "God will produce a happy outcome." Yet this attempt to preserve their sense of well-being actually put them in jeopardy. It actually made them more vulnerable to harm within the world.

Therefore, within each person there is a certain protective mechanism that does not allow them to experience too much pain or too much uncertainty. And yet this is the very mechanism that endangers humanity and prevents it from solving its problems while the problems are small. It is in a sense the very mechanism that makes life more difficult and more hazardous.

Yet denial is not simply the result of a built-in survival mechanism. It is also the result of people's preoccupations. It is also the result of what they have given their allegiance to. Let Us explain this.

If you give your allegiance to your ideas and to your preferences, then by the very nature of your approach, you are at variance with the realities of life. You are insisting that life give you what you want, and you will either deny or neglect that which proves that your emphasis is incorrect.

This preoccupation with happiness, this preoccupation with allegiance to one's ideas and beliefs, is a very hazardous approach. It sets out only to acknowledge and to identify with certain elements of life, certain aspects of life, and seeks to thwart everything else.

For example, [people want] to become wealthy, comfortable and happy, but they do not recognize the course that this is producing for them—the loss of vitality, the loss of relationship, the loss of their inner life. They also do not want to take into consideration that perhaps this is not the best thing for them or for the world. They have set their minds upon one goal, and they will not consider the costs. They will not consider what this really means, and they will pursue their goal relentlessly, not realizing that it is costing them everything and that in fact it may not be meant for them at all.

The idea of Knowledge is fearful to them. The idea that there are grave problems in the world is something they do not want to have to contend with. They are preoccupied with themselves and with their own goals, yet as a result they will not find their true Self, their true purpose and their true meaning in life. And they will not recognize the very circumstances of life that will determine the outcome of their existence and the future of humanity.

This is fundamentally taking a position without intelligence. In the Greater Community, intelligence is defined as the willingness, the desire and the ability to adapt and to create. That is the definition of intelligence. It is not the size of your brain. It is not how many calculations you can do in a minute. It is the desire, the willingness and the ability to adapt and to create. You cannot create if you cannot adapt though many people attempt to do this every day.

The real creative impulse comes from a direct engagement with the world, having to create something needed in the world, something that you are endowed to create, something that you have the skills to produce. This is intelligence. Intelligence is the ability to recognize a problem and to immediately address it. There is no other real and meaningful definition of intelligence.

The demonstration of intelligence is the ability to solve problems in a creative way and to improve the condition of existence both for yourself and for others as a result. And yet denial, in all of its forms and manifestations, demonstrates a profound lack of intelligence. When you avoid or resist what reality is presenting to you, you are not exercising your intelligence. You are forfeiting your intelligence, and with your intelligence you forfeit the ability to adapt and to create.

Here the pursuit of happiness becomes the root of all evil, not because it is inherently bad but because people become obsessed with it to the exclusion of everything else, and what they forfeit for

their pursuit is so great and so meaningful and so important for their
well-being and their fulfillment.

Many people will go away from the Greater Community. They have
their own ideas. They have their own objectives. They do not want
life to interfere with their plans. They will simply block this from
their awareness, or they will deny that it exists. Or if they cannot
deny that it exists, they will turn it into something pleasurable,
something good, something that they can identify with, something
that supports their personal plans and objectives.

This is happening in the world today. Many people think, "Oh, the
visitation from other forms of intelligent life is a great spiritual
event"—something that will fulfill their ideals, something that will
give them the sense of enlightenment, hope and peace that they are
seeking in their own lives. Yet even these goals, which in a sense
represent the true purpose of life, are miscalculated and
misinterpreted here.

To see the real possibility for peace—developing equanimity,
bringing greater harmony into the human family—you must work
with reality as it really is. You cannot superimpose your ideals or
your values, for life will not respond to this and you will lose touch
with both your real nature within yourself and the reality of life
around you. You will become estranged from life and from yourself,
and the very ideals that you thought would give you the greater
rewards of life will actually rob you of them.

There are many people in the world today who hope and believe that
the presence of the Greater Community here will bring peace and
equanimity and true resolution to human life. They do not want to
see the real situation. They only want to see what they want to see,

and this is not seeing. They only want to think what they want to think, but this is not thinking.

They are not exercising their intelligence here. They are not calling upon Knowledge within them to reveal the real truth. They are not opening their eyes to see things as they really are. This is a form of denial. This is going away from reality. This is avoiding the meaning, purpose and nature of life.

Therefore, when We say that people will go away from the Greater Community, this can manifest itself in many different ways. Many will simply turn away, believing that this does not exist, and for them there will not be enough evidence in the world to convince them. Unless their lives are overtaken, they will deny and avoid the reality that the Greater Community is in the world and is casting a great influence there.

Others will consider that it is a possibility, but their conclusions will only be made to reinforce their ideas and their beliefs. They do not want their world view to be threatened or challenged. They only want life to confirm it, and so they will use the evidence that the Greater Community is in the world to confirm their world view, whatever it may be. They will acknowledge that it is a reality, but they will construe it to serve their personal interests and aims.

They will turn and look, but they will not see, for they will only see their thoughts and their beliefs, unable to see beyond them. This represents denial and avoidance—an inability to engage with life as it really is, an inability to open the mind and to consider something new, an inability to be vulnerable to life, an inability to begin anew in developing a new set of strengths and abilities.

HUMAN RESPONSES TO THE
GREATER COMMUNITY

Many people will go away. Other people will go against the Greater Community. Unable to go away or to deny its existence, they will struggle against it. They will believe that the visitors are here to destroy them. They will believe perhaps that the visitors represent demonic forces and will attempt to interpret their presence here based upon old religious teachings in the world.

In a sense, they are exercising avoidance as well because they cannot recognize that the visitors are sentient beings like themselves, driven by their own needs and preoccupations, like themselves. They will turn them into demons, into the agents of Satan.

They will interpret the reality of the Greater Community from their own religious perspective, but they will not see. They will fight against the Greater Community, insisting that humanity be left alone to its own devices, but they will not understand that humanity is at a new threshold and that the presence of the Greater Community represents the evolution of life within this world. They will fight to maintain their religious ideas. They will fight to maintain their own self-identity as they know it without accepting the possibility that there is a new panorama for growth and development.

They will struggle against this reality. They will see it from their own retreated position. Yet they will not understand what they are dealing with. They too will not be able to see even though they are looking. They will be governed by fear and by anxiety.

The third possible response is to go towards the Greater Community, to recognize that it is a reality, to recognize that it is new, to recognize that it needs and requires a new approach and a new understanding. There will be a few people in the world who will recognize it and who will make a sincere attempt to comprehend its meaning. If they can be successful, if they can learn a Greater Community Way of Knowledge, they will be in a position to educate and to guide others and will themselves be a positive force for advancement within the world.

Yet they too face great difficulties, but they must learn to see the situation with new eyes and with a new understanding. They must develop their perception and discernment. They must be able to learn about life in the Greater Community, to comprehend the meaning and the intent of the visitors. They must have the ability to see that the visitors are not angels and are not demons but are real sentient beings like themselves. They must move beyond the dichotomy of good and evil in order to see clearly and objectively.

They will also have to contend with the tremendous denial that will exist and the fear and hostility that will exist all around them. Either people will not want to know or they will only see things fearfully and defensively. They will have to contend with these prevailing attitudes and beliefs, which in some ways will present even a greater obstacle than the presence of the Greater Community itself.

They will have to learn to distinguish between what they believe and what they know. They will have to recognize the superstitions that exist even in their own thinking and evaluations. Their learning requirements will be enormous, yet they will have an opportunity for discovery, for creation, for adaptation, that no one else around them will have.

Therefore, there are three possible responses to the Greater Community. These are the same three possible responses that one can have to any new experience in life. These are the three possibilities that anyone can have to confronting difficulty or adversity in life.

The presence of the Greater Community represents difficulty, adversity and opportunity. Yet who is in a position to recognize this? Who can see this? Who can see things as they really are? Who has the courage to look? Who has the ability to discern the difference between reality and their own perception? Who has the patience and perseverance to learn a Greater Community Way of Knowledge?

There are very powerful forces in the world that keep humanity in a state of ignorance. In some cases, they attempt to do this as their intention. In other cases, they do this inadvertently because they are ignorant.

Governments within the world attempt to keep their populations obedient and compliant. This is done intentionally. They believe it is up to them to solve the great threshold problems and that the average person is not equipped or able to do this. They give themselves the sole authority and responsibility to solve the great problems of humanity. But without the will of the population, how can they do this? They do not believe in Knowledge. They only believe in persuasion and manipulation.

The religious institutions in the world today want to preserve their ancient beliefs. They want to preserve their authority. They want to preserve a traditional interpretation of divinity and human purpose and destiny.

For them, the Greater Community represents such a challenge and such a threat that they are more prone to be in denial of it completely. And if they do become aware of it and are able to interpret it wisely, will they have the courage and integrity to educate people, to educate their followers and their congregations?

These are very serious questions. The answer to them can be found by looking inside yourself, at your own tendencies, at your own beliefs. All of the tendencies that I have spoken of so far exist within you because you have been in denial about things in your life in the past. You have struggled against change and adversity. And, at times, you have gone towards something that was new and that required a new approach.

You who are reading this book have demonstrated all three of these possible responses. Even as you read this book, even as you face the challenge and the opportunity that We are presenting here, you can feel these tendencies within yourself. It is all there. And you most certainly will see them all around you in the people that you know and in the tenor, and emphasis and priorities of the public.

Read your newspapers. You will see where human priorities exist. People are fascinated by murder and mayhem but do not want to contend with the greater events that are happening in life. They do not want to face the fact that the food supply in the world is diminishing, that topsoil is diminishing, that environmental systems are breaking down, that increasingly there is less opportunity in life and greater adversity.

They do not even want to recognize the possibility that the Greater Community is in the world. Perhaps they will think, "Well, we don't need one more problem like this!" There is a fundamental inability here to see life as it really is and to differentiate between what is a small problem and what is a great problem. This inability is supported by the powerful institutions in the world today.

It is only because of the courageous acts of individuals and small groups that humanity has any hope of keeping pace with its changing circumstances. There needs to be more of these individuals. It cannot simply be the responsibility of one or two gifted people here and there. The need for education must be felt within each person. You cannot rely upon your institutions alone, for they may be unwilling or unable to provide the greater education that you need. It is your responsibility. It is your response.

If you turn away from the future, it will overtake you. If you fight the future, it will defeat you. Yet if you can move towards the future and prepare yourself for the future, then you will be equipped not only to deal with it directly, but to use it to produce beneficial results for yourself and for others. This is what is necessary now.

Within you, you have a great nature and you have a weak nature. Your great nature is represented by the reality of Knowledge within you. Your weak nature is your tendency to attempt to live without Knowledge and to rely upon your own ideas and preferences to guide you. Here you must choose, not only once but again and again, to find and to claim your greater nature and to receive the greater power and responsibility that this gives to you.

If you seek to escape and go live in a world of fantasy, giving all of your attention to your relationships, to your hobbies or to your personal goals, you will not be in a position to contribute to life, and life will seem to be a great adversity to you.

If you struggle against change and new revelations, you will be struggling against yourself, for Knowledge within you seeks to move you forward into the future by enabling you to engage with the present in a real and productive way. Yet if you hold to your ideas, if you cling to your beliefs and associations, you will not be able to respond to Knowledge. Life to you will become like a battleground, and happiness, peace and equanimity will be unknown to you.

There is another problem. That is the problem of influence. This is the problem of humanity's lack of skill and awareness of the mental environment. Today the Greater Community presences are attempting to establish themselves in the world. They are here to gain resources from the world. They are attempting to cast influence over human thinking.

Part of their agenda is to take the brightest and most freethinking individuals, those who are perhaps the least traditional or conventional in their approach, and to pacify them. Here We see, for instance, a spiritual emphasis on peace and harmony and retreat from life. And yet this is not a retreat to the monastery or the convent where real spiritual focus and activity are carried out. Rather, it is more like a retreat from life itself.

There is some spiritual teaching in the world today [that] does not have a Divine source. It is the product of Greater Community intervention. It motivates people to seek happiness and comfort beyond all things, setting them into a process of retreat from life and retreat from themselves.

While these teachings promise enlightenment, unbounded happiness, equanimity and uninterrupted joyfulness, they in fact neutralize the deeper inclinations of the people who are affected and put them into a position where they cannot see, they cannot know and they cannot act according to Knowledge. Their desires, their preferences, their hopes are so indulged that they cannot see or know anything else.

HUMAN RESPONSES TO THE
GREATER COMMUNITY

It is a remarkable thing that with the world becoming ever more demanding, calling for resolution, calling for positive engagement, calling for contribution, that so many people who are in a position to provide these things are becoming pacified and disabled. They retreat to their little hamlets in the mountains or on the beach. They go away from everyone and everything that they find to be distasteful. They seek to isolate themselves and insulate themselves in a world without tribulation, in a world without difficulty.

And yet they wonder why there is such tribulation within themselves. Perhaps they are taught that it is part of their spiritual unfolding when in reality it is the conflict that they are experiencing that is the result of the inability to engage with life within themselves or life within the world. They suffer, but their suffering is justified. They want to surrender their power to a greater power, but they do not have the wisdom or discernment to know who to surrender themselves to or what this really means.

So they give it all away to be guided, but they do not know who is guiding them. They want to be free of responsibilities of life. They want someone else to make the decisions for them. They think that being like little children, carried along, led along by the hand, is the way to live life and to be genuine within life. They forfeit their authority. They lose connection with their soul, all the while believing that they are living a truly spiritual life.

They are not in a position to face the Greater Community. They are not in a position to understand the Greater Community. They are not in a position to use their own authority to call upon their own strength, to set aside their preferences, to risk their happiness, to do something vital and necessary in life. They have lost the will to engage with life. They have given over their authority.

I can assure you that the Creator does not will this. This is not the way. The focus of the Creator and the Unseen Ones is to make people strong, responsible and capable. It is not to generate some kind of spiritual welfare where people hope and expect that everything will be provided for them.

I can assure you that the Greater Community forces who are interacting with humanity will take full advantage of these tendencies and will use them for their own benefit. They will study these individuals. They will neutralize their deeper tendencies. They will take advantage of their naiveté. And they will direct their good intentions.

Perhaps at this point you are thinking, "My God! Is this possible? How can this be?" But when you gain skill and understanding of the mental environment, you will see what an opportunity this creates for the visitors and how relatively easy it is for them to take advantage of it.

Do not trust any spiritual teaching that does not emphasize your authority, that does not emphasize the reclamation of Knowledge within you, that does not call you into the world to respond and to act, to contribute, to learn and to give. Do not respond to any spiritual teaching that robs you of your responsibility to do this and that does not cultivate genuine and practical wisdom within you.

This you must discern for yourself if you are going to be amongst those courageous individuals who will choose to face life and to engage with life, who will choose to become strong in The Way of Knowledge and who will choose to develop wisdom.

HUMAN RESPONSES TO THE
GREATER COMMUNITY

As We have said, it is the tendencies of humanity rather than the intentions of the visitors that will be the most difficult and discouraging things to deal with. For there is a preparation to learn how to interpret, contend with and relate to the Greater Community presences in the world. They are not all powerful. They are not omnipotent. They are relying upon human weakness to establish themselves.

But where human strength can emerge, they will find that humanity will be more than a match, and they will have to adjust their agenda, and they will have to change their approach, and they will have to learn to respect the rights, privileges and dominion of human existence.

Yet you must earn their respect. You must demonstrate your abilities. You must establish your boundaries. You must gain your discernment. You must exercise your authority. Even if you are the only person you know who is doing this, you must do this.

Look to life. Become a student of Knowledge. Let the greater power emerge within you. It will revitalize you. It will give you courage and strength and perseverance. It will lift you above demoralization and discouragement. It will give you the Light of life. It will give you what the Creator wants you to have, and it will enable you to do what the Creator wants you to do. It will enable you to rise above the fog of human denial, human ambivalence and human hostility. It will take you out of the realm of belief into the realm of certainty, wisdom and strength.

CHAPTER 14

DEVELOPING CERTAINTY, STRENGTH AND WISDOM

The coming of the Greater Community may seem overwhelming, but really it represents the greatest possible opportunity that humanity could have at this time. Humanity needs something to enable it to overcome its internal bickering and conflicts, to rise to a greater occasion, to restore its integrity, to preserve its resources, to unite its people, to establish its common needs and common bonds within the human family. Only the world's emergence into the Greater Community could provide such an impetus and such a requirement.

Here everyone will find themselves to be in the same situation. What city you live in, what country you live in, what language you speak, how you dress, your religious customs and rituals are now all being overshadowed by a greater need and a greater requirement in life.

Yet for this great benefit to be realized, and for the opportunity to be recognized and to be fully responded to, there must be a greater education in the world. There must be an education that lifts people beyond their tribal identities, beyond their natural allegiances, beyond their limited scope and understanding of life and beyond all that separates them and keeps them small and [self-obsessed].

A great education is being given into the world in a Teaching called The Greater Community Way of Knowledge, for the Creator would not leave humanity unprepared for the Greater Community. And the Creator would not leave humanity without the means for realizing the greater purpose that has brought each person into the world. It is for this reason that this Teaching is being provided. Its primary focus is to provide the means for gaining certainty, strength and wisdom.

It is no longer enough to believe in a Higher Power. It is no longer enough to believe in the integrity of your own government or in the infallibility of your religious teaching. People seek security in believing in these things. They seek resolution through these allegiances. But each person has a greater allegiance to Knowledge. This represents their direct relationship with the Creator. And though they still will need governments and religious institutions, rituals and systems of belief in order to organize their thinking and to uplift their activities, they have a greater allegiance to Knowledge.

This represents your fundamental allegiance in life. It is by building this allegiance and this relationship that you will be able to give yourself into the world with wisdom, with clarity and with abiding strength.

The Greater Community represents a formidable challenge for the human community, but a redemptive one. If you respond to the Greater Community with fear and apprehension alone, you will not understand the great benefit and opportunity that it provides.

Life is truly redemptive if you can take advantage of its great opportunities and rise to meet its great occasions. Life becomes defeating and overwhelming when you are either unwilling or unable to do this.

Clearly, you can see that humanity needs to become stronger and more united, more responsible and more intelligent in its behavior and in its perception. The Greater Community will provide the necessary impetus for this to be established. But this can only be established if enough people develop in The Way of Knowledge, if enough people become certain, strong and wise. This is not required for everyone, but it is required for many, many people. In fact, the requirement is much greater now than it has ever been, which means more people will have to respond than have ever been called upon before.

This is why you are reading this book. Certainly, this book is not giving you everything you want, but it is giving you everything you need. And it will satisfy the greater desires of your heart and your Being. Time will demonstrate this. Preparation will make it real for you. That is why you are here.

This is the greater purpose and the greater mission that has brought you into the world, and it has brought you into the world to serve a world in transition, a world that is emerging out of its isolation into a Greater Community of life. This is a human community that needs to become stronger, more integrated, with greater capacities and abilities.

The Greater Community Way of Knowledge provides a step-by-step means for reclaiming your relationship with Knowledge, for developing wisdom about the world and the Greater Community, for learning how to utilize your past and your current abilities in a new way. Its emphasis is on developing certainty, strength and wisdom.

The need for certainty is enormous. You live in a very uncertain age because people's old alliances and allegiances to their beliefs and institutions are breaking up now. Tribal identities are giving way to international communities. Local living is giving way to more global involvement. Everyone is becoming slowly more interdependent.

In the midst of this, ancient cultural and tribal hostilities are erupting all around the world. People are trying to reassert their national identities, and they are doing so, but the reality is that they cannot be isolated, that they cannot be what they ever were before, for the world is changing now. It is emerging into a Greater Community.

In response to the great uncertainty that pervades human experience today, many people are attempting to relive their old religious traditions, to go back in time, to try to recreate an early era that they feel was more pure, more wholesome and more complete. Others become disillusioned and discouraged and fall prey to the many preoccupations and addictions that afflict humanity. Still others create wonderful and magnificent prescriptions for humanity, believing that humanity is at the threshold of a golden age of peace and prosperity. Everyone clamors to gain security in their ideas, in their allegiances, in their relationships and in their personal pursuits because they are living in a world of increasing uncertainty and change.

It is the world's emergence into the Greater Community that is fueling this accelerating change, that is fueling the rapid advancement in technology, the collapse of tribal cultures, the integration of the human community. It is a very difficult time to live in. It is filled with conflict, hostility, confusion and personal degradation.

Yet you cannot stop this movement, for this is the evolution of the world. This is the destiny of humanity. And though there will be much struggle and much contention in the years to come, humanity is turning a great corner in its experience. Its isolation is over. Its world's resources are in serious decline. The Greater Community is in the world, attempting to establish itself here, attempting to generate its own influence and gain allegiance from people who fall under the spell of these influences.

It is a grave time, a serious time, a difficult time. But it is a time that calls for a greater strength and ability. It is a time of redemption. It is a time of renewal. It is a time to become stronger than you as a person and humanity as a race have ever become before. It is a great time. It is a time for greatness to come forth.

It is what your Being calls for even if your mind is afraid. It is what your true nature can respond to even if your ideas are threatened. It is a time for greatness to emerge from within you even if you do not know what it is. It is a good time. It is the right time. It is the time for certainty.

Where can real certainty be found? Many people rely upon the conviction of their beliefs or upon the power of their will to make things happen, but this is not real certainty. This does not have the foundation of true Divinity behind it. Personal will, personal conviction do not have the power of Knowledge within you.

Belief is weak and fallible. No matter how adamantly it is adhered to, it is subject to manipulation, and it exists without a solid foundation. That is why it leads to abuse. That is why it promotes manipulation. That is why it is cruel in its enforcement. It lacks an inherent stability that one must truly have in life in order to be productive and creative.

The world does not need a new set of beliefs to which people must adhere to strictly. The world does not need people to indulge themselves in their will power, trying to garner more wealth and opportunities for themselves at the expense of everyone else.

People everywhere need real certainty. They must look within themselves, and they must look to their primary relationships to provide this certainty.

Real certainty lives within you. You can only find it in one place. Only Knowledge within you is certain of your true nature, of your purpose and of your destiny. Only Knowledge within you can discern what is beneficial and what is not beneficial in your experiences in the world. Only Knowledge within you can discern the forces in your mental environment that are influencing you even now. Only Knowledge can liberate you from the constraints of your past conditioning to give you a new beginning and a new life.

Only Knowledge knows where you are going and what you must achieve. Only Knowledge knows who you must be with, who you must unite with, and who you must learn to avoid. Only Knowledge knows the meaning of your mission here and the reality and identity of those who have sent you into the world. Only Knowledge knows the real situation in the world. This is the foundation of certainty within you.

Yet people are afraid. They are afraid of certainty. They protect their little pleasures and their ideas with such anxiety, and yet they are asked to give up so little to receive so much. People are afraid of certainty. They are afraid that it will commit them in life, which it will. They are afraid of how their life might change and what they might lose and how others might disapprove of them. And they cower in the corner afraid of the great gift that the Creator has endowed them with.

They are ambivalent. They want the fruits of Knowledge, but they do not want to go through what they have to go through to receive and to produce these fruits. They want relief from the vicissitudes of life. They want relief from the degradation of ambivalence and indecision. They want freedom from manipulation and coercion. And yet they are afraid to trust something so fundamental within themselves.

Yet what is their great need? Their great need is for certainty—not the certainty that they find by believing in ideas or institutions or by creating heroes and heroines to believe in, but the certainty of Knowledge.

Knowledge is the only part of you that can produce peace and can sustain peace, within yourself and within the world. For there is no division in Knowledge. There is no contention in Knowledge. There is no "your Knowledge" and "my Knowledge." There is only Knowledge.

We may have different perceptions. We may interpret things in our own ways, but what we know will always unite us. That is why Knowledge is the great peacemaker in the world, and that is why Knowledge is the great need in the world.

Yet Knowledge produces more than peace and a foundation for cooperation. It is the source of real human strength. It is the Fire that enables you to act bravely and decisively in life. It is the source of your courage that can propel you forth into unknown and new circumstances. It gives you the power to explore. It gives you the ability to adapt. And it gives you the inspiration to create.

The Greater Community Way of Knowledge teaches how to reclaim Knowledge. It provides the program for following the Steps to Knowledge. Its focus is to build this greater foundation within you.

Its focus is to enable you to build this greater foundation within you by receiving the great gift that has been given to you, by learning how to distinguish it from the other forces and other trends within your mind and by learning to follow its guidance and to express its grace and power effectively and appropriately.

Here you learn forbearance. Here you learn patience. Here you learn compassion. Here you cultivate your discernment because all of these must be developed in order to become a man or a woman of Knowledge.

Knowledge is stimulated each day in the preparation. It is called upon each day. Here you learn step by step what Knowledge is, how it expresses itself through you, how it enhances and activates your nature and how it guides you and leads you in the direction that you must follow. Here you are able to undo all the binds that hold you and all of the dilemmas and falsehoods that confuse you and that debilitate you.

This is a Teaching in certainty. That is what people need. That will produce the foundation for action, for cooperation and for a greater responsibility to be assumed and to be demonstrated.

Though it is a difficult proposition, humanity will have to become united in the future—not because it is a good idea, but because it is a necessity for survival. In the Greater Community, it is a necessity. As long as humanity is a race of divided and contentious nations, it possesses a great weakness; it is easy to exploit from the outside.

Only a united humanity can become strong and self-determining in the Greater Community. If it continues to be weak and divided, it will not be able to amass the strength, the will and the determination that it needs. It will not be able to develop a group mind experience that is necessary in developing interactions with other races of intelligent life who are visiting the world now and who will visit the world in the future. It is the result of humanity's weakness and lack of unity that has given the Greater Community forces in the world such an advantage and has encouraged them to use tactics that really do not serve the best interests of humanity.

As We have said, it is a great truth in life that if you do not take responsibility for your life, someone else will. If you do not learn to command your life, someone else will. If you do not make full use of your resources and utilize them properly, someone else will. If you do not claim authorship in your life, someone else will. This is an unavoidable truth of life. You cannot escape it. Believe what you may, see things the way you want to see things, it is unavoidable.

That is why certainty must be learned—not false certainty, not the pretense of certainty, not adamancy in one's beliefs, not a commitment to one's personal goals, not a reliance on one's will power. This is only the power of the thinking mind. You need the power of the knowing Mind, the power of Knowledge.

The Greater Community Way of Knowledge teaches the way of certainty by providing a marked contrast between what is certain and what is uncertain within you and by teaching you how to build a foundation in Knowledge, day by day, step by step. It teaches you how to engage with life wisely; to learn how to see things in a new way; to gain a greater vantage point on the mountain of life; to see with clarity, to see with discernment, to see with open eyes, and to see with the discernment of Knowledge itself.

This is certainty. Nothing else is certain. No set of beliefs, no set of ideals, no philosophy is certain. They are only helpful or they are not helpful. They only enable you to engage in life more meaningfully or they prevent you from doing so. They either help you see, know and act or they provide obstacles to doing this.

The second great need is the need for strength. This is not simply physical strength—how much you can lift, how much you can push, how much you can endure. This is a strength of how much you can hold, how much you can consider, how much you can see, how much you can know. This is the strength of a great capacity in life and a great determination. This is the result of becoming a man or a woman of Knowledge.

Before this happens, people identify with their ideas, with their desires and with their fears—all of which are weak and changeable and easily manipulated from the outside. They have no foundation beyond this, and therefore they are profoundly afraid of change. They are fearful of everything that happens. They attempt to counteract their fear by having unfounded hopes and fantasies about what life is and what life could be. And yet their hope does not have strength and foundation. It is merely a set of wishes and is established only to offset the grave anxiety that they feel deeper within themselves.

The idea that the world is emerging into the Greater Community may seem terrifying to them, and to offset the terror they will create a wonderful explanation for it and a grand result for themselves. But there is no strength in this approach. It is inherently weak and fallible. It has no foundation in truth. It is not connected to Knowledge within yourself. It is simply a complex set of ideas and behaviors that are fundamentally built upon fear and inability. They masquerade as being strong, as being certain, but they have no foundation at all. They are vaporous, without substance, without meaning and without enduring strength.

When people do not know, they believe. They identify with their beliefs and their ideas. They identify with what they own, what they possess and what they can manipulate. This is a desperate attempt at living. It is filled with fear, tension and hostility. And yet it is weak and easily influenced and manipulated by others.

The great need for strength, then, is the need to develop a real capacity for Knowledge. Here there are two learning requirements. The first is to develop a desire for Knowledge based upon a growing understanding of what it is and why it is essential. The second is developing a capacity to experience Knowledge and to experience what Knowledge will reveal to you and what Knowledge will do through you and with you.

Developing desire, developing capacity—this represents the day-to-day study and training in The Way of Knowledge. For at this moment you do not have sufficient desire, and you do not yet have the capacity to become a man or woman of Knowledge. Though you have made some strides along the way, and you are moving perhaps in the right direction, you do not yet have what it takes to become what you must become.

That is why study in The Greater Community Way of Knowledge builds your capacity day by day. And it enhances and develops your desire for Knowledge by showing you what Knowledge is and by giving you a direct experience of the reality of Knowledge within yourself so you can see that it has been a saving grace within your life and come to appreciate its tremendous strength and wisdom. Here you develop strength by developing determination and by developing capacity.

One of the essential things that must be learned in developing capacity is the ability to deal with uncertainty—not hiding from it, not pretending it does not exist, not trying to overcome it with a set of ideas or beliefs or projections, but by learning how to face new situations with an open mind.

Here you learn to escape the ongoing battle to try to assert yourself and to reassure yourself. It is only your thinking mind you are trying to assert and to reassure, for without Knowledge, it has no foundation. It is profoundly afraid. This is a hopeless struggle and one for which you suffer every day.

Learning The Way of Knowledge provides an escape because it provides the foundation you need and teaches you how to develop the strength that you must have in order to advance. Here you learn to become strong by having to be strong and by having the resources within yourself to recognize your strength and to apply it directly. Here you are able to move forward without a rigid system of belief, without relying upon your thinking mind's determination because now you have a greater strength, a greater resource within you to call upon.

This is not a journey that you will take alone, for as you take the Steps to Knowledge, you will develop a foundation and you will develop a resource within yourself that will stimulate Knowledge within others. This will provide the foundation for developing relationships of Knowledge, an entirely new kind of relationship for you to experience—a relationship based upon certainty, a relationship that has real strength, a relationship where people do not deny their natures in order to be together, but instead must realize their natures and enhance them.

This is a relationship of Being to Being, not belief to belief or need to need. These relationships have all the strengths and capabilities of Knowledge. They can unite dissimilar people in a way that is entirely natural for them and complementary.

Yet these relationships cannot be established without real certainty and without real strength. They cannot be established unless one can move beyond their former thinking and their former motivations.

Here you must learn to become free in your own mind and become responsible for your own mistakes. Though you do not generate all of your own emotional states, you must learn to deal with them. This generates strength and capability. Here you slowly learn to become the master of the ship by realizing that you are on a ship, that the ship has a special cargo, that you have somewhere to go and something important to do, and that you must learn to harness the winds and cut through the waves of life to gain your direction and to reach your destiny.

The third need is for wisdom. Wisdom is something you must develop and learn. Whereas Knowledge is endowed within you, wisdom you must develop on your own with the help of others.

Wisdom is the result of developing discernment, discretion and a capacity and a desire for Knowledge. Wisdom is learning how to see what is really there, how to recognize what is important and what is not important, and how to know in which direction you should move based upon the development of your perception and understanding and upon the strength of Knowledge within you.

Clearly, if you look at your own life objectively and the lives of those who are close to you, you will see the great need for wisdom. With wisdom, you will not gamble your existence on momentary urges, needs, pleasures or ambitions. You will not gamble the precious years and time that you have within the world, pursuing things that can only give you momentary meaning and pleasure.

With wisdom, you will choose something greater and deeper within yourself. You will forego many things that captivate other people in order to reach deeper within yourself and deeper within life around you. Here you will not settle for ideas. You will not settle for pleasing moments. You will not settle to believe or follow certain groups. You will gain your strength from a deeper well within you and preserve yourself for the greater meaning and the greater mission you have come here to serve and to express.

You will not be fooled by appearances. You will learn to recognize the influences in your life and establish a relationship with them that enables you and strengthens you. You will not follow everyone else out of a desire to belong to the group. You will follow a different way, a different calling, a real calling that is sounding throughout the world today. And when you meet others who are responding to this calling, you will have the basis of real relationship. And when you meet those who share your destiny and your specific calling in life, you will have the foundation for real union and real companionship.

You will look the same. You will perhaps dress the same. Perhaps you will live in the same house or the same town. But there will be a tremendous transformation that will have occurred within you. A complete shift in your experience, in your perception and in your values will have slowly taken place within you.

As a result, you will feel more yourself, more connected, more complete and more whole, and yet you will be living without all of the assumptions that gave you a false sense of security before. You will be anchored in the truth within yourself instead of tied to the perceptions of your society or the demands of others.

This is the real and genuine freedom. It is being offered to you, but you must develop the strength, the capacity and the desire for it. And you must take the steps to achieve it—not the steps that you create for yourself, but the steps that are given you from the Creator, for the Creator knows the way to Knowledge. The Creator knows how to engage you, re-engage you with your greater purpose and mission in life.

Do not think you can create these steps for yourself. Do not think that you can build a spiritual path based upon an eclectic approach to life, for an eclectic approach will only give you what you prefer, and what you prefer may well not be what you really need.

Wisdom is rare within the world. Everyone has a little bit of wisdom about a few things. But to become really wise, that is something else. There is a great need for this. There is a great need for men and women not to waste their time and their resources [in order] to gain a greater discernment and understanding and to call upon a greater power within them.

How will you know you are doing the right thing? How will you know you are engaging with the real power and ability? How will you know that you are finding Knowledge rather than simply following your old beliefs? How will you know you are choosing the right direction in life, the right person to be with, the right situation to become involved with, the right form of employment? How will you understand the influences that are affecting you mentally, that are stimulating your emotions? How will you understand the great events that are shaping the world and the greater forces that are operative there?

You must become wise. Wisdom now is not simply for a rare and gifted individual. It is not simply for a saint or an avatar or a great spiritual teacher. It is for you. It is for people like you, who must become wise.

The hope for humanity rests upon you, not alone, but upon you with others like you—the ones who respond, the ones who can receive, the ones who can prepare, the ones who can begin anew, the ones who can break free from the restraints of the past, the ones who can feel the emergence of life, the ones who can feel the presence of the Greater Community.

Perhaps this feeling within you is very small and intermittent, but that is enough to begin. That is enough to take the first step into a greater life, into a greater reality.

The Greater Community Way of Knowledge teaches how to cultivate, develop and to express certainty, strength and wisdom. It is not a certainty, strength and wisdom that someone made up. It is not the product of an institution. It is not the result of a set of wonderful ideals or beliefs. It is the living certainty, strength and wisdom that live within Knowledge within you.

These are the fruits of Knowledge. These are the results of Knowledge. This is the Creator's Will and Genius, for the Creator does not come into your life and punish you. The Creator does not come in and take everything away from you. The Creator does not strip you bare of all of your happiness and involvements. The Creator does not come and send lightning bolts down upon the Earth to destroy evil. This is a primitive idea.

No, the Creator is much more intelligent. The Creator puts the gift within you, and the gift works from within you outward. Here everything is re-employed instead of destroyed. Here everything is transformed instead of cast away. Here your thinking mind and your body are given a new meaning, a new purpose, a new value. Here nothing is repudiated. Everything is simply redirected.

The Creator knows how to transform you and your life. The Creator knows what is required to prepare for the Greater Community. The Creator knows what you need to find meaningful relationships, meaningful employment, to find greater health and vitality, greater meaning and value.

But do not appeal to a distant God in a fathomless sky, for the means for achievement live within you, within your Knowledge. They are here to prepare you for a greater life. They are here to teach you what Knowledge means within the Greater Community, as well as within your world. And that is why The Greater Community Way of Knowledge is being sent. That is why it is here.

You will learn The Way of Knowledge. And you will learn to become certain, strong and wise by taking the Steps to Knowledge, for you must take the steps to find Knowledge.

The way is now clear, for the need is great. You know enough to begin. Take one step today, and you will be able to take another step tomorrow. Take that step, and you will be able to take the step that follows. This is how you find your way Home. This is how you build a life of certainty, strength and wisdom.

CHAPTER 15

DEVELOPING GREATER
HONESTY

It is necessary that We talk about honesty within the context of preparing for the Greater Community and learning how to follow and live The Way of Knowledge. It could be said that the experience of Knowledge is the experience of profound honesty. This is the result of wanting to know the truth above and beyond all other considerations. It could be said that learning The Way of Knowledge is learning the way of honesty—going beyond the honesty of what you feel and think into the honesty of what you truly know.

To begin, [you] must be honest with [your] inclinations, at least insofar as to realize that [you] must gain a greater freedom, ability and participation in life. You must have this honesty just to begin. Many people are not yet this honest. You must have greater honesty to be able to look at the Greater Community presence in the world and to gain the vantage point to see what it really is and what is really happening.

Within this book, We are not giving you all the answers. We are not telling you everything, for there are certain things that you must find out about on your own. For We do not want to engender belief. We want to engender Knowledge.

It is enough for you to know that you have competitors in the world who are vying for control of this world, who are establishing influence here and who are fulfilling their own objectives and mandates in doing this. They are not part of your spiritual cosmology. They are just sentient beings from another world. In fact, they represent several groups of sentient beings from other worlds who are here to find resources and establish alliances.

To know more, you must go deeper yourself. We open the door, but you must go through. It is not necessary for you to know their names or what world they come from. That would be meaningless at this point. This information is reserved for the serious student of Knowledge.

Why do We withhold this information? Because We value your integrity, and We want you to develop your integrity. We value your potential for honesty, and We want you to develop your honesty. We value your strength and your determination, and We want you to develop your strength and determination. Otherwise, you would read this book and have a whole new set of things to believe in. But belief is not what We are seeking to engender or to embellish here.

You need a certain perspective, that is true. You need a certain orientation to be looking in the right direction. We are pointing in the right direction. We are giving you the orientation. But you must make the journey. It is not enough simply to know about the presence of the Greater Community or to accept the possibility that they are here. You must come to know what this really means.

We are promoting Knowledge, not ideas alone, but ideas are necessary to take you to Knowledge, to aim you in the right direction, to bring you to the threshold of Knowledge. That is the greatest service ideas can provide for you. But beyond this threshold, ideas cannot go. You venture [forth] without a solid construct of ideas into the pure realm of experience in Knowledge.

To get there, you must become really honest with yourself. This is necessary to engage in the process of discerning what you want from what you know. You may be well acquainted with what you want, but do you know what you really want? Do you know what is really essential for your Being? Do you know what has brought you into the world? Do you know what you must fulfill here?

You may have ideas about these things, but do you really know? You may say, "Well, I am here to bring peace. I am here to help people," but these are only generalizations. Your purpose in coming here is more specific than that. Your mission in being here is more specific than that.

We know you do not yet know these things fully. If you are honest with yourself, you will recognize you do not yet know these things. That is good. It is good to be so honest. It is good to have an honest evaluation. It is good to know what you know and what you do not know. Maybe you only know a few little things. Maybe you only have a few pieces to the puzzle, a few clues to the mystery, but that is enough to begin.

The problem is when people think they know what they really do not know because they cannot distinguish between their ideas and what is truly known within them. They cannot distinguish between their thinking mind and their knowing Mind.

Some people say, "Well, I am very intuitive," but that is not it. Being intuitive is simply being more sensitive. It does not mean you have found the reality of Knowledge within yourself. It does not mean that you have come close enough to Knowledge to know what Knowledge is and what it is attempting to do in your life. You have not come close enough to realize that what Knowledge is and who you really are, are the same.

These realizations all represent tremendous thresholds in The Way of Knowledge. Anyone who takes the Steps to Knowledge will be approaching these thresholds, and there are more than one of them. Each threshold will require a greater honesty and a clearer self-evaluation.

At the outset, there is considerable confusion, for though you know something that is real within you and you know there is something important for you to do in life, you do not want to be superstitious. You do not want to have wild ideas. You do not want your approach to be merely self-seeking. You do not want to be governed by fear or ambition.

So you are unsure that you are doing the right thing, and you do not know where it is taking you, and you do not know what it will require, but you have the honesty. You have the response to yourself, the response-ability to Knowledge, to take the next step. Knowledge only asks you to take the next step. It does not ask you to realize what you cannot realize, to accomplish what you cannot yet accomplish or to become what you cannot yet become. It only asks you to take the next step.

For many people, though, they do not have the self-confidence to simply take the next step. They want to know the whole picture, and since Knowledge will not reveal it all to them, they invent it for themselves, or they garner it from other people's inventions. They fill in all the spaces with their ideas and their beliefs until they have a complete explanation.

Perhaps you have done this yourself to a certain degree. You can certainly remember talking to someone who seemed to have all the answers, but did they really know? Perhaps they were very firm in their conviction, perhaps they felt very strongly about what they were seeing and feeling, but did they really know? Were they honest enough with themselves to know the difference between what they believed and what they know?

You will be with people who even say, "I know this to be true! This is the truth. I know it!" But if you reflect upon this carefully, you might see that they really do not know it, but they defend their ideas even with their life. People will lay down their lives for their ideas, can you imagine? Sacrifice your life for an idea?

To lay down your life for something real and genuine and permanent, yes, that may have merit under extreme circumstances, but to lay down your life for an idea? Unless that idea is imbued with Knowledge, it does not have reality. Even if everyone believes in it and relies upon it, without Knowledge, it does not have reality.

These things that I am speaking of represent realizations. Each realization is a threshold in and of itself, but over the course of life there are great thresholds over which you must pass if you are to fully realize who you are and why you are here.

These great thresholds require tremendous self-evaluation and re-evaluation. They take honesty to a whole new level, for it is not enough to admit to what you think or feel or believe. The great honesty is feeling what you know. It is being united with what you know. To become united with what you know, you must become aware of what you know. You must accept what you know. You must discern what you know from the other preoccupations in your mind, from the other forces in your mind and from all of the persuasion and conditioning that have shaped you and formed you thus far.

Here there is a tremendous process of sorting out. It is like going through your closet at home with a commitment to only keep what is really being used and is really useful and is really valuable. Everything else, you get rid of. And you might end up with a pretty empty closet, but that creates space for new things to happen.

When you learn to sort out your mind, which can only be done in stages, you create a lot of space in your mind. Your mind is no longer filled to the brim with ideas and beliefs and memories. You have sorted things out because at every threshold you must sort things out even more. And in practicing The Way of Knowledge, you learn to become still while over time things that are not real or are not meaningful to you now just fall away. This creates a lot of space and openness in the mind, a lot of space and openness for Knowledge to fill.

It is a sobering realization at the outset that for the beginning student of Knowledge—and everyone who begins the preparation in Knowledge is a beginning student of Knowledge—much of what you believe, much of what you idealize and much of what you give your energy to are really not that important.

The sense of loss that this can engender can be immediately offset by the fact that you will have an opportunity to get in touch with what is really important, to feel what is really meaningful, to identify what is really valuable. It is by doing this that you finally begin to experience yourself as being meaningful. You start to experience yourself as being valuable, for your experience of yourself is the result of what you identify with and give yourself to.

If you give yourself to little things, you will feel little. If you give yourself to great things, you will feel great. There is no way around this. If you are feeling inadequate, if your life feels inadequate, it is because you need to identify with greater things within yourself and give yourself to greater things in life. A simple prescription, but not easy to accomplish. Why is it not easy to accomplish? Because of this issue of honesty.

Here it is necessary to realize that there are two minds within you. There is the mind with which you think and there is the Mind with which you know. Our emphasis is to bring your thinking mind together with the knowing Mind, in service to the knowing Mind, for this is the thinking mind's true relationship with Knowledge. And this is what gives your thinking mind true efficacy and value.

But until Knowledge is discovered, the thinking mind seems to be the only mind, and it sets up a whole defense mechanism to protect itself from destruction, from uncertainty, from invalidation and from hopelessness. It is weak and fallible, and so it tries to build great defenses against life. But this is not who you really are.

You need the thinking mind to negotiate the physical world and to function within the mental environment, but the thinking mind is really a mechanism to serve a greater Mind and reality within you. As you learn to identify with the greater reality, you learn to see that the mind is a medium. You learn to see that it is a temporary thing. It is not eternal, and it is only relevant to your life here in this world at this time.

When you leave this world and return to your Spiritual Family, you will not need this thinking mind, but right now you do need a thinking mind. So the important question is, "What does this thinking mind serve?" It either serves itself or it serves someone else or it serves the greater power of Knowledge, for the thinking mind can only serve.

This is a great truth in The Way of Knowledge and a liberating one at that, for with this understanding, you can shift the allegiance of your mind. By shifting the allegiance of your mind, you realize that you are not your mind, that you are greater than your mind. How can the mind be changed if it is all that you are?

Your mind will be transformed as you learn The Way of Knowledge. It will not be denied. It will not be repudiated. It will not be destroyed. It will not be condemned or maligned. It will be re-employed. It will be transformed. It will become a great instrument of communication. That is the ultimate purpose and value of the mind.

When the mind serves the Spirit, then the body can serve the Spirit and everything serves the Spirit. This is a complete transformation of your experience.

Its fundamental reality is honesty. You can be honest to your mind. You can be honest to another person and their mind. But can you be honest to Knowledge? This means that what you say and what you think and what you do, do not violate Knowledge.

The only way you can have this experience is to follow the Steps to Knowledge, learn to receive Knowledge and to experience Knowledge and learn to recognize what Knowledge really is and why it is here. There is no other way.

Fundamentally, all religious practice, all spiritual focus must be on the reclamation of Knowledge. We put it into these terms so that you may understand it more clearly and may see it without all of the conditions and preoccupations of religion as it has come to be known within your world.

Raw spirituality is Knowledge. The essence of spiritual life is living a life of Knowledge. Here what you believe, what you think, how you evaluate, what you perceive, what you choose become a great instrument of Knowledge within you. Here your true Self emerges and is able to use the vehicle of your mind and the vehicle of your body to give great things into the world. Then when you are done, you go home to your Spiritual Family and you are done.

The world's teaching about spiritual enlightenment is full of error. While it is true there must be great breakthroughs in life, and this might represent an enlightening experience, the true state of enlightenment is beyond the world.

You are here to contribute, not to gain rewards for yourself, but you will receive great rewards as you find the nature of your contribution and learn how to experience it and express it with wisdom in life.

What is enlightenment in the world? Even if you were able to grow beyond all of the limitations of human experience, you would still be a beginner in the Greater Community. That is like graduating from middle school and going to high school. Yes, you have graduated, but you now find yourself in a new class, where you are the beginner.

That is why We are teaching The Greater Community Way of Knowledge, because you need an education in both worldly spirituality and Greater Community Spirituality. There is only one

Teaching that can prepare you for this and give you this education together, and they must go together now because the world is emerging into a Greater Community.

Human wisdom alone is not enough. Learning how to function in human affairs wisely, though highly valuable and rarely achieved, is not enough, for humanity is no longer alone. This is its great problem. This is its great opportunity. This is its great requirement. This is its great need.

As you read this book, it will be an exercise in honesty for you. Let Us clarify what this means. Real honesty is being accountable to Knowledge. Yet because Knowledge is so unknown within the world, this is a very difficult definition to use. You might read this book and think, "I can't relate to this. I don't relate to these ideas. I don't agree with these ideas."

Some people will read this book and have that response. They will say, " I don't agree with this. I don't relate to this," but what are they really saying? What they are really saying is that they cannot relate their old ideas to this new information. They are saying, "This new information does not correlate with my current ideas or with my current experience."

This should be a motivation to discover. This should be a motivation to move into new territory to learn new things. But what usually happens is people use this as an excuse to dismiss the new information, to prevent themselves from having the new experience. Instead of saying, "I need to learn this. I haven't learned this yet, and I need to learn this," they say, "Well, I don't relate to this," and so they pass it by.

Being accountable to your ideas is not honesty. That is deception. You must be accountable to something greater within you, which will motivate you to go beyond your ideas, to outgrow them if it is necessary.

We are presenting a New Revelation in this book—a new spirituality; a new experience of being alive in the world; a new foundation for experiencing certainty, strength and wisdom. We are not here to embellish what has already been learned. We are not here to validate everything that is being believed in the world. We are here to provide a New Revelation and all that that entails. It is a Revelation based upon reality, not upon hope and fear. It is a Revelation based upon what is actually occurring within the world, not upon human ideals or human anxieties.

So if someone reads these words and says, "Well, I don't relate to this. I don't agree with this," We say, "That is fine. Take the next step." We do not expect people to believe everything We are saying, but We want to give them the opportunity to experience it for themselves. It is the experience that counts. If people believe in what We are saying but do not know it, it is not worth anything. It is no good. Yes, it may bring them to a greater realization, but they must go beyond their ideas to enter into this realization.

We are talking about honesty here—a greater honesty than what people usually think of when they think of honesty. When people think of honesty, they think of revealing what they think or revealing what they have done. That is only the beginning. Those are only the baby steps in honesty.

If you encounter something new in life, then you must go deep within yourself and ask yourself, "Is this important for me to learn?"

And you must not listen to your mind, for your mind will simply reassert its old ideas. You must listen deeper. You must listen at the level of your heart, your Being. This is honesty.

You might find that you need to do something you do not want to do. You might find you need to learn something that is in contrast or in conflict with your current ideas or beliefs. You might find that you need to experience something you have never experienced before.

When people encounter something new and they say, "Oh, I don't relate to this," they are simply shutting the door on it. They are not asking the deeper question. They are not really reflecting upon it. They are simply following the dictates of their thinking mind in the moment.

Their thinking mind is not interested in a greater education. It is primarily concerned with its own survival because without Knowledge, it is afraid and it is vulnerable in the world. What the thinking mind really needs is Knowledge because this is its real foundation. This is what it is meant to serve. But without Knowledge, it can only serve its own interests, which are primarily concerned with protecting itself.

That is why the thinking mind without Knowledge is primarily governed by fear. It gains its stability by the strength of its ideas and by its convictions concerning its ideas. Though this gives it reprieve from its own anxiety, it does not open the way for its liberation.

Some people might read this book and say, "Well, I can relate to what is being said, but I do not understand." We say, "That is good." Real understanding is the result of real preparation and participation. The real answer to the great questions is not a set of words or an idea. It is a means for finding out.

You will need to find out what the Greater Community is. You need to find out what Knowledge is. You need to find out what following The Way of Knowledge, learning The Way of Knowledge and taking the Steps to Knowledge [means]. You must find these things out for yourself. You must make the journey. The journey is what matters.

People want answers because they are lazy, because they do not want to take a journey. They simply want to fortify their ideas. Their mind is like a prison, and they want to add more bricks and mortar to it. They want to make the walls thicker, stronger, to keep the world out. But they pay the price by keeping themselves in. Their ideas are like a great buffer.

This is not a proper use of the mind. This is not utilizing intelligence. This is not being intelligent. Remember, intelligence is the willingness, the desire and the ability to adapt and to create. To create, you must adapt, which means you must change and grow, which means your thoughts must be changeable. No matter how useful they may seem at the moment, they must be changeable, and you must be able to change them. If they are fixed like concrete, then they will bind you, they will imprison you, they will prevent you from seeing and knowing what you really want to see and know.

The mind must be stirred constantly because it is like concrete. If you stop stirring the concrete and adding the water, it hardens and then you cannot work with it. People's minds become like hardened concrete. You cannot work with them. They are entirely fixed in the way they think.

Their Beings are prisoners within their own creation. They have walled themselves in. They cannot hear the Creator speaking to them now. They can only hear their own thoughts. They cannot hear the deeper minds of others calling to them. They can only hear their own thoughts. They cannot face life as it really is. They can only see life according to what their mind will reveal to them. They are slaves to what should serve them, for the real purpose and function of the mind is to serve the Being, is to serve Knowledge. For them, honesty is simply being obedient to their ideas, being consistent in their thinking.

Take to heart what We are telling you here. Ask yourself deeply what is important, but do not be satisfied with immediate answers, for you must go deeper. You must stop living at the surface of your mind and penetrate to its depth, to its core, for that is where the reality is. What is at the surface of the mind is layers and layers of conditioning— walls, blocks, shields, scar tissue. The mind is like a machine at its surface until it has become liberated by Knowledge.

That is why many people act and react in predictable ways. They are governed by forces they do not even recognize. They never think to question their ideas. They never think to really question their values. They do not want to deal with the uncertainty of doing so. They do not want to risk what they have even though they have so little.

When you are honest with yourself, this means being honest with Knowledge. If you do not know what Knowledge is, then you must find the way to Knowledge. You find the way to Knowledge by calling upon Knowledge, by going beyond your thoughts and beliefs, going beyond what you can relate to or what you believe in or what you have experienced thus far.

The preparation in Steps to Knowledge will enable you to do this, for it does not appeal to your beliefs about certainty, strength and wisdom. It teaches you how to appeal to Knowledge. This is different from seeking some psychic force outside yourself. This is different from opening your mind to whoever wants to dominate it in the mental environment. This is coming home to Knowledge within yourself.

Being true to yourself means being true to Knowledge, to what is deeply known, to what is the real meaning and current of your life. You can only develop this ability by taking the Steps to Knowledge, by opening your mind so that Knowledge can emerge there, by learning to still the mind so that you can learn to see through its mechanisms, by learning how to direct the mind and to develop its great capacities.

Here the mind learns to serve. Here it gives up its pretense of being the master. Here the whole pursuit of mastery changes, for in the world there are no masters. This is true because in the Greater Community, there are no masters. This is true because Knowledge is the master. It is the master in you. It is the master that the Master Creator has placed within you. It is your connection to God, to divinity, to truth, to purpose, to everything that is meaningful in life.

How can you be the master when Knowledge is the master? You can only express the master. You can only accept the master. You can only let the master transform you, revitalize you and redirect your life. This is mastery in a real sense, but it is a very humble form of mastery.

This is being honest. This is knowing what is great and what is small. Your body is small. Your mind is small. Your Being is great. We are bringing you to what is great so that what is small may have real expression. Then the body becomes greater and the mind becomes greater because they represent something greater. They demonstrate something greater. They are the vehicles for something greater.

This is what is needed in the world, and this is what is needed in the Greater Community. This is what will give humanity strength and preeminence in the Greater Community. It will not be your technology, for that is still in very primitive stages of development. It will be something greater, something more important.

What is technology in the Greater Community? Eventually, you reach the limits of what you can do technologically, for there are limits. Then you try to develop strength in the mental environment, which is a great, great environment.

But without Knowledge, you still do not have a great foundation. You still cannot discern the truth. You still cannot know fully what you are doing or the meaning of things. We are giving you this Greater Community perspective so that you may gain a greater honesty within yourself, so that you may learn what being true to yourself really means, what it requires and how it can be achieved.

We are giving you a different vantage point from which to see—to see something you could not see before; to see what is there; to see beyond your fears and your wants and your preferences; to see beyond all of the social conditioning that has shaped you thus far; to see beyond the prevalent attitudes and the mythology of your age; to see with clear eyes, not anyone else's eyes, but your eyes; to see with Knowledge within you.

Some people may read this book and say, "Well, I'm not getting enough information." They think We are here to provide more for them to believe in. They are looking for information. They want facts and figures, dates and places. They want to know how many worlds in the Greater Community are inhabited; they want to know how many races have visited our world; they want to know their systems of propulsion; they want to know their names and their languages; they want information.

This information will be useless if you do not have the Knowledge to recognize it and know what it means. Go into your library. There is more information there than you can possibly assimilate. There is so much information that people do not know what to do with it. There is so much information about the presence of the Greater Community— so many sightings, so much evidence. If you look for it, if you are open to finding it, it is there. The problem is that people do not know what to do with it. They cannot understand it. They do not know how to discern what it means. You could have a million sightings of Greater Community craft in your skies, but without Knowledge you would not know what it means.

Do not seek for information. That is not your need. We are giving you something of far greater value. We are giving you the key to realization, to understanding. Then when you look at the information, you can learn how to discern what it means. You can see beyond appearances. You can see beyond persuasion. You can see beyond manipulation—the manipulation of your governments, the manipulation of the religious institutions, the manipulation even of the Greater Community forces who are interacting with humanity at this time.

If you want information, then you are not yet being honest with yourself. That is not your greater need. You need to have the ability to discern what you are looking at. You need to have the greater intelligence within you to know what trail to follow, what clues are important and how to put them together.

Yes, We know the names of the visitors. We know where they have come from. It would be utterly meaningless to you, a bunch of incomprehensible words. It is the relationship between them that is valuable. That is important. You can fill in the names later if it ever becomes necessary.

You know people's names. You know where they were born, some of them, but do you know who they really are? Do you know what their life is really about? Do you know what they are destined to do? Do you know their deeper inclinations? Do you know why they are here?

Therefore, consider the Greater Community and ask yourself these same questions. Either your mind will fill in the answers, you will get the answers from somewhere else, based upon someone else's ideas, or you will find the way to Knowledge where you can know.

The Way of Knowledge is the way of honesty, and it is the way of relationship. It is the way of gaining a greater participation and a greater perception and understanding of life. But beyond this, it is a complete transformation of your mind and your being in the world, for you have come to serve the world in its present needs and you have come to serve the world's needs for its future. For you are here now and you are connected to its future.

CHAPTER 16

RELATIONSHIPS, DESTINY AND CALLING

You have come here for a greater purpose. You were born with the Knowledge of what you must do, what you must accomplish, who you must meet and where you must go. It is time to find this Knowledge and begin to live it.

The Knowledge that you possess is directly connected and responsive to the evolution of the world, and though you have spent most of your life developing yourself as a person—developing your personal skills and being conditioned by your society and its institutions—this Knowledge lives within you at this moment.

When I say you have come to the world for a great purpose, do not think of grandiose roles for yourself. Do not think you are going to become a great emancipator or a great healer. Rather, your role will be more mundane and more hidden, but it will be quite specific, and it will be vital in the larger scheme of things.

You cannot figure this out on your own because you only hold part of the puzzle to the reality and the meaning of this greater purpose for you. To find the rest of the parts, to complete the picture, you must find those key individuals who are destined to participate with you in your greater purpose and mission.

Understanding this, you can see why there is an incessant quest for relationship. Even though people's romantic endeavors have produced enormous pain and cost, they keep trying to establish a real connection somewhere. Why else would they continue something that has so little success and such great costs?

Despite all of the fantasy surrounding romantic relationships, in spite of all of the misunderstanding regarding this, there is a genuine motivation to connect with certain people for a certain purpose. And though, for most people, this drive is largely unconscious, it is very powerful nonetheless.

You must find those key individuals with whom you share a destiny. They hold the rest of the pieces of the puzzle to the mystery of your life. That is why you cannot find the way on your own. You can begin on your own. You can advance. But you cannot fulfill what you are here to do on your own.

As We have said, Knowledge will bring important people into your life to assist you. Not all of them represent the key people that We are speaking of, but they will all play an important role in your development. However, there are a few key people that you must meet. Knowledge within you will attempt to bring them to you or bring you to them. It will attempt to bring you together in any way that is possible. Likewise, Knowledge within them will attempt to do the same.

But Knowledge does not overwhelm the person. It is not a tyrant. It does not dominate. It does not rule in a harsh manner. Rather, it gives its influence and attempts to keep the person moving in a positive direction, in the direction they are meant to go.

Not everything that happens to you is predetermined, but there are certain things you must do and certain people you must meet and certain activities you must participate in. How this can come about can happen in many different ways, but certain key elements must be there. You cannot replace these. You must find your purpose, your people and your mission in life.

In many forms of spiritual teaching and practice, people are encouraged to be concerned about their destiny beyond the world, for example, whether they will go to Heaven or Hell, or whether they will elevate to another level and so on and so forth. There is a wide variety of ideas and beliefs associated with this, but for many this is a primary focus. But this is not Our focus, and this is not the focus of Greater Community Spirituality.

When you leave this world, you will go home to your Spiritual Family. They are watching over you now, and they are waiting for you when you return. You must return there; you have no choice. You cannot stay in the world forever; over that you have no choice.

It is what you are able to accomplish here that will make all the difference. It will make the difference in terms of your development and in terms of your Spiritual Family advancing. Your Spiritual Family is comprised of individuals who are directly connected to you at the level of Knowledge, who share a specific set of missions and accomplishments with you. Your Spiritual Family will ultimately join with other Spiritual Families, like the rivers joining together on their way to the sea.

What distinguishes one Spiritual Family from another only has to do with the nature of accomplishment and the activities that must be carried out in manifest life. There is no opposition between Spiritual Families; they are all working towards the same goal. But the Creator realizes that individuals work better in small groups to which they can become accountable, and so this is part of the Greater Plan for the reclamation of all separate beings.

The critical questions are: What is your destiny in the world? What are you here to do and how will it be accomplished? These are the critical questions for you, and these should be the critical questions in all spiritual traditions.

Yes, there is a reward in the afterlife. If you are successful here, you will bring great success with you to your Spiritual Family. And if you are not successful here, then you will return and realize that you must come back and try again. The reward in a sense is that you will not have to come back and try again. We think that is a very worthwhile reward.

Therefore, focus on the question about your destiny in the world. Your heritage is established. Your destiny beyond this world is established. You are blessed in the sight of the Creator, for the Creator only knows who you really are. You must find out who you really are while you are in the world and allow Knowledge within you to express itself and contribute to the world through you.

This is the only mastery that is possible here, and this is the mastery that is needed. If you can accomplish this, you will seem masterful compared to others, but you will come to understand that you are not the real master. The master is working through you and with you and for you and for others and for the whole world. This is the mastery.

It could be said that The Greater Community Way of Knowledge is The Greater Community Way of Relationship. For the way out of isolation and self-absorption is to develop meaningful and purposeful relationships with people, with possessions, with places, with everything. This is what ends Separation. This is what restores meaning and value to all things that have been degraded before.

Ultimately, your spiritual advancement is the ability to join in greater and greater panoramas of relationship. You cannot simply unite with everything. You must begin to unite incrementally. Though it is believed by many and hoped by many more that you can simply jump from your isolated state into the Mind of God and disappear there, but it is really not like that. It is that you are able to join together in serving people. You are able to join with Knowledge. You are able to join your mind and your body together. You are able to establish meaningful relationships with people and purposeful relationships with people. It is all a transformation of relationship.

Before this, people attempt to use people to fulfill their ideas or to fortify their self-identity. Relationship is more a form of usury than companionship. People bond together for financial advantage, for beauty, for pleasure, for excitement, but they rarely know one another.

The great transformation occurs when you can establish relationships based upon Knowledge and based upon purpose. This is an entirely different foundation for relationship and one that is sound and strong and will yield for everyone involved a greater wisdom and a greater ability.

In Greater Community Spirituality, there are no great individuals. There are no heroes and heroines. But there are great relationships and there are great communities. What makes a great relationship is the greatness that each person can bring to it—not their ideals and their aspirations and their ambitions, their wealth and their possessions, but the greatness of their Being and what they can produce and create in life together.

Knowledge within you knows that you cannot accomplish your task alone, and it also knows that you cannot accomplish your task with whomever you choose. There are only certain people who can really help you, who you really need, and you do really need them.

They have a responsibility to find you, and you have a responsibility to find them. They have a responsibility to be ready to participate with you in an intended way as you have a responsibility to participate with them in the intended way.

It is your ability to join in relationships that represent Knowledge and real purpose in life that is a great accomplishment because these relationships will give to the world around them. They will yield far more than they take. They will create; they will produce; they will serve. They represent the real promise for humanity. And though they might seem mundane on the outside, within themselves there is a spiritual Fire burning now so hot and so bright that it will be able to illuminate others who come into proximity to these relationships.

You already have great relationships, so take heart. The Unseen Ones are with you. They will not interfere in your personal life and only under very, very rare circumstances will they reveal themselves to you. But the greatness of this relationship is already with you.

They are not here to give you everything that you want. They are not here to make your life wonderfully comfortable and easy. They are not here to smooth your way so that there are no bumps in your road. Instead, they are here to remind you of your purpose, of your decision to come into the world and of the greater nature and gift that you possess that must be discovered and reclaimed.

You cannot use them to gain advantages in life; you cannot employ them to help you fulfill your personal goals. They cannot be used and manipulated. That is how great they are. They in a sense are a model for the relationship that you need to establish with those key individuals that you are destined to meet.

There is a great deal that must be taught concerning relationships— the establishment of relationships of Knowledge, the maintenance of relationships of Knowledge and the fulfillment of relationships of Knowledge. To learn more about this, you must read Our forthcoming book, Relationships and Higher Purpose. But for now it is important to gain a perspective and a basic understanding that in The Way of Knowledge, you will not journey alone. Certain others who are sharing this mysterious and great path with you will be called to abide with you and to assist you.

There will be no heroes. There will be no avatars. There will be no perfect beings. There will only be students of Knowledge at different levels of accomplishment.

The real master is Knowledge. That is the work of the Divine within your life and within the world, working behind the scenes to reclaim the separated through Knowledge.

It is critically important that you realize that you have a destiny within the world and that the meaning and nature of this destiny is determined by where you have come from and where you will ultimately go, for that is where your mission is set. That is where your goals are established. But they are meant to be expressed and carried out right here in the world—in the world of mundane things and mundane situations, the world of conflict and difficulty, beauty and opportunity.

How will you find your destiny? Well, your destiny can only be known. You may have any idea you want about it. You may formulate any belief. You may build a complicated system of ideas based upon your preferences and your past experience, but this is not destiny.

Destiny happens in a whole different part of you. It is something you cannot eradicate from your Being. You cannot change it; you cannot alter it; you cannot make it do what you want it to do in the moment. It is there like a blueprint within you. It will require the involvement of others in a very specific way, for you must learn that you can do nothing alone and that everything that is created, by anyone at any time in any place throughout the Greater Community, is the result of this kind of relationship.

In this world, many people are preoccupied with marriage, partnership like this, but that may not be their greatest need. Their yearning for relationship is genuine, but their interpretation may be in error. You need to be able to unite with others to produce great things because alone you cannot produce great things.

Everything is the product of relationship. Everything that is created is the product of relationship. Everything that is contributed is the product of relationship. That is why The Way of Knowledge is The Way of Relationship.

People are very pessimistic about relationships based upon their past experience and based upon what they see demonstrated within the world. And so they try to think, "Well, I have to do it on my own. I must learn to be complete within myself. I cannot rely upon anyone else." Though understandable, this reaction cannot produce success.

The key is to become a man or a woman of Knowledge, for your great relationships will be built upon your ability to do this. This is what you bring to the relationship of destiny.

For even should you find that person you are destined to meet, if you are not ready to participate, or if they are not ready to participate, or if you both are not ready to participate to carry out and to fulfill what you came here to do, it will produce great conflict for you. It is better that you do not find each other until you are ready and that you concentrate instead upon becoming ready—ready for each other and ready for the life that you are meant to live and the gifts that you are meant to give.

Here you will not remove yourself from society and meditate for long hours, trying to break through the fabric of the mind. That is only meant for a very few people who have a very specific purpose. The fact that it has become popular or socially acceptable in certain places does not mean that it is the way for you.

As We have said, the world's emergence into the Greater Community will forever change humanity's understanding of religion and spirituality. It will change the context. Now you must find a greater God and a greater religion and a greater spirituality.

It is a spirituality of community. In the Greater Community, what can an individual do? What kind of power can they yield? What kind of influence can they have? It is a different environment.

The social development that has occurred there has generated group mind. Tremendously powerful it can be if it is used wisely with Knowledge. Without Knowledge, like anything else, it becomes destructive and manipulative.

Your destiny in life requires the development of others, specifically those others with whom you are meant to be engaged. You, therefore, practice in The Way of Knowledge, not just for yourself, but for them as well. They practice not just for themselves, but for you as well. You are now relying upon each other to become successful.

This is how things happen in life. This is part of the Greater Plan. People must be taken out of their self-obsession and self-absorption into meaningful relationship in order to understand their true nature and their purpose for being in the world. This is fundamental.

It is now made even more urgent by the presence of the Greater Community, for they recognize that individual power is insignificant unless you are dealing with individuals of Knowledge. And those individuals will not be individuals alone for long, for they must join with others because Knowledge always leads people to join in meaningful relationships. Yes, they are still individuals, but now they have a greater Being and a greater identity. They are greater than the sum of their individual parts.

This represents a formidable power in the Greater Community. These individuals together cannot be manipulated. Their mental environment cannot be dominated. Regardless of what you might do to convince them or to persuade them, to induce them or to discourage them, because of the strength of Knowledge in their relationships, they are beyond your influence. You cannot see them, but they can see you. You cannot discern them, but they can discern you.

Perhaps this does not seem important to you yet at this moment. Perhaps you will say, "Well, that is not what I need right now." But it is what you will need. It is what the world will need. And in effect, you do need it right now because you do need to offset the influences that are guiding your life. You do need to reclaim your authority. You do need to exercise your authority. You do need to find your authority. And you need to find those people who can help you do this because you cannot journey in The Way of Knowledge alone. How can one person alone undo their own conditioning and offset the conditioning of the world? People have tried, but that is not the way.

Men and women of Knowledge join together in alliances and in communities of Knowledge. They have their great allies. They require these relationships in order to be strong and focused. They cannot carry out their activities alone, for they need the cooperation and support of others. They need to be known and recognized by someone else.

This confirmation amplifies their ability and confirms the true nature of their Being and their purpose. Everyone in the world needs this confirmation, but you must be prepared in order to understand it and to utilize it properly.

There are strong relationships needed in the world. The potential is here. Humanity has always had strong relationships, but they have been too rare. There have been too few of them. This needs to grow in people's experience. The fear, the doubt, the hostility, the cynicism need to be dispelled by a demonstration of true union and true ability. These relationships you cannot establish with everyone, for you are only destined to have them with certain people, but that will be a challenge in and of itself.

Yet it is bringing Knowledge into the experience of daily life and into the greater comprehension of the world that will make the critical difference. This is what will engender the courage, the selflessness and the ability to meet the problems of the world and the greater problems you will encounter in the Greater Community.

Your true heritage is built upon real relationship. Your true destiny is built upon real relationship. And your calling in the world will be built upon true relationship. Yes, you will find the people you need, but you must be ready. That is the emphasis. Right now you are not ready. Perhaps they are not ready either.

They will not come to you by chance though your meeting may be very circumstantial. Being with them may not be easy because you will both have to get beyond your personality in order to deal with the reality of your relationship.

Before this can happen, you will have to gain the discernment to know what a relationship of destiny is and to distinguish it from a relationship of preference and desire. You can have strong preferences. You can have strong desires. You can build seemingly strong relationships based upon this, but these relationships are not really strong, and they will fail within the context of a real life. They will not have the foundation or the substance to support the revelation of Knowledge.

How will you know who to be with and who not to be with? You will know. To gain a deeper understanding of this, it is essential to become a student of Knowledge and to learn the teaching on relationships within The Greater Community Way of Knowledge.

In this sense, what has been accomplished in the Greater Community far exceeds what has been demonstrated here in the world. It is not simply technology or the ability to get around, the ability to travel from one world to another. That is all machinery. But the ability to develop real and meaningful relationships and communities, this is something that is rare in the Greater Community but has been achieved at very high levels.

Most societies in the Greater Community are not communities of Knowledge. They are communities of law. They require a very strict obedience, conformity, a highly regulated life for their members. You would find living in most of them to be quite intolerable.

And yet they have power. It may not be the power of Knowledge, but they have power—power in the physical realm and power in the mental environment. They gain their cooperation through force and through enforcement, not through Knowledge.

The communities of Knowledge that exist in the Greater Community are small and withdrawn. Their allegiance is natural. Their power is unique.

We share these things with you to give you an understanding and a perspective about the nature of power in the world and how Knowledge functions within the world—quietly behind the scenes. This gives you an idea of how you will function in the future.

For as you learn to become wise, you will not want recognition. You will only want recognition from those who can truly know you. You may want your works to be recognized and to be studied and to be utilized, but you yourself will not want recognition.

You have a destiny within the world. It will require great relationships. Your ability to find these and to participate in them will be the result of your preparation in The Way of Knowledge.

Take heart, then. There is something great for you. Great things are happening in the world. Yes, they are risky, but they are also promising. Take heart. You will not travel this journey alone, but you must prepare and you must be patient. You will not be able to find your way all at once.

From where you stand today to the full experience of your destiny in the world, there are many, many steps, and you do not have a great deal of time. That is why you feel this sense of urgency. And if this sense of urgency is denied, you will feel depression.

Look into your heart, then, and you will know. You will respond at a deeper level and not all at once. The calling is subtle, but it is continuous. The opportunity is hidden, but it is there. The reality is beyond your vision, but it can be seen.

Knowledge will take you there, but first you must find Knowledge. You must unite with Knowledge. You must learn how to become wise and discerning with Knowledge. You do not simply give yourself up with Knowledge. You bring your strength to Knowledge, and you learn how to become stronger.

This is bringing all aspects of yourself together in their rightful order. It is entirely natural, but in order to do it, you must unlearn what has been unnatural. This is what is set out before you now.

We emphasize the reality of the Greater Community because this is the greater context for realizing who you are, why you are here and what you must do. You cannot create a context yourself and be able to understand these things.

Here you must look into the world and you must look into yourself. Rather than trying to impose your values upon the world, trying to impose your goals upon life, trying to extract the rewards you want from life itself, you come into a dynamic relationship with life.

Here you stop resisting being in the world. Here you outgrow your ambivalence about being here. Here you gain a real foundation.

It is remarkable that many people in the world today have not really decided to be here. It is like they have one foot out the door. That is why so many people live in fantasy. That is why so many people have disengaged from reality. That is why so many people are lost within their own minds. That is why so many people are disassociated and alone and isolated.

The Way of Knowledge brings you into contact with what is great and small—what is great within you and what is small within you, what is great within the world and what is small within the world. It sets a clear distinction that you can experience. It makes things clear because things are clear when you can see them clearly.

You know, there is a prevailing attitude in the world today that everything is quite relative to your perspective and viewpoint. People will say, "Well, that's just one way of looking at it. There are other ways to look at it." And while this holds true, it does not represent the truth. In other words, different viewpoints do yield different perceptions, but there is actually something beyond your viewpoint in order to see and to know.

This relativistic thinking then is so pervasive. It keeps people from recognizing what is essential within themselves and the world. It keeps them in a constant state of doubt and speculation about their own experience. It makes the obvious seem to be mixed in with everything else. They cannot tell what is real from what is unreal, what is genuine from what is not genuine. They think it is all their perception.

They do not realize that they need to become connected to what is happening in the world. They need to become connected to what is happening deep within themselves at the level of Knowledge. This is the foundation for relationship. This is the foundation for community. This is the foundation for being able to accomplish anything with anyone.

In The Greater Community Way of Knowledge, you are prepared to discover your destiny, your purpose and those key relationships that you will need to make your life fulfilling and complete here. This will take you away far beyond where you have ever gone before. In a way, what you have done before will not be what you rely upon now.

Instead, there will be a greater current pulling you forward. You will continue to have good days and bad days, days when you feel clear, days when you feel unclear, days when things are in focus, days when things are out of focus. But something will be driving you forward. It is connected to life. It is connected to the Greater Community. It is connected to who you are. They are all connected. They are all in dynamic relationship.

You can experience this. You must experience this. This is calling to you. This is waiting for you. This is meant for you.

You have a relationship with the world's emergence into the Greater Community. This is the greater context you will need to fully realize why you are here and what you must do. Without this context, it will not be clear to you. This is when people fill in all the gaps with their own ideas. This is when people create their ideology because they cannot see things as they really are.

Therefore, The Way of Knowledge must take you to that vantage point where you can see. In order to get up the mountain of life, you must have strong relationships, true companions who can take this journey with you. You will make it possible for each other to advance.

The journey now is before us. The Greater Community is here. Humanity must become strong. There must be greater demonstrations of relationships of Knowledge within the world. There must be more contribution. There must be greater mental and physical health. There must be preparation for the future. These are all calling to you now. Become still and you can feel it.

I can say it in many, many different ways. I can illustrate it in many, many different ways. But it is the same calling and the same force. It is the call for Knowledge. It is the calling of Knowledge.

Stay with this. Respond to this. Keep this within your sights. Begin to prepare in The Way of Knowledge. You cannot get there without the preparation. You must take the Steps. Take these Steps and you will not journey alone, for the Unseen Ones will be with you and others will come to join you in your great journey homeward to Knowledge.

CHAPTER 17

Beginning the Preparation

The message that We are presenting in this book is of the greatest importance, and yet you must find out for yourself. You must discover what you know, and you must be able to see the world clearly. You must be able to see with your own eyes—not the eyes of your culture, not the eyes of your religion, not the eyes of your family, not the eyes of your friends, but with your own eyes and with the greater Mind that is within you.

What We are presenting in this book is obvious if you can see it, but if you cannot see it, it is not obvious. If you cannot relate to it, then it is beyond your reach. If you cannot consider it, then you are lost to it.

This is not some subtle event happening in the world. This is something that is permeating the mental environment in human civilization. This is a phenomenon that is occurring all around the world. But the governments of the world keep it hidden. They are trying to understand, but they do not realize their own vulnerability. The religions of the world cannot account for it, and may not even hold it to be real.

So where do you go for validation? Where do you go for instruction? How do you find your way? How can you come to know the meaning of the world's evolution and your fundamental relationship with it?

For this, you must assume a greater authority in life. You must realize that no one else can do this for you. The preparation is being provided. It is being made available to people all around the world. It is something they must study on their own. Yes, they will need help along the way, but they must assume the responsibility to become educated about the Greater Community and to learn the way to Knowledge.

We are giving you, then, tremendous responsibility and authority within your own life, more than you have ever assumed before. And yet We are giving you this right and this recognition with the understanding that it requires a tremendous amount of preparation and responsibility.

You cannot simply mindlessly assume [you have] it and carry on because you will not find your way. And instead of learning the reality of life and the meaning of your position in the world, you will simply generate your own beliefs and ideas, which come largely out of your imagination and your social conditioning.

The way is not hard, but it is different, and it requires a lot of honesty. Here you must step aside from the persuasions of your friends, your family and the institutions with which you may be allied or involved and develop your own vision and understanding, not based upon what you want, or what you are afraid of, or what other people expect of you, but based upon Knowledge within you.

We are confident that if you can make this approach, and cultivate your honesty, and develop your skills, and patiently learn The Way of Knowledge as it is being offered to you that you will be able to see with your own eyes, and you will be able to have your own experience.

In time, you will realize how necessary this is for you and for the world in which you live. This will give you a sense of mission, a sense of direction in life, and you will begin to realize your real gifts and where they must be given.

Everyone in the world has an important role to play. If they can find this foundation within themselves and develop the necessary honesty and discernment, they will find their contribution and they will find it in the world.

There must be service in the world at every level of human activity, but if it can be rendered with this greater understanding—this understanding of the world's emergence into the Greater Community, the need for humanity to gain greater cooperation and integration, the need to develop intelligence, the need to care for people—then humanity will be able to make great strides and will find a new foundation within a larger arena of intelligent life.

The conditions are perfect for this. The conditions require this. It is not simply an option anymore; it is a vital necessity. Just like finding Knowledge within you is a vital necessity. Allow your life to become vital and necessary and you will begin to feel that you are vital and necessary. This is where you discover your power. This is where you tap into your greater energy. This is where you dispel all self-abuse and all negative attitudes towards yourself.

Here you take a humble yet real approach to the meaning and value of your existence, for you see that there is something you can do here, given what you have and given what you have developed already, and that you do not have to become a superman or a superwoman, but instead become a man or a woman of Knowledge. It is possible for you to do this. It is needed for you to do this. It is necessary.

Just take the first step. Knowledge does not ask you to leap off the cliff into the unknown. That is not The Way of Knowledge. The Way of Knowledge is to follow step by step, follow the path before you, keep your eyes open, keep your ears open, try to keep your mind free of assumptions, come to recognize your blind sides and your weaknesses. Build your strengths and you will advance and progress.

Though you may not see the advancement day in and day out, you will notice a fundamental shift in your awareness and your experience: a deepening of your sensitivity, a sharpening of your abilities, greater objectivity about your life and abilities, strengths and weaknesses and a clearer understanding of other people's intentions and their own problems that they must overcome within themselves.

As you journey forth, you will develop greater compassion, for you will realize that this requires tremendous focus and strength—a focus and strength that you actually have and must now utilize. You will understand why others falter and why others are ambivalent, even to receive the gifts that the Creator has given to them.

You will understand why people look but do not see. You will see all the mechanisms of denial, and you will begin to see the degree of social conditioning and the extent of influence that is now being perpetrated in the mental environment [on] people everywhere.

Here you will work and fight for your own freedom internally, and you will want to provide freedom [for] others—freedom from manipulation, freedom from influence, freedom from the past, freedom from the wretched conditioning that so many people labor under today.

BEGINNING THE PREPARATION

You will want freedom, but you will want something even greater than freedom, and that is the ability to be connected to the world, to be fully involved in life and to bring the greater endowment of Knowledge that you have, and all the gifts that are associated with it, into active demonstration in the world.

All of this is waiting for you. Indeed, it is calling for you. It is saying, "Come, come! Awaken out of your preoccupations. There is something important for you to do."

And if you are broken down by the side of the road, and you do not know what to do or where to go, or you are not sure of your strength, or you are doubting your ability or your value, this is the calling that will get you moving again. For your life must be moving. If it is not moving, it will begin to sink. That is not good.

Feel your life moving and you will begin to sense a direction. You cannot sense a direction standing by the side of the road looking up and down and all around and wondering what you should do. You actually have to experience yourself moving and making progress.

The practice in Steps to Knowledge will get your life moving in a real way, in a real direction. And your life will be moving in harmony with your true nature and your true purpose. As a result of taking these Steps, you will begin to experience your true nature and your true purpose, but they can only be experienced if you are moving in this direction, if you are actually moving in the direction you are meant to move in.

Society will want you to move in other directions. Perhaps the people with whom you are engaged will want you to move in other directions. Your past conditioning will try to move you in other directions. But you must move in the real direction.

Knowledge within you knows where you must go, who you must meet and what you must accomplish. It will never give up on you. It will never be defeated. As long as you are in this world, it will continue to exert its influence to provide this movement and this direction.

And yet Knowledge within you knows that you cannot do it alone, that you need others to assist you and that you need a method of preparation. Because you cannot take the journey to Knowledge alone, you will need to share your deeper inclinations with others, but you must not simply share them with anyone. Here you must discern who can hear and who cannot hear. This is something that you can feel within yourself.

There are many people that you like and care for, perhaps, but that does not mean that all of them can really hear your deeper inclinations and can relate to them. In fact, if you share them with everyone, you will be shocked perhaps to see that many people are threatened by this or afraid of it or do not trust it or will even actively belittle or condemn what you are telling them.

In your personal life, you can have many friends, but in your deeper life, you need true allies and companions. This means that you must be able to share The Way of Knowledge with others—not to try to convince them, not to try to persuade them, but to see if this calling is being experienced by them.

As We have said, there is a great calling in the world—a calling to prepare, a calling to look over the horizon to see what is coming in your future, a calling to gain a new foundation and a new understanding. This calling is being sounded throughout the world, but there are many, many people who do not feel it and have not heard it.

You cannot persuade them. You will exert enormous energy and effort trying to do so. Only if they have heard it and have felt it and can identify it within themselves will they be able to hear what you are telling them. Here you are simply confirming something that they know.

Yet if you tell people who do not have this spark within themselves, they will fight you; they will disagree; they will become threatened; they will not understand what you are talking about; they will think that you are obsessed with something; they will become afraid. Even if their beliefs can accommodate the ideas that you might present to them, if they do not have this spark within themselves, there will not be a resonance between you.

Therefore, you must choose carefully. Do not try to win people over. It is only if a person has this spark within themselves. It is only if they have felt this calling, this uneasiness, this restlessness within themselves that you can reach them at another level.

Then they will need support because they may not believe in what they are experiencing. They will need some assistance because they may not understand what they are experiencing. They need some sense of confirmation so that they can give greater credence and credibility to this deep but mysterious inner experience: this responsiveness to the world, this sense of calling, this sense that there is something greater for them to do and to be and to demonstrate.

As We have said, We are not here to generate belief. We are here to activate Knowledge. Have this be your approach as you share The Way of Knowledge with others. You do not need people's opinions. You do not want to have to deal with their ideas and beliefs. You want to find the spark. You want to find the spark within yourself. You want to find the spark in them.

Even as I say these words, even at this moment, perhaps there is someone you can think of who could really respond to this, with whom you could really share something very precious, very sacred and very rare. Perhaps you are thinking, "Oh yes, I know someone. I know someone who could really hear this." Share your experience with them. Share this book with them.

This book is a calling for people who have felt this spark. This calling and this book are for people who have a greater possibility and a greater destiny.

Perhaps everyone else is not ready, but there are many people in the world today who are ready. They will look in vain into their romantic relationships, into their hobbies, into their art, into all kinds of interests, but they are looking because they need this calling. It is vital for them. It is lifegiving. It is essential.

You will see this spark in people. Look for it. Review your relationships and ask yourself, "Is this person ready to learn about the Greater Community and about The Way of Knowledge? Is this other person ready to learn about the Greater Community and about The Way of Knowledge?" If you ask this with a clear mind, more often than not you will be able to see clearly who is ready and who is not. It is a feeling. It is something you know.

While it is true sometimes people will surprise you, yet often you will have an inclination that someone has something mysterious going on in their life, and they are ready to learn more, and they need some assistance. Just like you are ready to learn more, and you need some assistance. This is how Knowledge is shared. This is how Knowledge is built within relationships.

Consider this: Knowledge within you is not trying to overtake you. It is not trying to win you over with praise or threats of destruction. It is not threatening you with eternity in Hell. It is not trying to control or manipulate you. Rather, it is a growing light within you, forever burning, forever calling, forever giving its beneficial influence.

This is how the Creator works in the world. This is how Knowledge functions within the individual. And this is how you can become over time an emissary for Knowledge. And the calling will sound through you and with you. It will happen naturally. Knowledge will speak to this person but not to that person. And Knowledge will call out to these people but not to those people—because Knowledge knows who is ready.

As you learn to become close to Knowledge, you will know who is ready and who is not. If someone is not ready, then bless them. Do not condemn them. It is okay. For earlier in your life, you were not ready either. You could not hear the message. You could not respond. You were too self-preoccupied. You were too governed by your ideas and beliefs. So there should be no condemnation in your approach.

Yet you will have a natural desire to share The Way of Knowledge with others because you need relationships of this type. You need relationships that are capable of expressing Knowledge and supporting Knowledge. This is vitally necessary for you, for you need a witness. You need the confirmation. You need to be known by at least one person.

If you are to play a great role in life, if you are to fulfill your purpose in being here, if you are to discover the greatness within yourself, then you must have this approach. You must take these chances. What do you have to risk?

All people really have to risk is their idea of themselves. People are terrified to challenge their ideas of themselves because they think without their self-created ideas of themselves, they would be nothing. They would have no focus, no purpose and no meaning and that they would sort of go into a state of self-annihilation.

What is really at risk? What are people really protecting? If you reduce it down to its essential elements, people are really protecting an idea of themselves—just an idea. You could say, "Oh, they are protecting their money. They're trying to keep money and love in their life and that is why they acted dishonestly. That is why they compromised themselves." But ultimately it is all an attempt to protect an idea about oneself.

Having fixed beliefs, being adamantly attached to one's ideals and beliefs and assumptions—it is all to protect just an idea of yourself. So really nothing is at risk because an idea of yourself is really nothing. It is just a substitute for Knowledge. It is an attempt to be who you are without knowing who you are. It is an attempt to have purpose in life without knowing your purpose in life. It is an attempt to have meaning and value without really knowing your meaning and value. How can this succeed?

Share The Way of Knowledge with others. But share it with those people who are feeling the spark. Maybe they will not accept your gift at first, but they will think about it. Perhaps their first response will not be welcoming, but they will be touched.

Share this book with them, for this book is a calling. It is sounding the calling. It is resonating the great calling that is happening in the world. It is one of the few books in existence that can prepare you for the future. It is one of the few books in existence that will really recognize your meaning and your value and your purpose in life within the context of the world's evolution. It is one of the few books in existence that can begin to teach you about the Greater Community and its imminent importance to you.

Share this book with those who are ready to receive it. Let them struggle with the message. Let them find its importance and its value within themselves. Do not argue with them. Do not debate with them. Simply give them this book. Everyone must go through some struggle to overcome their ambivalence and to learn to discern where Knowledge really exists within them.

This book is only about Knowledge. It is only about truth. It is only about being connected to reality in the world. If you find its ideas to be radical, it only tells you how far behind humanity is in understanding its condition and its need for preparation. If you think this book is far-fetched, then that only shows you how your social conditioning has retarded your understanding, your ability and your vision.

This book is not far-fetched. This book is not radical. It is sound. It is true. It is absolutely fundamental. But because people in the world have not found this soundness, they have not found what is true, they have not found what is fundamental, then what is fundamental seems radical. It seems far out. But it is not.

Share this book with people. Let them struggle with the book. Do not have them struggle with you. This book is a calling. To respond to a calling, you must find what is real within yourself. You cannot simply engage with it at the level of ideas and beliefs. You must feel it deep within yourself.

While We are here to present new ideas, Our fundamental aim is to activate Knowledge. In this, this book is an initiation into The Way of Knowledge. It is a confirmation of who you are, why you are here and what you most deeply know.

And yet it is a challenge because it challenges all of the ideas, all of the assumptions that disable people from having this fundamental and primary experience. It challenges the ambivalence; it challenges the pessimism; it challenges the obsessions that are endemic in human society.

It only honors Knowledge, nothing else. It only asks for Knowledge, nothing else. It is a calling. Those who can hear, will hear. But they must hear more clearly; they must develop their hearing; they must find the strength to trust what is most deeply known within them.

It is time now to begin the preparation for the Greater Community. It is time now to begin the preparation in learning The Way of Knowledge. Yet how can this be done? Should you go to the university? Should you go to the therapist? Should you go to your best friend? Should you peruse the library and see what kind of books you can find?

Yes, you will find writings and teachings that validate the reality of Knowledge, but you will not find any books or teachings that will validate the reality of Knowledge within the context of the world's emergence into the Greater Community. That is because humanity is at a great turning point, and a turning point requires a New Revelation, a new Teaching and a new foundation.

The vast majority of what is available to you has been created in a state of isolation. There is no recognition of the Greater Community. There is no recognition of humanity's future in the Greater Community. There is no recognition that the Greater Community, more than anything else, is what will determine what humanity must face and contend with.

Read the predictions for the future in books everywhere, and you will find human beings postulating a future for human beings alone. There is no recognition that you are emerging into a larger arena of life. It is totally isolationist thinking. If there were no Greater Community, and if the Greater Community were not in the world, that would be adequate. But this is not the case.

Therefore, these teachings, no matter how valuable they may be in their content and in their intention, are not adequate. Humanity is at a turning point. What was valuable yesterday, what worked yesterday now has to be reassessed. Something new has to be given to enable humanity to take the great steps ahead.

All religious traditions in the world need something new to give them this vantage point, to give them this power so they can continue to be viable and relevant. That is why The Greater Community Way of Knowledge is being presented into the world. It is not here to replace the religions of the world but to give them new life and to give them relevancy and purpose within the context of the world's emergence into the Greater Community.

This Teaching, which has never been available before in the world, is now being introduced. It is not being advertised over the television. It is not on billboards across the country. Instead, it is being presented through this book and books like it. It is being shared from person to person. It is being transmitted through meaningful relationships.

It is being given to empower humanity, to redirect humanity's awareness and focus, to educate humanity about the Greater Community and to call upon the inherent strength of humanity so that human beings everywhere can come to find their meaning and their value and their purpose in life and can make a real contribution to the world in its current needs.

You are very fortunate to have this book. You are very fortunate to be able to hear these ideas. Even if you have difficulty understanding them or relating to them, you are a person of great fortune to be able to receive them.

You are one of the first to hear the great Message. You are one of the first to have the opportunity to begin a Greater Community education. You are one of the first to have the privilege to be able to learn what spirituality means in the Greater Community and how it will clarify all of your questions about spirituality here on Earth.

It is time to begin the preparation. That is the only way that you will understand fully what is being presented here. And that is the only way that you will be able to experience it for yourself.

I know My words are not enough. I know that the perspective I am sharing is not quite enough. People must have this experience themselves—not just a fleeting experience here and there, but a clear experience.

It must be very crystal clear to them that the world is emerging into the Greater Community and that people must find the way to Knowledge in order to prepare. This cannot simply be a hope or an expectation, an ideal or a belief. It must be a certainty based upon a real experience. How will you gain this real experience? By taking the Steps to Knowledge. By learning a Greater Community Way of Knowledge.

As We have said, the answer to great questions is a means of preparation. When you ask, "Who am I? Why am I here? What must I accomplish? Who must I meet?" these are great questions. Would a few words suffice to answer them? If you think that words alone would be an answer to these questions, then you do not know what you are asking for. You have no idea what you are requesting.

The only way to find the answer is to be given a means of preparation that can take you up the mountain of life, that can provide the steps, that can give you the perspective that you need, that can enable you to refocus your mind and your energies in a true direction.

If you ask Me, "How will I know what I need to know?" I say, " I will take you up the mountain where you can see for yourself." You may say, "Well, just give me the answer!" and I say, "There is no answer until you see for yourself, and the only way you can see for yourself is to reach that vantage point where you can look above the trees out over the lay of the land and gain a real perspective about where you are and what is happening."

You must get there. There is no other way. Having beliefs, having ideals, having grand visions of life, having high experiences—that is not it. That will never work. Many people dedicate themselves to having these things, thinking that that will be adequate, but they never have the foundation inside, and they never get far enough up the mountain to see what is happening on the outside.

Therefore, the answer to your need to know, your need to realize who you are, why you are here, what you must accomplish and who you must meet can only be answered by giving you a preparation that will enable you to find out for yourself.

Here you will find out without heroes, without gurus, without falling down on your knees to worship some individual. Here you must find the way, but you will not journey alone, for you will need others to help you.

And you will need one of the few people in the world who can instruct you in The Way of Knowledge, in a Greater Community Way of Knowledge. They are there and you will find them when you really need them. But in order to find them and in order to recognize them, you must prepare.

Many people want the great results of spiritual awakening, but they are unwilling to take the journey. They simply want the answers. They think the answers can be given in words or in concepts or can be revealed in having high and happy experiences. They will not make the journey, and so they will not find out. And they will never develop the skill and the power and the ability to live such an awakened life because they will not take the journey.

Life is a journey. It is trying to get from one place to another. Knowledge knows where you need to get to. It knows what you need to recognize. It knows the skill and ability you need to cultivate along the way.

It is time to prepare. The Greater Community Way of Knowledge is the only Teaching in the world that can prepare you for the Greater Community. It is the only Teaching in the world that can present to you what Knowledge and Wisdom really mean within a larger arena of intelligent life. It is the only Teaching in the world that can activate your Knowledge and give it full expression within the context of the world's evolution.

It is a New Revelation. It is a new gift to humanity. It is the gift humanity now needs in order to emerge out of its isolation and face the realities, the difficulties and the opportunities that await it in the Greater Community.

The Creator would not leave you alone or unprepared for the Greater Community. The Creator would not leave you without a means for discovering the greater purpose that has brought you into the world.

Receive this gift. Hear this calling. Find your deepest response. Go beyond your thinking and your ideas. Go beyond your preoccupations and attachments.

There is something great living within you. It is needed within the world now. It is being called for at this moment. It is a calling to awaken.

EPILOGUE

*C*ontact with intelligent life in the universe is a world event like no other. It is the next great step in the development and evolution of the human family. It is unstoppable. It is inevitable. It is happening now. Here we must choose to either undertake the preparation and education for the Greater Community and, in so doing, ensure the freedom and sovereignty of our world, or continue to fight and struggle with each other, blind to our common future and blind to the Intervention now present in the world. It comes down to the decision of each person: the decision to be aware or to be unaware, the decision to prepare or to be blind to a future now racing towards us.

Remarkably, you are in the world at this time. You are coming to learn about humanity's emergence into the Greater Community, and you have found this book, a book of Revelation from the Creator of all life. It is no coincidence that this is the case. We each have been sent into the world at this time to serve the needs of our time and of a world in transition. Indeed, some in the world today have a Greater Community connection and lineage that extends beyond this life alone.

The revelations of Preparing for the Greater Community have been given to activate this awareness in you, to call forth the deeper Knowledge that you carry and to provide you with the education and preparation you will need to be a contributor to an emerging world. In time, this will bring true clarity, inner certainty and direction to your life, for now you are moving with the greater movement of the world itself.

Now you can gain a greater understanding of the true context for your life and the mysterious and perhaps inexplicable calling that has brought you to this point. This understanding will naturally call forth the gifts you carry, the gifts you brought with you from your Ancient Home to serve the world at this time.

The door to the Greater Community is opening now. Never before has this door opened to the human family. Now it is time to pass through this threshold and prepare for a greater life in a greater universe of worlds.

GUIDELINES FOR PREPARING FOR THE GREATER COMMUNITY

As revealed to
Marshall Vian Summers
on June 19, 2008
in Boulder, Colorado

1. Begin to read the Allies of Humanity Briefings and study them deeply.
2. Read everything you can about the Greater Community within the Teaching, The Greater Community Way of Knowledge.
3. Learn what you can about the presence of foreign forces in the world.
4. Encourage human unity, emphasizing humanity's vulnerability to Intervention and to persuasion in the universe and that humanity has little or no defense established yet to deal with influences from the Greater Community in which you live.
5. Support the disclosure of the extraterrestrial presence—disclosure from governments, disclosure from the Intervention itself and disclosure from the public, who has already been impacted in so many ways.
6. Think of yourself as living within a Greater Community of intelligent life, a Greater Community where life has evolved and where technology has accelerated, but a Greater Community where the limits of physical life are still impinging on everyone who exists in the physical universe.
7. Do not fall prey to persuasion and inducements from any extraterrestrial presence who is active in the world interfering in human affairs. Do not believe that anyone is going to come here to save or to rescue a struggling humanity, and [recognize] that

those who claim to do so are here for their own purposes—to take advantage of humanity's weakness, divisions and superstitions.

8. See humanity and yourself as the native peoples of the world who are now facing Intervention. What must the native peoples do to secure their boundaries and to determine how and when and where engagement with the outside should occur for the benefit of the native peoples of the world?

9. Do not believe that any other race has claim to this world, or is genetically bonded to the race of humanity, or is humanity's parents or guides in any respect. This is a falsehood that is being presented by those forces who are intervening in the world today.

10. Understand why humanity's Allies are not present in the world and that they have a policy of non-intervention, only sharing their wisdom and insight for those who seek to know about life beyond this world.

11. Prepare yourself for the Great Waves of change that are coming to the world so that you may be in a strong position to navigate these Great Waves of change and to be of service to others. This will be supporting humanity and preparing it for its future within a Greater Community of intelligent life.

12. Do not let anyone persuade you that those forces who are intervening in the world are here for the benefit of humanity. This represents confusion on the part of the human family and deception on the part of those forces who are here already.

13. Understand that humanity must establish a boundary to space, and that attempts at intervention and persuasion will be ongoing, and that humanity—because it is divided and because it is ignorant about the realities of life in the universe—is especially vulnerable to outside persuasion and intervention.

14. Look to see if you have had any contact with extraterrestrial forces yourself, either through the mental environment or

through direct physical contact. Be courageous in asking yourself, "Have I had any direct contact with an extraterrestrial force? And if so, what was the nature of the contact and what occurred?"

15. Denounce war as a weakening of the human family in the face of the Greater Community. Emphasize unity and cooperation in humanity facing the Great Waves of change and in preparing for its great encounters with the Greater Community in which it exists.

16. Share the Allies of Humanity Briefings with as many people as possible and send the Declaration of Human Sovereignty to your friends and associates and to government leaders. The more people who can know about this, the stronger humanity will be and the more able it will be to ward off intervention and persuasion in order to set its own course to become a free and advancing race in the universe.

17. Do not believe that the taking of human beings by extraterrestrial forces holds any benefit for humanity. Understand that these abductions are only for the purpose of breeding a hybrid being capable of influencing governments and commerce and religious institutions, and to also create a network of supporters for the Intervention itself. This is a gross violation of your rights and well-being, and a tremendous threat to the future and freedom of humanity.

18. Recognize that advanced technology does not equal advanced ethics and morality. Use humanity as a good example of this. Do not think that those who have gained the ability to travel in space represent any advancement in ethics or morality or religion or spirituality. Do not think that they can teach you anything in this regard, for in many cases, you are more advanced than they are in your awareness of the reality of God and the nature of your own spirituality.

19. Understand that to be free in the universe, humanity will have to meet three requirements: unity, self-sufficiency and discretion. Humanity will have to achieve these goals to a very great degree. At present, none of these are being cultivated adequately. This represents the emphasis and focus for uniting humanity in its own defense and preparing it to emerge into a greater arena of life.

20. Understand that the Intervention that is here in the world today is here to break down human unity. It is here to break down humanity's ability to be self-sufficient, and it is here to learn as much about human nature, human behavior and human society as possible, thus undermining your discretion and exposing your weaknesses.

21. Look to the stars with clarity and sobriety. It is a challenging but wondrous environment in the universe, but you must be strong and determined in order to emerge into this larger arena.

22. Learn The Way of Knowledge and build your foundation in Knowledge so that it may protect you against persuasion and Intervention and that it may guide you forward in service to humanity—to prepare humanity to become more united and more determined and more capable of responding and functioning within a Greater Community of life.

23. Understand that God has provided a warning and a preparation for the Greater Community so that humanity may safely pass through this great threshold and bring about a greater unity and cooperation amongst the human family, and prepare itself for both the reality and the spirituality of life in the universe.

24. Do not think that any race will physically come here and rescue humanity. It is humanity itself that must build its unity and its cooperation, its strength and its determination. Educating people about the reality and the spirituality of life in the universe is an essential preparation to support this advancement. Any races

who come here and claim that they are here to save or to rescue humanity represent a great danger and a great deception.

25. Maintain your confidence in yourself and in the power and the potency of the human family. Do not lose confidence in human leaders or institutions, regardless of their fallacies or their errors. Humanity has the hidden strength to ward off Intervention and persuasion and to emerge into a Greater Community of intelligent life as a free and self-determined race. Never allow anything to displace this faith and this confidence, for there are many forces in the world today who are seeking to do just that.

26. Recognize to what degree you may have a Greater Community heritage and reality within yourself. The possibility is that you have lived in other worlds and that your experience of the Greater Community is part of your foundation. Accept this as a possibility, and allow the revelations regarding this, whatever they may be, to emerge in your mind over time. You are a citizen not only of this one world, but of a Greater Community of intelligent life, and this represents, in a greater context, the meaning and the power of your relationships and spirituality.

27. Understand that humanity has a destiny in the Greater Community, a destiny as a free and self-determined race. But in order to achieve this and fulfill this destiny, humanity must become united; it must cease war and conflict; it must learn to limit the damage it is creating in the Earth to create a sustainable and self-sufficient existence here in this world.

28. Understand that humanity will not be able to go out and exploit and plunder the Greater Community, for beyond this solar system, the lands and the regions and the routes of travel are owned by others. Humanity will have to learn to become self-sufficient within the sphere of its own influence within this solar system. If it can achieve this, then it can ward off

Intervention and influence from the outside and establish itself as a free and self-determined race in the universe.

IMPORTANT TERMS

The New Message from God reveals that our world stands at the greatest threshold in the history and evolution of humanity. At this threshold, God has spoken again, revealing the great change that is coming to the world and our destiny within the Greater Community of life beyond our world, for which we are unaware and unprepared.

Here the Revelation redefines certain familiar terms, but within a greater context and introduces other terms that are new to the human family. It is important to understand these terms when reading the texts of the New Message and hearing the Voice of Revelation.

GOD is revealed in the New Message as the Source and Creator of all life and of countless races in the universe. Here the Greater Reality of God is unveiled in the expanded context of life in this world and all life in the universe. This greater context redefines the meaning of our understanding of God and of God's Power and Presence in our lives. The New Message states that to understand what God is doing in our world, we must understand what God is doing in the entire universe. This is now being revealed for the first time through a New Message from God. In the New Message, God is not a divine entity, personage or a singular awareness, but instead a pervasive force and presence that permeates all life and is moving all life in the universe towards a state of unity. God speaks to the deepest part of each person through the power of Knowledge that lives within them.

THE SEPARATION is the ongoing state and condition of being separate from God. The Separation began when part of Creation willed to have the freedom to be apart from God, to live in a state of

Separation. As a result, God created our evolving world and the expanding universe as a place for the separated to live in countless forms and places. Before the Separation, all life was in a timeless state of pure union. It is to this original state of union with God that all those living in Separation are ultimately called to return—through relationship, service and the discovery of Knowledge. It is God's Mission in our world and throughout the universe to reclaim the separated through Knowledge, which is the part of each individual still connected to God.

KNOWLEDGE is the deeper spiritual Intelligence within each person, waiting to be discovered. Knowledge represents the eternal part of us that has never left God. The New Message speaks of Knowledge as the great hope for humanity, an inner power at the heart of each person that God's New Message is here to reveal and to call forth. This deeper spiritual Intelligence exists beyond our thinking mind and the boundaries of our intellect. It alone has the power to guide each of us to our higher purpose and destined relationships in life. The New Message teaches extensively about the reality and experience of Knowledge.

THE ANGELIC ASSEMBLY is the presence of God's Angels who have been assigned to watch over our world and the evolution of humanity. This Assembly is part of the hierarchy established by God to support the redemption and return of all those living in Separation in the physical reality. Every world where sentient life exists is watched over by an Angelic Assembly. The Assembly overseeing our world is now translating the Will of God for our time into human language and understanding, which is now being revealed through the New Message from God. The term Angelic Assembly is synonymous with the terms Angelic Presence and Angelic Host in the text of the New Message.

THE NEW MESSAGE FROM GOD is a communication from God to people of all nations and religions. It represents the next stage of God's progressive Revelation for the human family and comes in response to the great challenges and needs of humanity today. The New Message is over 9000 pages in length and is the largest Revelation ever given to the world, given now to a literate world of global communication and growing global awareness. The New Message is not an offshoot or reformation of any past tradition and is not given for one tribe, nation or group alone. It is God's New Message for the whole world, which is now facing Great Waves of environmental, social and political change and the new threshold of emerging into a Greater Community of intelligent life in the universe.

THE VOICE OF REVELATION is the united voice of the Angelic Assembly delivering God's Message through a Messenger sent into the world for this task. Here the Assembly speaks as one Voice, the many speaking as one. For the first time in history, you are able to hear the actual Voice of Revelation speaking through God's Messenger. It is this Voice that has spoken to all God's Messengers in the past. The Word and the Sound of the Voice of Revelation are in the world and are available for you to hear in their original audio form.

THE MESSENGER is the one chosen, prepared and sent into the world by the Angelic Assembly to receive the New Message from God. The Messenger for this time is Marshall Vian Summers. Marshall is a humble man who has undergone a long and difficult preparation to receive God's New Revelation and bring it to the world. He is charged with the great burden, blessing and responsibility of presenting this Revelation to a divided and conflicted world. He is the first of God's Messengers to reveal the reality of a Greater Community of intelligent life in the universe. The Messenger has been engaged in this process of Revelation since the year 1982.

THE PRESENCE refers to different but interconnected realities: the presence of Knowledge within the individual, the Presence of the Angelic Assembly that oversees the world or ultimately the Presence of God in the universe. The Presence of these three realities offers a life-changing experience of grace and relationship. All three are connected to the larger process of growth and redemption for us, for the world and for the universe at large. Together they represent the mystery and purpose of our lives, which the New Message reveals to us in the clearest possible terms. The New Revelation offers a modern pathway for experiencing the power of the Presence in your life.

STEPS TO KNOWLEDGE is an ancient pathway of spiritual practice now being given by God to the world for the first time. Steps provides the lessons and practices necessary for learning and living the New Message from God. In beginning the Steps, you embark on a journey of discovering Knowledge, the mysterious source of your inner power and authority, and with it the essential relationships you are destined to find. Its 365 daily "steps," or practices, lead you to a personal revelation about your life and destiny. In taking this greater journey, you can discover the power of Knowledge and your experience of profound inner knowing, which lead you to your higher purpose and calling in life.

THE GREATER COMMUNITY is the larger universe of intelligent life in which our world has always existed. This Greater Community encompasses all worlds in the universe where sentient life exists, in all states of evolution and development. The New Message reveals that humanity is in an early and adolescent phase of its development and that the time has now come for humanity's emergence into the Greater Community. It is here, standing at the threshold of space, that humanity discovers that it is not alone in the universe, or even within its own world.

THE GREATER COMMUNITY WAY OF KNOWLEDGE is a timeless tradition representing God's work in the universe to reclaim the separated in all worlds through the power of Knowledge that is inherent in all intelligent life. To understand what God is doing in our world, we must begin to understand what God is doing in the entire universe. For the first time in history, The Greater Community Way of Knowledge is being presented to the world through a New Message from God. The New Message opens the portal to this timeless work of God underway throughout the universe in which we live. We stand at the threshold of emerging into this Greater Community and must now have access to The Greater Community Way of Knowledge in order to understand our destiny as a race and successfully navigate the challenges of interacting with life in the universe.

THE INTERVENTION is a dangerous form of contact underway by certain races from the Greater Community who are here to take advantage of a weak and divided humanity. This is occurring at a time when the human family is entering a period of increasing breakdown and disorder, in the face of the Great Waves of change. The Intervention presents itself as a benign and redeeming force while in reality its ultimate goal is to undermine human freedom and self-determination and take control of the world and its resources. The New Message reveals that the Intervention seeks to secretly establish its influence here in the minds and hearts of people at a time of growing confusion, conflict and vulnerability. God is calling us, as the native peoples of this world, to oppose this Intervention, to alert and educate others and to put forth our own rules of engagement as an emerging race. Our response to the Intervention and the Greater Community at large is the one thing that can unite a fractured and divided human family at a time of the greatest need and consequence for our race.

THE GREAT WAVES OF CHANGE are a set of powerful environmental, economic and social forces now converging in the world. The Great Waves are the result of humanity's misuse and overuse of the world, its resources and its environment. The Great Waves have the power to drastically alter the face of the world— producing economic instability, runaway climate change, violent weather and the loss of arable land and freshwater, threatening to produce a world condition of great difficulty and human suffering. The Great Waves are not an end times or apocalyptic event, but instead a challenging period of transition to a new world reality. The New Message reveals what is coming for the world and provides a preparation to enable us to navigate a radically changing world. God is calling for human unity and cooperation born now out of sheer necessity for the preservation and protection of human civilization. Together with the Intervention, the Great Waves represents one of the two great threats facing humanity and a major reason why God has spoken again.

HIGHER PURPOSE refers to the specific contribution each person was sent into the world to make and the unique relationships that will enable the fulfillment of this purpose. Knowledge within the individual holds their higher purpose and destiny for them, which cannot be ascertained by the intellect alone. These must be discovered, followed and expressed in service to others to be fully realized. The world needs the demonstration of this higher purpose from many more people as never before.

SPIRITUAL FAMILY refers to the small working groups formed after the Separation to enable all individuals to work towards greater states of union and relationship, undertaking this over a long span of time, culminating in their final return to God. Your Spiritual Family represents the relationships you have reclaimed through Knowledge during your long journey through Separation. Some members of your Spiritual Family are in the world and some are beyond the world. The Spiritual Families are a part of the mysterious Plan of God to free and reunite all those living in Separation.

ANCIENT HOME refers to the reality of life and the state of awareness and relationship you had before entering the world, and to which you will return after your life in the world. Your Ancient Home is a timeless state of connection and relationship with your Spiritual Family, The Assembly and God.

MENTAL ENVIRONMENT is the environment of thought in which we live that exists parallel to the world of physical form that we more readily perceive. Within this environment are unseen entities and thought forms that influence our thinking, emotions and actions. It is critical that we become aware of the Mental Environment and learn to both shield ourselves in it and exert a beneficial influence upon it. This is because alien intelligences are in our world and are capable of exerting a new and more powerful influence in the Mental Environment than humans have ever exerted upon one another.

GREATER COMMUNITY PERSPECTIVE is a perspective about our lives and the world informed by the awareness of the Greater Community. This perspective is the natural result of being educated by the New Message regarding what life is like in our region of space, why Intervention is occurring in our world now and what this means for humanity. With this perspective comes an expanded sense of gratitude, tolerance and compassion for humanity and a natural desire to support human unity, self-sufficiency and the awareness of our commonalities, not our differences, as a human family.

THE STORY OF THE MESSENGER

Marshall Vian Summers is the Messenger for the New Message from God. For over three decades he has been the recipient of a Divine Revelation given to prepare humanity for the great environmental, social and economic changes that are coming to the world and for humanity's contact with intelligent life in the universe.

In 1982, at the age of 33, Marshall Vian Summers was called into the deserts of the American Southwest where he had a direct encounter with the Angelic Presence, who had been guiding and preparing him for his future role and calling. This encounter forever altered the course of his life and initiated him into a deeper relationship with the Angelic Assembly, requiring that he surrender his life to God. This began the long, mysterious process of receiving God's New Message for humanity.

Following this mysterious initiation, he received the first revelations of the New Message from God. Over the decades since, a vast Revelation for humanity has unfolded, at times slowly and at times in great torrents. During these long years, he had to proceed with the support of only a few individuals, not knowing what this growing Revelation would mean and where it would ultimately lead.

The Messenger has walked a long and difficult road to receive and present the largest Revelation ever given to the human family. Still today the Voice of Revelation continues to speak through him as he faces the great challenge of bringing God's New Revelation to a troubled and conflicted world.

Read more about the life and story of the Messenger
Marshall Vian Summers:
www.newmessage.org/story-of-marshall-vian-summers

Read and hear the original revelation *The Story of the Messenger:*
www.newmessage.org/story-of-the-messenger

Hear and watch the world teachings of the Messenger:
www.newmessage.org/messenger

THE VOICE OF REVELATION

For the first time in history, you can hear the Voice of Revelation, such a Voice as spoke to the prophets and Messengers of the past and is now speaking again through a new Messenger who is in the world today.

The Voice of Revelation is not the voice of one individual, but that of the entire Angelic Assembly speaking together, all as one. Here God communicates beyond words to the Angelic Assembly, who then translate God's Message into human words and language that we can comprehend.

The revelations of this book were originally spoken in this manner by the Voice of Revelation through the Messenger Marshall Vian Summers. This process of Divine Revelation has occurred since 1982. The Revelation continues to this day.

Hear the original audio recordings of the
Voice of Revelation, which is the Source of the text contained
in this book and throughout the New Message:
www.newmessage.org/experience

Learn more about the Voice of Revelation,
what it is and how it speaks through the Messenger:
www.newmessage.org/voiceofrevelation

About The Society for the New Message from God

Founded in 1992 by Marshall Vian Summers, The Society for the New Message from God is an independent religious 501(c)(3) non-profit organization that is primarily supported by readers and students of the New Message, receiving no sponsorship or revenue from any government or religious organization.

The Society's mission is to bring the New Message from God to people everywhere so that humanity can find its common ground, preserve the Earth, protect human freedom and advance human civilization as we stand at the threshold of great change and a universe full of intelligent life.

Marshall Vian Summers and The Society have been given the immense responsibility of bringing the New Message into the world. The members of The Society are a small group of dedicated individuals who have committed themselves to fulfill this mission. For them, it is both a burden and a great blessing to give themselves wholeheartedly in this great service to humanity.

The Society for the New Message

Contact us:

P.O. Box 1724 Boulder,
CO 80306-1724
(303) 938-8401 (800) 938-3891
011 303 938 84 01 (International)
(303) 938-1214 (fax)
society@newmessage.org
www.newmessage.org
www.marshallsummers.com
www.alliesofhumanity.org
www.newknowledgelibrary.org

Connect with us:

www.youtube.com/thenewmessagefromgod
www.facebook.com/newmessagefromgod
www.facebook.com/marshallsummers
www.twitter.com/godsnewmessage

Donate to support The Society and join a community of givers who are helping bring the New Message to the world:
www.newmessage.org/donate

About the Worldwide Community of the New Message from God

The New Message from God is being studied and practiced by people around the world. Representing more than 90 countries and studying the New Message in over 30 languages, a worldwide community of students has formed to both receive the New Message and support the Messenger in bringing God's New Message to the world.

The New Message has the power to awaken the sleeping brilliance in people everywhere and bring new inspiration and wisdom into the lives of people from all nations and faith traditions.

Learn more about the worldwide community of people who are learning and living the New Message and taking the Steps to Knowledge in their lives.

Read and hear the original Revelation *The Worldwide Community of God's New Message:*
www.newmessage.org/theworldwidecommunity

Join the free Worldwide Community site where you can meet other students and engage with the Messenger:
www.community.newmessage.org

Learn more about the educational opportunities available in the Worldwide Community:

Community Site - www.community.newmessage.org/
New Message Free School - www.community.newmessage.org/school
Live Internet Broadcasts and International Events -
www.newmessage.org/events

Encampment - www.newmessage.org/encampment
Online Library of Text and Audio -
www.newmessage.org/experience

BOOKS OF THE NEW MESSAGE FROM GOD

God Has Spoken Again

The One God

The New Messenger

The Greater Community

The Journey to a New Life

The Power of Knowledge

The New World

The Pure Religion

Steps to Knowledge

Greater Community Spirituality

The Great Waves of Change

Life in the Universe

Wisdom from the Greater Community I & II

Secrets of Heaven

Relationships & Higher Purpose

Living The Way of Knowledge

Lightning Source UK Ltd.
Milton Keynes UK
UKHW011318200522
403286UK00001B/11